Post Traumatic Stress Disorder

Post traumatic stress disorder develops after exposure to one or more terrifying event that has caused or threatened to cause the sufferer grave physical harm. This book discusses how trauma-focused cognitive therapy can be used to help children and adolescents who suffer from post traumatic stress disorder.

Cognitive therapy is frequently used to treat adults who suffer from PTSD with proven results. *Post Traumatic Stress Disorder* provides the therapist with instructions on how CT models can be used with children and young people to combat the disorder. Based on research carried out by the authors, this book covers:

- assessment procedures and measures
- formulation and treatment planning
- trauma-focused cognitive therapy methods
- common hurdles.

The authors provide case studies and practical tips, as well as examples of self-report measures and handouts for young people and their parents, which will help the practitioner to prepare for working with this difficult client group.

Post Traumatic Stress Disorder is an accessible, practical, clinically relevant guide for professionals and trainees in child and adolescent mental health service teams who work with traumatised children and young people.

Online resources:
The appendices of this book provide worksheets that can be downloaded free of charge to purchasers of the print version. Please visit the website www.routledge mentalhealth.com/cbt-with-children to find out more about this facility.

Patrick Smith is a Lecturer in Psychology at the Institute of Psychiatry, King's College London, and Consultant Clinical Psychologist at the South London and Maudsley NHS Foundation Trust.

Sean Perrin is a Lecturer in Psychology at the Institute of Psychiatry, King's College London, and team leader for the Child Traumatic Stress Clinic at the South London and Maudsley NHS Foundation Trust.

William Yule is Emeritus Professor of Applied Child Psychology at the Institute of Psychiatry, King's College London; Consultant Clinical Psychologist; and Founding Director of the Child Traumatic Stress Clinic.

David M. Clark is Professor of Psychology at the Institute of Psychiatry King's College London; and Director of the Centre for Anxiety Disorders and Trauma, South London and Maudsley NHS Foundation Trust.

CBT with Children, Adolescents and Families
Series editor: Paul Stallard

'The *CBT with Children, Adolescents and Families* series, edited by Professor Paul Stallard and written by a team of international experts, meets the growing need for evidence-based treatment manuals to address prevalent psychological problems in young people. These authoritative, yet practical books will be of interest to all professionals who work in the field of child and adolescent mental health.' – *Alan Carr, Professor of Clinical Psychology, University College Dublin, Ireland*

Cognitive behaviour therapy (CBT) is now the predominant treatment approach in both the NHS and private practice and is increasingly used by a range of mental health professionals.

The *CBT with Children, Adolescents and Families* series provides comprehensive, practical guidance for using CBT when dealing with a variety of common child and adolescent problems, as well as related family issues. The demand for therapy and counselling for children and adolescents is rapidly expanding, and early intervention in family and school settings is increasingly seen as effective and essential. In this series leading authorities in their respective fields provide detailed advice on methods of achieving this.

Each book in this series focuses on one particular problem and guides the professional from initial assessment through to techniques, common problems and future issues. Written especially for the clinician, each title includes summaries of key points, clinical examples, and worksheets to use with children and young people.

Titles in this series:

Anxiety by Paul Stallard
Obsessive Compulsive Disorder edited by Polly Waite and Tim Williams
Depression by Chrissie Verduyn, Julia Rogers and Alison Wood
Eating Disorders by Simon Gowers and Lynne Green
Post Traumatic Stress Disorder by Patrick Smith, Sean Perrin, William Yule and David M. Clark

Post Traumatic Stress Disorder

Cognitive Therapy with Children and Young People

Patrick Smith, Sean Perrin, William Yule and David M. Clark

Routledge
Taylor & Francis Group

LONDON AND NEW YORK

First published 2010
by Routledge
27 Church Road, Hove, East Sussex BN3 2FA

Simultaneously published in the USA and Canada
by Routledge
270 Madison Avenue, New York NY 10016

Transferred to digital printing 2010

Routledge is an imprint of the Taylor & Francis Group, an Informa business

Typeset in Times by
RefineCatch Ltd, Bungay, Suffolk
Printed and bound in Great Britain by
TJI Digital, Padstow, Cornwall
Paperback cover design by Andy Ward

This publication has been produced with paper manufactured to strict
environmental standards and with pulp derived from sustainable forests.

British Library Cataloguing in Publication Data
A catalogue record for this book is available from the British Library

Library of Congress Cataloging-in-Publication Data
Post traumatic stress disorder : cognitive therapy with children and young people /
   Patrick Smith . . . [et al.].
       p. ; cm.
   Includes bibliographical references and index.
   1. Post-traumatic stress disorder in adolescence–Treatment.   2. Post-traumatic
   stress disorder in children–Treatment.   3. Cognitive therapy for teenagers.
   4. Cognitive therapy for children.   I. Smith, Patrick, Dr. [DNLM:
   1. Cognitive Therapy–methods.   2. Stress Disorders, Post-Traumatic–therapy.
   3. Adolescent.   4. Child.   WM 170 P856 2009]
   RJ506.P55P66 2009
   618.92′8521–dc22   2009010027

ISBN: 978–0–415–39163–4 (hbk)
ISBN: 978–0–415–39164–1 (pbk)

Contents

Illustrations

Figures

Boxes

Acknowledgements

With grateful thanks to our colleagues and collaborators, especially: Tim Dalgleish, Richard Meiser-Stedman and Troy Tranah.

Special thanks to Anke Ehlers for invaluable detailed comments on an earlier draft.

Thanks to staff and patients at King's College Hospital Accident and Emergency Department; to the South London and Maudsley NHS Foundation Trust; and to all the young people and families who have attended the Child Traumatic Stress Clinic, Maudsley Hospital, London.

Patrick Smith would like to thank the Psychiatry Research Trust, Kraupl Taylor Fellowship, for funding while this treatment was being evaluated.

Permissions

Box 2.3, p.17
Extract from Scheeringa, M.S., Zeanah, C. H., Drell, M. J. and Larrieu, J. A. (1995), Two approaches to diagnosing posttraumatic stress disorder in infancy and early childhood, *Journal of the American Academy of Child and Adolescent Psychiatry*; extract from Scheeringa, M., Zeanah, C. H., Myers, L. and Putnam, F. (2003), New findings on alternative criteria for PTSD in preschool children, *Journal of the American Academy of Child and Adolescent Psychiatry*, copyright © (1995, 2003), by permission of Lippincott, Williams & Wilkins.

Figure 2.1, p. 23
Reprinted from *Behaviour Research and Therapy, 38,* 4, Ehlers, A. and Clark, D.M., A cognitive model of post traumatic stress disorder, copyright © (2000), with permission of Elsevier.

Appendix A, pp. 176–78
Material from Foa, E.B., Johnson, K. M., Feeny, N. C. and Treadwell, K. R., The Child PTSD Symptom Scale: a preliminary examination of its psychometric properties, copyright © (1991), *Journal of Clinical Child & Adolescent Psychology*, by permission of Taylor & Francis.

Appendix A, pp. 179–81
Material from Meiser-Stedman, R., Smith, P., Bryant, R., Salmon, K., Yule, W., Dalgleish, T. and Nixon, R., Development and validation of the Child Post Traumatic Cognitions Inventory (CPTCI), copyright © (2009), *Journal of Child Psychology and Psychiatry,* by permission of Wiley-Blackwell Publishing.

Every effort has been made to obtain permission to reproduce extracts from other sources. Any omissions brought to our attention will be remedied in future editions or reprints.

1

Introduction

Cognitive therapy for PTSD with children and young people

Since publication of Beck's seminal key text (Beck *et al.* 1979) on cognitive therapy for depressed adults, there has been rapid development of cognitive therapies for a range of disorders across a range of ages. This growth of effective treatments has come about in part because treatment approaches are theoretically based. That is, the careful evaluation of cognitive behaviour therapy (CBT) in randomised controlled trials has been preceded by equally careful evaluation of the cognitive models on which they are based.

The development of CBT for children and adolescents has lagged behind that for adults, but the overarching approach has been the same. Theoretical models of the disorder(s) specify maintaining factors; these are empirically tested in naturalistic or experimental studies; interventions aimed at reversing key maintaining factors are piloted; and finally, comprehensive CBT programmes which incorporate a variety of techniques to target key maintaining factors are tested in controlled trials.

This book is a reflection of the last stage in that process. It has its origins in a therapist guide which was used in a preliminary randomised controlled trial to evaluate cognitive therapy for young people with post traumatic stress disorder (PTSD, Smith *et al.* 2007), treatment being firmly based on Ehlers and Clark's (2000) cognitive model of PTSD, suitably adapted for children (Meiser-Stedman 2002). The book is intended as an accessible, practical, clinically relevant guide for professionals working with traumatised children.

Who is this book for?

The book is aimed primarily at professionals and their trainees who work with traumatised children in child and adolescent mental health service (CAMHS) teams. This will include clinical psychologists, psychiatrists, social workers, nurses, occupational therapists, family therapists, and others. Most will be gained from this book by those who have some prior CBT experience, although formal post-qualification CBT training is not required. Regular supervision will be helpful in implementing this treatment approach. It is hoped that this will be a useful resource for those who are experienced in working with children with PTSD, but also as a guide for less experienced trainees. The important point is that this treatment should be implemented by trained and qualified mental health workers in the context of a safe and professional approach to working with children and families – usually within a CAMHS setting.

> CBT should be provided by suitably trained and supervised mental health practitioners.

Who can benefit from cognitive therapy for PTSD?

The model on which this treatment is based has empirical support for the 7 to 16 years age group, while the randomised controlled trial evaluating its effectiveness was carried out with 8 to 18-year-olds. Participants in the trial – and those in most of the basic research testing the applicability of the cognitive model – had developed PTSD as a result of single-incident traumatic events such as road traffic accidents and exposure to violence. Primarily then, the approach described here is intended for 7 to 18-year-olds who have developed PTSD as the primary disorder following a one-off trauma.

However, with some adaptation, this treatment is helpful for a broader range of young people. First, it may be used with those who have developed PTSD symptoms relating to more than one traumatic event, following multiple traumatic exposure. In this case, the same principles of treatment will apply, but additional sessions are usually needed in order to process multiple trauma memories. Second, the principles of this treatment approach may be used with children younger than seven years old, including pre-schoolers. Adaptations include more family involvement, less reliance on verbal processing of trauma memories, and a more behavioural approach to working with traumatic reminders.

What is cognitive therapy for PTSD?

The form of cognitive therapy for PTSD described in this book shares many characteristics with the wider family of CBT interventions that are used successfully across a range of disorders and ages. The approach is based on

Ehlers *et al.* (2005) cognitive therapy treatment programme for adults. Treatment components overlap to some extent with other CBT approaches, but differ in a number of key respects.

Cognitive therapy is theory based. The central idea in cognitive theories is that feeling, thinking and behaviour are all interrelated; changes to thoughts will influence feelings and behaviour. Put another way, idiosyncratic appraisals of events (the meaning we give to things) are critical in the regulation of affect and behaviour (Bolton 2005). The cognitive theory of PTSD (Ehlers and Clark 2000) is a detailed and elaborated, disorder-specific example of this central idea, and is described in Chapter 2. When working clinically, cognitive models or theories enable formulations to be developed: presenting problems are understood and explained using the overarching framework of the model. As described in some detail in Chapter 4, this cognitive formulation is a 'working hypothesis', subject to change or refinement as further information is gathered. It is also individualised for each client – it is a unique way of understanding each particular young person's problems. Thorough knowledge of the model is therefore crucial to understanding a client's problems, and in developing strategies to help. That is, CT for PTSD is far more than a collection of techniques. Cognitive models are sometimes construed as 'roadmaps'. The model, or map, may suggest many different starting points or routes to change – but it is not prescriptive about how one gets there, about the means of transport. Cognitive theory shows the way, while cognitive therapy uses all sorts of ways to get there, pragmatically encompassing a wide variety of helpful techniques, some of which overlap with, or are drawn from, different therapeutic traditions. The important point to bear in mind here is that therapists must have a thorough grounding in the principles and models of the disorder, as well as skills in implementing the various treatment components with young people, if they are to effectively help their young patients.

> CT for PTSD is based on a clear theoretical model which informs the intervention.

As with CBT in general, the therapeutic relationship in CT for PTSD is characterised by warmth, genuineness and accurate empathy. Maintaining high levels of empathy is crucial in carrying out PTSD work with young people, and therapists should be alert to the possibilities of either becoming overwhelmed by the intense nature of the traumatic material, or hardened to it over time. However, the therapeutic relationship in CT for PTSD goes beyond being empathic and supportive: it also characterised by being active, goal-oriented, highly collaborative, and by taking an empirical, scientific approach to problems. Collaboration starts at assessment. Here, the therapist and young person will agree joint goals which will give a clear direction in treatment. Collaboration continues when developing an individualised formulation and a treatment rationale which is shared with the young person, at a level appropriate to their development. During the treatment phase, a strong therapeutic alliance is nurtured. The stance taken is one of actively working together as a team towards agreed goals. A trusting relationship is needed. For example, as will be seen in later chapters, the young person's attempted solution in dealing with PTSD symptoms is often part of the problem, and young people must be able to trust their therapist if they are to drop these old unhelpful habits and test out new ways of responding to difficulties. 'Collaborative empiricism' in CT for PTSD refers to the scientific approach that is taken within sessions. That is, a problem is defined and relevant data are gathered (through self or parent report, or from questionnaires); hypotheses or predictions are made and then tested out in behavioural experiments or site visits; data are monitored and hypotheses are revised in the light of the new findings that have been discovered together. Empiricism and experimentation are emphasised throughout. Therapist and young client are working together as a scientific team, jointly discovering new information that will help to alter old unhelpful ways of thinking and behaving.

> CT for PTSD is based upon a therapeutic relationship which is empathic, supportive, goal oriented, and promotes collaborative empiricism.

Put this way, CT for PTSD can appear rather cold, level-headed and overly rational. But this sort of therapy, done well, is none of these things. First, children's level of felt or displayed emotion in sessions may be intense. Therapists are often working with very high affect, especially at the beginning of treatment. Although expression of strong feelings in itself is not necessarily an aim of therapy, the important point in CT for PTSD is that the all-important cognitions, so central to maintaining the disorder, are invariably associated with strong emotions: cognition and emotion go hand in hand. Second, CT for PTSD is active, energetic and at times fun for young people. It is characterised by discovering new information and learning new ways of responding and behaving, hopefully in a manner that is engaging and interesting. Of course it can be hard at times, but the overall attitude in CT for PTSD is a positive one, looking forward and opening up new possibilities for change.

Finally, there is also a strong education element to CT for PTSD with young people. This is apparent first of all in the initial emphasis on psychoeducation for children and parents about the nature of PTSD and its treatment. It comes to the fore in some of the behavioural experiments used to demonstrate the unintended consequences of suppressing thoughts and feelings. Education and new discoveries are of course part of the collaborative empiricism that is a theme throughout sessions. There is also some explicit skills learning for particular problems during the course of CT for

PTSD, as described in Chapter 5. Kendall (2006) has thus characterised the role of the therapist in CBT for young people as a coach/educator – someone who is supportive and encouraging, providing opportunities for the young client to try out new strategies, and giving feedback to help them develop new skills. The education element to CT for PTSD is explicit at the final session, where young people are helped to reflect on what they have learned during the course of therapy and to write out a 'blueprint for the future', an individualised relapse prevention plan, based on the new discoveries and skills they have learned during therapy.

> Psycho-education and learning through doing are core elements of CT for PTSD.

Developmental aspects to cognitive therapy for PTSD

The cognitive model of PTSD (Ehlers and Clark 2000) was developed with adults in mind, but has empirical support for children as young as seven years old (Bryant *et al.* 2007). Ongoing work (Meiser-Stedman *et al.* 2007) suggests that at least some aspects of the model may apply to even younger children. This research, and our clinical experience, shows that while the principles of the cognitive model do indeed apply to young children, the nature of the idiosyncratic misappraisals differ between adults and children. That is, subjective meaning seems to play a central role for children, as it does for adults, although the kinds of attributed meaning will be different. From an individual case consideration, Bolton (2005) is reassuring on this point. Rather than being concerned with general questions about the child's cognitive developmental level, the therapist needs instead to ask the question: 'What cognition is involved in the maintenance of the problem in this particular case?' If cognitions and appraisals are involved in the problem for a particular child, then they will need to be addressed; if not, then there is no need. The emphasis is firmly on the assessment of cognitive factors in individual cases.

A related question concerns the developmental level needed to engage in CT for PTSD (Stallard 2002). Reynolds and colleagues specified a number of cognitive abilities needed to engage in a typical CBT programme (such as the ability to distinguish between thoughts, feelings and behaviour; the capacity for logical thinking; memory abilities; a theory of mind). In a series of experiments they found that children as young as five years old show some abilities for many of these tasks (e.g. see Quakley *et al.* 2003, 2004; Doherr *et al.* 2005). They conclude that many young children could engage in cognitive therapy when given age-appropriate materials. The materials used in this CT for PTSD programme include handouts and leaflets, worksheets and diaries, and age-appropriate metaphors and experiments.

For very young children, the materials differ, with more use of play, drawing and cartoon strips to reconstruct trauma narratives. While the components of CT for PTSD are often very appealing to children and young people, clinical skill and experience are needed to engage young people and to adapt and implement these sorts of techniques successfully according to the child's developmental level.

> CT for PTSD can be used with children younger than seven years of age if appropriately tailored to the child's development.

A course of cognitive therapy for PTSD with young people

Following detailed assessment, a typical course of CT for PTSD with young people will last between 10 and 12 sessions. The first of these is a cognitive assessment, leading to a shared formulation and agreed treatment goals. The final session is a look towards the future, leading to an individualised written blueprint for relapse prevention. The intervening eight to ten sessions will comprise an individually customised treatment package combining some or all of the CT for PTSD components detailed in Chapter 5.

Sessions are generally held weekly. If less frequent, then some of the momentum in therapy is lost – new learning is not consolidated and new skills are forgotten. For this reason, appointments are scheduled well in advance and reminders given the day before. If appointments are missed, then it is helpful to double up appointments for the following week. Sessions vary in length, but are generally around 90 minutes. Longer sessions may be needed when carrying out imaginal reliving, especially in beginning sessions or when doing substantial work with parents.

> CT for PTSD typically involves 10 to 12 weekly sessions.

Each session begins with listing the topics to be covered (setting an agenda), usually followed by a brief check in with the child's symptoms and problems in the preceding week, referring to the Child PTSD Symptom Scale (CPSS) which the young person completes weekly. Homework review is done early in each session. Depending on the progress of homework, some tasks may be carried forward as new homework for the following week. The main topic for the session will fill most of the remainder of the time: this may be, for example, carrying out reliving or writing, continuing with cognitive restructuring, or designing behavioural experiments. In the spirit of collaborative empiricism described above, feedback from the young person is sought throughout. Towards the end of the session, it is useful to summarise what has been done, and some young people will like to write brief notes as a reminder. The session finishes by setting new homework tasks. These will have arisen naturally from the main topic of the session and will be agreed and set jointly with the young person at the end of the session. The diaries or worksheets that are needed for homework will be handed out, and the young person keeps a note of what they have planned to do before the next session.

Parents or carers will always be seen if available. The varied and important roles that parents and carers may play in CT for PTSD are described more fully in Chapter 5. These may range from supporting the child in attending therapy sessions or completing homework assignments, to being a more active collaborator in treatment (helping to reconstruct trauma narratives, for example), to engaging in separate treatment for themselves. Each CT session will follow a similar format and will typically involve:

- agenda setting
- symptom assessment
- homework review
- main session topic
- agreeing homework task(s).

2

PTSD in children and young people

Until relatively recently, it was believed that children were largely resilient to the psychological effects of exposure to trauma. However, research over the last 15 years or so has established that the effects of major stressors, such as encountered in disasters, war, or other life-threatening experiences, may be severe and long lasting. Post traumatic stress disorder (PTSD) is just one of a broad range of adverse outcomes. Other potential reactions include depression, other anxiety disorders, and prolonged grief.

Graham was involved in a boating accident just before his twelfth birthday. His father, sister and Graham were rescued after hanging on to the wreckage for several hours, but his younger brother was swept away and drowned. Prior to the accident, Graham was well adjusted and happy. He was seen in clinic four months after the accident. A detailed personal and family history was taken from his parents along with an account of the accident and Graham's subsequent behaviour.

Graham was seen later on his own. He said he did not know how to describe how low his mood was. Much of the time, he felt that life was not worth living and he had thought of ways of killing himself. He described how it took more than an hour to get off to sleep. He would lie in bed, not reading or listening to music, but thinking about how he and his brother used to be happy. Thoughts of his brother triggered a host of upsetting images of the accident.

On systematic questioning, Graham said that upsetting thoughts and pictures of the accident popped into his head every day. He had bad dreams every night. These woke him up and it then took him a long time to get back to sleep. Graham had occasional flashbacks in which he experienced the 'up and down' sensation of being in the water, he became cold and felt as if it were happening all over again. Graham felt that he could not do anything about the intrusive recollections, although he tried very hard not to think about the accident. He avoided talking about the accident and his reactions to it, but now felt emotionally cut off from close friends and family. He saw less of his friends and had lost interest in hobbies. Graham was much more aware of danger and got scared very easily – he felt jumpy and was snappy with others. He missed his brother and felt bad that he had not helped him more. Graham felt that he would never be happy again.

Graham's reactions to the dreadful accident are in many ways typical of those of children aged over eight years, although complicated by the grief he felt at the loss of his brother. Clinical experience, surveys and clinical descriptive studies show that children's reactions to life-threatening traumatic events are broad and diverse. However, characteristic post traumatic stress symptoms tend to cluster, roughly speaking, into three main groups: intrusive recollections, avoidance and emotional numbing, and physiological over-arousal.

> Post traumatic stress symptoms include intrusive trauma recollections, avoidance and increased arousal.

Intrusive recollections

Intrusive and distressing recollections of aspects of the traumatic event are the cardinal symptoms of post traumatic stress. Recollections may occur in any sensory modality, but visual images are most common. These may be snapshots (often of the worst moment or 'hotspot'), or moving images. Children may report auditory intrusions, such as the sound of screaming, or cars crashing, or gunshots. Olfactory intrusions are rare, but usually evoke intense emotion when they occur. Occasionally, children will report what have been called 'proprioceptive intrusions' – i.e. the sense that their body is moving in the same way that it did at the time of the event (as in the example of Graham above). Some children who sustained injury will re-experience physical pain when reminded of the trauma, despite there being no organic cause.

The language that children often use to describe these symptoms suggests that the subjective experience of intrusive recollections is quite different from that of deliberate recall of ordinary autobiographical memories. For example, children might talk of 'seeing' (rather than remembering) the event; or of 'hearing' the same sounds that were heard at the time of the event. That is, intrusive recollections have a strong here-and-now quality – visual images being particularly vivid and detailed. When asked directly, many children are able to describe this unusual (and frightening) quality to their trauma memories.

Intrusive recollections can occur at any time during the day. Sometimes, there may be very obvious reminders present. At other times, intrusions seem to pop into mind 'out of the blue', with no obvious external triggers. As described later, triggers are often very low level sensory cues which are difficult to spot. This can give rise to the subjective experience of out-of-the-blue intrusions. Children often report that they can keep intrusions at bay as long as they remain busy, but that upsetting recollections intrude into consciousness as soon as they relax, such as when trying to drop off to sleep.

When asleep, intrusive recollections may occur in the form of frightening vivid nightmares. Sometimes, these nightmares are straight replays of the event – with the child often waking up at the worst moment. Otherwise, dreams may be variations on what actually happened. The dream might be worse than the events that occurred in reality (for example, a child who survived a non-fatal car crash dreams that her parents were killed in the crash); or they may be events that the child wished had happened (for example, a teenager who was viciously assaulted by a gang of youths dreams that he fought back, rather than running away).

In contrast to other forms of intrusions, flashbacks appear to be less common in children. Some degree of dissociation – in which the young person feels that they have lost touch with their surroundings – occurs during flashbacks. Some care is needed in assessment here, because young people often use the word 'flashback' to report what we have described above as intrusive recollections. That is, direct enquiry about the extent of dissociation is usually needed in order to distinguish intrusions from true flashbacks.

Not all children will report intrusions, nightmares or flashbacks. Some children experience intense distress or strong bodily reactions in the face of traumatic reminders. This occurs, for example, when the young person has sustained a head injury which resulted in temporary loss of consciousness at the time of trauma. In this case, although no memory for the events after the loss of consciousness can have been laid down, the young person may show distress and physiological reactivity when encountering cues that were present before the loss of consciousness.

Very young children may not be able to report the sorts of symptoms described above. Instead, re-experiencing in the young child may be expressed in repetitive and trauma-thematic play. Parents of young children might report that trauma-related activities have increased since the trauma: a child who was involved in a car crash might play with his toy cars much more. Such play may not have the enjoyable, flexible, imaginative flavour that was present pre-trauma; it is instead characterised by being repetitive, sometimes with aggressive themes. For example, the child involved in a car crash may repeatedly smash his toys together, over and over again. This sort of play and drawing may be equivalent to intrusive recollections in older children. Alternatively, it might reflect an attempt by the child to better understand the event or to gain mastery over their recollections. Likewise, while vivid nightmares involving the theme of the trauma are common in children of all ages, younger children may experience an increase in dreams which are not about the traumatic event as such, but which are nonetheless frightening: dreams involving monsters, being chased, getting lost, or other threats to the self or loved ones. On waking from nightmares, young children may become panicky, run to their parents' bedroom and find it difficult to describe or recall what has been dreamt. Parents often find that they are unable to get the child back to bed and it is not unusual to learn from the parents that their traumatised child has not slept alone in months or even years.

> Intrusive recollections, nightmares and flashbacks are cardinal symptoms of post traumatic stress disorder.

Avoidance and emotional numbing

Unsurprisingly, many children try to cope with these upsetting intrusive recollections by pushing them out of mind, or by staying away from any trauma reminders or triggers. For example, children often report that they try hard to get rid of intrusive memories when they arise, or try to recall pleasant memories instead, or try to keep themselves busy in order not to recall the trauma. Children might also be very clear that they are fearful and avoidant of trauma reminders. Overprotective parents might shield children from reminders, or discourage discussion of the trauma. Some child survivors experience a pressure to talk about their experiences, but paradoxically find it very difficult to talk to parents and peers. Often, they do not want to upset the adults, and so parents may not be aware of the full extent of their child's suffering. Peers may hold back from asking what happened in case they upset the child further; the survivor often feels this as rejection.

When avoidant coping becomes ingrained or pervasive, children may lose interest in seeing friends, or in continuing with previously enjoyed activities or hobbies. Of course, changes in preferred playmates and activities are part of normal childhood development, and so care needs to be taken if symptoms are being assessed several months or years after the event. Older adolescents may feel that no one else can really understand what they have been through – they feel different to and cut off from peers to whom they were previously close. Survivors have learned that life is very fragile. This can lead to a loss of faith in the future, a sense of foreshortened future or a premature awareness of their own mortality.

> Children may try to avoid intrusive trauma memories, talking about the trauma, or events and activities associated with it.

Physiological over-arousal

The third symptom cluster concerns physiological hyperarousal. Arousal symptoms are common in traumatised children of all ages and quite straightforward to assess. Trauma survivors are usually very alert to danger in their environment and continually on the lookout – hypervigilant – for potential threat. Hypervigilance is sometimes evidenced by excessive checking of locks and doors, overprotectiveness of others and frequent reassurance seeking. Children may report feeling continually 'on edge', 'wound up' or 'jumpy' – for example, in response to loud noises. Many children are much more irritable and angry than previously, both with parents and peers. Increases in arguments are common and parents are often bewildered that previously easy and placid children are now snappy and overly sensitive. Difficulties in concentration may occur, especially in schoolwork. Children might experience memory problems at school, both in mastering new material and in remembering old skills such as reading music. Sleep disturbances are very common: fears of the dark and waking through the night are widespread. Not surprisingly, difficulties around bedtime are common in younger children. Parents of younger children often report an increase in somatic complaints such as headaches and stomach pains.

> Increased arousal may be demonstrated by hypervigilance, irritability, poor concentration and memory and sleep disturbance.

Diagnostic issues

Historically labelled as 'traumatic neurosis', 'railway spine' or 'shell shock', reactions approximating what we now call PTSD have been documented since before the beginning of the last century (Young 1997).

DSM-IV *criteria for PTSD*

In its current form, PTSD was first recognised as a distinct disorder in the third edition of the American Psychiatric Association's *Diagnostic and Statistical Manual (DSM-III)* in 1980, in response to the realisation that many young servicemen returning from the horrors of the Vietnam War were presenting with a syndrome that was proving very difficult to treat.

Initially it was thought that children would not present with such symptoms, but by the time of publication of *DSM-III-R* in 1987 it was recognised that some young people might do so. From the outset, a major problem for child mental health was that the PTSD diagnosis was developed as a result of working with adult patients. Twenty years ago, there were very few studies of the clinical presentation of child reactions to life-threatening events, or of the natural course that such reactions followed. Some of the symptoms identified in adults were therefore developmentally inappropriate for children, making it more difficult for children to reach criteria for a diagnosis. The fundamentals of the diagnosis remain the same in the latest revision to the *DSM* criteria (APA 1994), although it is now recognised that children may show different reactions at the time of exposure, and in the manner in which intrusive symptoms present (see Box 2.1).

Box 2.1 *DSM-IV* criteria for post traumatic stress disorder

A. The person has been exposed to a traumatic event in which both of the following have been present:

1   The person experienced, witnessed, or was confronted with an event or events that involved actual or threatened death or serious injury, or a threat to the physical integrity of self or others.

2   The person's response involved intense fear, helplessness, or horror. Note: In children, this may be expressed instead by disorganized or agitated behaviour.

B. The traumatic event is persistently re-experienced in one (or more) of the following ways:

1   Recurrent and intrusive distressing recollections of the event, including images, thoughts, or perceptions. Note: In young children, repetitive play may occur in which themes or aspects of the trauma are expressed.

2   Recurrent distressing dreams of the event. Note: In children, there may be frightening dreams without recognizable content.

3   Acting or feeling as if the traumatic event were recurring (includes a sense of reliving the experience, illusions, hallucinations, and dissociative flashback episodes, including those that occur upon awakening or when intoxicated). Note: In young children, trauma specific reenactment may occur.

4   Intense psychological distress at exposure to internal or external cues that symbolize or resemble an aspect of the traumatic event.

5   Physiological reactivity upon exposure to internal or external cues that symbolize or resemble an aspect of the traumatic event.

C. Persistent avoidance of stimuli associated with the trauma and numbing of general responsiveness (not present before the trauma), as indicated by three (or more) of the following:

1   Efforts to avoid thoughts, feelings, or conversations associated with the trauma.

2   Efforts to avoid activities, places, or people that arouse recollections of the trauma.

3   Inability to recall an important aspect of the trauma.

4   Markedly diminished interest or participation in significant activities.

5   Feelings of detachment or estrangement from others.

6   Restricted range of affect (e.g., unable to have loving feelings).

7   Sense of a foreshortened future (e.g., does not expect to have a career, marriage, children, or a normal life span).

D.   Persistent symptoms of increased arousal (not present before the trauma), as indicated by at least two of the following:

1   Difficulty falling or staying asleep.

2   Irritability or outbursts of anger.

3   Difficulty concentrating.

4   Hypervigilance.

5   Exaggerated startle response.

E.   Duration of the disturbance (symptoms in B, C, and D) is more than 1 month.

F.   The disturbance causes clinically significant distress or impairment in social, occupational, or other important areas of functioning.

Specify if:

Acute: If duration of symptoms is less than 3 months.

Chronic: If duration of symptoms is 3 months or more.

With delayed onset: Onset of symptoms at least 6 months after the stressor.

Of the three *DSM-IV* symptom clusters, it is Cluster C which remains the most adult oriented. Clinical experience suggests that many young people who present with cardinal intrusive symptoms, physiological over-arousal and clear impairment in functioning fail to reach the *DSM-IV* diagnostic threshold because they present with insufficient avoidance symptoms. This is especially true of very young children (discussed below).

PTSD as described by *DSM-IV* requires symptoms of trauma re-experiencing, avoidance and increased arousal.

The *DSM-IV* criteria for PTSD require that symptoms have been present for at least a month. This was based on the finding that although in the first few weeks after a traumatic event the majority of adults might manifest a large number of distressing symptoms, many of these initial reactions would resolve within four weeks. However, this meant that the clinical presentation of people with significant and impairing traumatic stress reactions in the first month post trauma could not be characterised within the *DSM* framework. A new diagnosis, acute stress disorder (ASD), was therefore included in *DSM-IV*.

In addition to dropping the requirement for a post-trauma latency of four weeks, the ASD diagnosis differs in a number of important ways from the PTSD diagnosis. The core symptom clusters of intrusion, avoidance and arousal are retained, but the number of symptoms required in each cluster is fewer in ASD. In addition, a diagnosis of ASD also requires the presence of dissociative symptoms, such as numbing, reduced awareness, derealisation, depersonalisation and dissociative amnesia.

Among adults, ASD appears to be a good predictor of later PTSD (Harvey and Bryant 1998). However, the emphasis on dissociation in ASD has been called into question. Although adults with ASD are indeed more likely to go on to develop later PTSD, the early dissociative responses seem to add very little to the predictive utility of the diagnosis (Harvey and Bryant 2002). Early PTSD symptoms predict later PTSD symptoms just as efficiently as an ASD diagnosis (Brewin *et al.* 2003).

Recent evidence suggests that the same may be true of children. Prospective longitudinal studies have shown that those children who present in the first few weeks with many PTSD symptoms are indeed those who are more likely to go on to develop chronic PTSD. However, just as with adults, the additional requirement of having dissociative symptoms does nothing to improve the diagnostic prediction (Kassam-Adams *et al.* 2004; Meiser-Stedman *et al.* 2005, 2007). Given these empirical findings, the diagnosis of acute stress disorder may well be radically altered in *DSM-V* (due for publication in 2012).

> Acute stress disorder (ASD) defines significant traumatic stress reactions during the first four weeks post trauma.

ICD-10 *World Health Organization criteria for PTSD*

The World Health Organization's official system for diagnosis of psychiatric disorders is contained in the tenth revision of the *International Classification of Disease (ICD-10)* (WHO 1991). The procedure for making diagnostic decisions using the *ICD* differs from the clear algorithm approach in the *DSM*. Under *ICD*, the clinician is required to compare and match the presentation of the patient with a clinical exemplar. While the symptoms of PTSD in both classification systems are broadly similar, the emphasis in *ICD-10* is on intrusive and distressing recollections as cardinal symptoms; avoidance and emotional numbing are seen as less important. This means that the threshold for diagnosis in children is lower under *ICD-10* (see Box 2.2).

Box 2.2 *ICD-10* criteria for post traumatic stress disorder

Arises as a delayed or protracted response to a stressful event or situation (of either brief or long duration) of an exceptionally threatening or catastrophic nature, which is likely to cause pervasive distress in almost anyone (e.g. natural or man-made disaster, combat, serious accident, witnessing violent death of others, or being the victim of torture, terrorism, rape, or other crime).

Predisposing factors such as personality traits (e.g. compulsive, asthenic) or previous history of neurotic illness may lower the threshold for the development of the syndrome or aggravate its course, but they are neither necessary nor sufficient to explain its occurrence.

Typical features include episodes of repeated reliving of the trauma in intrusive memories ('flashbacks'), or dreams, occurring against the persisting background of a sense of 'numbness' and emotional blunting, detachment from other people, unresponsiveness to surroundings, anhedonia, and avoidance of activities and situations reminiscent of the trauma. Commonly, there is fear and avoidance of cues that remind the sufferer of the original trauma. Rarely, there may be dramatic acute bursts of fear, panic, or aggression, triggered by stimuli arousing a sudden recollection and/or re-enactment of the trauma or of the original reaction to it.

There is usually a state of autonomic hyperarousal with hypervigilance, an enhanced startle reaction, and insomnia. Anxiety and depression are commonly associated with the above symptoms and signs, and suicidal ideation is not infrequent. Excessive use of alcohol or drugs may be a complicating factor.

The onset follows the trauma with a latency period that may range from a few weeks to months (but rarely exceeds 6 months). The course is fluctuating but recovery can be expected in the majority of cases. In a small proportion of cases the condition may follow a chronic course over many years, with eventual transition to an enduring personality change.

This disorder should not generally be diagnosed unless there is evidence that it arose within 6 months of a traumatic event of exceptional severity. A 'probable' diagnosis might still be possible if the delay between the event and the onset was longer than 6 months, provided that the clinical manifestations are typical and no alternative identification of the disorder is plausible. In addition to evidence of trauma, there must also be a repetitive intrusive recollection or re-enactment of the event in memories, daytime imagery, or dreams. Conspicuous emotional detachment, numbing of feeling, and avoidance of stimuli that might arouse recollection of the trauma are often present, but are not essential for diagnosis. The autonomic disturbances, mood disorder, and behavioural abnormalities all contribute to the diagnosis, but are not of prime importance.

Similarly, the *ICD* is less prescriptive about the length of time since trauma that is required before a diagnosis can be made. Whereas under *DSM* four weeks must have elapsed since the trauma before a diagnosis can be considered, *ICD* notes that 'the latency period may range from a few weeks to months'. This means that there is not a separate ASD diagnosis for the initial four weeks post trauma in *ICD-10*.

ICD-10 diagnostic criteria are less prescriptive than those in *DSM-IV*, and there is less emphasis on symptoms of avoidance. The threshold for diagnosis is therefore lower under *ICD-10* than in *DSM-IV*.

Diagnostic issues in young children

Most of the studies on PTSD in children have been undertaken with children of seven or eight years and older, and far less is known about the manifestation of stress reactions in younger children. Indeed, the manifestation of traumatic stress reactions in children under the age of two (with limited language) presents particular challenges to clinicians. Two recent reviews have examined the impact of development on the presentation of reactions to trauma (Meiser-Stedman 2002; Salmon and Bryant 2002). These reviews address in some detail how language development, cognitive capacity in memory encoding and retrieving and family influences play important roles in young children's adjustment to trauma. But this still leaves the vexed question of when and how to diagnose PTSD in pre-school children, given that developmentally they simply do not show the sorts of symptoms expressed by adolescents and adults. One possible solution has been proposed by Michael Scheeringa and colleagues (1995, 2001, 2003, 2006). This group has developed and evaluated an alternative algorithm for diagnosing PTSD in pre-school children (PTSD-AA), based on parent report of observations of children's behaviour (see Box 2.3).

Box 2.3 Scheeringa *et al.* (1995, 2003)

Alternative criteria for diagnosing PTSD in very young children

A.   The person has been exposed to a traumatic event in which he or she experienced, witnessed, or was confronted with an event or events that involved actual or threatened death or serious injury, or a threat to the physical integrity of self or others.

B.   The traumatic event is persistently re-experienced in one (or more) of the following ways:

   1   Recurrent and intrusive recollections of the event (but not necessarily distressing), including images, thoughts, or perceptions. Note: In young children, repetitive play may occur in which themes or aspects of the trauma are expressed.

   2   Recurrent distressing dreams of the event. Note: In children, there may be frightening dreams without recognizable content.

   3   Objective behavioural manifestations of a flashback are observed but the individual may not be able to verbalize the content of the experience.

   4   Intense psychological distress at exposure to internal or external cues that symbolize or resemble an aspect of the traumatic event.

C.   Persistent avoidance of stimuli associated with the trauma and numbing of general responsiveness (not present before the trauma), as indicated by one (or more) of the following:

   1   Efforts to avoid activities, places, or people that arouse recollections of the trauma.

   2   Markedly diminished interest or participation in significant activities.

> Note: In young children, this is mainly observed as constriction of play.
>
> 3   Feelings of detachment or estrangement from others. Note: In young children, this is mainly observed as social withdrawal.
>
> 4   Restricted range of affect (e.g., unable to have loving feelings).
>
> 5   Loss of previously acquired developmental skills such as toileting and speech.
>
> D.   Persistent symptoms of increased arousal (not present before the trauma), as indicated by one (or more) of the following:
>
> 1   Difficulty falling or staying asleep.
>
> 2   Irritability or outbursts of anger, or extreme temper tantrums and fussiness.
>
> 3   Difficulty concentrating.
>
> 4   Hypervigilance.
>
> 5   Exaggerated startle response.
>
> E.   New cluster: one (or more) of the following:
>
> 1   New separation anxiety.
>
> 2   New onset of aggression.
>
> 3   New fears without obvious link to the trauma, such as fear of going to the bathroom alone, fear of the dark.

Under Scheeringa *et al.*'s PTSD-AA criteria, the requirement for distress or agitation at the time of trauma exposure is dropped; the number of symptoms for each cluster is reduced to one (i.e. the requirement for at least three symptoms of avoidance, often problematic in child PTSD, is abandoned); and an additional set of symptoms including new separation anxiety, new fears and new aggression is added.

Research with pre-school (sometimes pre-verbal) children presents considerable challenges, but carefully conducted studies from Scheeringa's group (1995, 2001, 2003, 2006) and others (Ohmi *et al.* 2002; Meiser-Stedman 2008) suggest that the PTSD-AA criteria are a sensitive, reliable and valid means of diagnosing very young children's traumatic stress responses.

Research in this area is at a very early stage, and it can be expected that the PTSD-AA criteria will be further revised in the light of new empirical findings. Nevertheless, at this stage, the PTSD-AA criteria provide a practical framework for clinicians working with very young children.

> Developmentally appropriate criteria for assessing trauma reactions in very young children are being evaluated.

Multiple exposure

Effects on presentation

The case of Graham cited earlier illustrates many of the reactions that can follow from a horrendous, single trauma. However, many children experience multiple traumatic events. In many cases, it may seem difficult to know which to concentrate on, both in assessment and in treatment. When the trauma involves physical or sexual abuse, it is important for the clinician to remember that the circumstances of the trauma are very different from those surrounding a one-off accident, assault or disaster. In the latter cases, while the child may have contributed a little to the lead-up to the event, in the case of child abuse the assaults are secretive, usually repeated, involve a major breach of trust between adult and child and frequently involve threats if the child discloses what has happened to anyone else. Thus, the reactions are inevitably going to be more complex, but it has still proved very helpful to construe those reactions within a PTSD framework as this has led to very effective interventions (Ramchandani and Jones 2003; Cohen *et al.* 2004).

Among child refugees and asylum seekers, it is almost the norm to find young people who have experienced multiple traumatic events. They and their families may have been harassed or tortured in their original homes. The child may have witnessed the murder of a parent or the rape of a relative. The whole family may have fled seeking asylum. The journey to a country of safety may have been both hazardous and dangerous. At times a young person arrives as an unaccompanied minor. They may not know where they have come to. Their expectations of reaching a place of safety may be shattered when the immigration authorities do not believe their claims. Waiting for a decision on the right to remain in the country is stressful in the extreme. Thus, refugees present a major challenge to any therapist trying to help them with their stress reactions. Fortunately, there is emerging evidence that adapting CT for PTSD can be helpful, as can using narrative exposure therapy (Schauer *et al.* 2005), a CBT technique that focuses on autobiographical memories.

> The nature and extent of traumatic experiences need careful assessment.

Prevalence of trauma and PTSD

There have been just a handful of epidemiological investigations of PTSD in children and young people; most have been of older adolescents. A key early community study of young urban Americans found a lifetime prevalence of

6 per cent by the age of 18 (Giaconia *et al.* 1995), somewhat lower than the 8 per cent lifetime prevalence reported for young adults in a large representative cohort study (Kessler *et al.* 1995). However, much lower rates have been reported more recently. A recent UK report, the *National Survey of Mental Health* (Meltzer *et al.* 2003) found a point prevalence of 0.4 per cent among 11 to 15-year-olds. In line with this, Copeland *et al.* (2007), in a very large, representative, multi-cohort, multi-informant study of 9 to 16-year-olds (the Great Smoky Mountain Study) reported a lifetime prevalence of 0.4 per cent, and a three-month prevalence of 0.1 per cent. These authors suggest that the developmental insensitivity of the *DSM-IV* diagnostic criteria (as discussed above) might account in part for these much lower rates. Future community-based studies will help to clarify the issue, but for now it seems likely that at any one point in time up to 1 per cent of children are likely to be suffering from PTSD (National Institute for Clinical Excellence 2005).

However, it is already clear that lifetime rates of PTSD among children and adolescents, even at the top end of the range of prevalence estimates above, are far lower than rates of children's exposure to traumatic stressors. Giaconia *et al.* (1995) reported that nearly half of her sample of 18-year-old Americans had been exposed to trauma. In the Great Smoky Mountain Study, more than two-thirds of young people had experienced at least one traumatic event by the age of 16 years (Copeland *et al.* 2007). It is also worth noting that traumatic events are not randomly distributed in the child population. Costello *et al.* (2002) showed that traumatic events (such as accidents, violence, rape) clustered together with lower magnitude stressors (such as parental separation or divorce) and vulnerability factors (such as family poverty, parental psychopathology). This clustering of stressors – traumatic or otherwise – is an important point to bear in mind when carrying out initial assessments with young people.

Taken together, epidemiological studies show that rates of PTSD in young people are far lower than rates of trauma exposure. In other words, at a community level, most children exposed to trauma do not develop PTSD. This implies that trauma exposure alone is insufficient to explain the development of PTSD.

> Estimates vary, but at any one time, up to 1 per cent of children will fulfil criteria for PTSD.

Incidence and course

This finding is borne out in carefully conducted studies of incidence (new cases) in trauma-exposed young people. Incidence rates vary widely depending on assessment methods and time elapsed since the event, as well as on the nature of the event. For example, following road traffic accidents, rates of 15 to 25 per cent are reported (Stallard *et al.* 2004; Meiser-Stedman *et al.* 2005), while rates of around 12 per cent have been reported for children exposed to interpersonal violence (Giaconia *et al.* 1995; Kilpatrick *et al.* 2003). Studies of the mental health of child refugees from war-torn countries find a much higher incidence of 63 per cent (e.g. Kinzie *et al.* 2006). PTSD in children has also been documented following large-scale disasters such as earthquakes, floods, hurricanes and terrorist attacks (Green *et al.* 1991; Pynoos *et al.* 1993; Vernberg *et al.* 1996; Pfefferbaum *et al.* 2004; Giannopoulou *et al.* 2006), with incidence raging from 10 per cent to 80 per cent. Overall, around 14 per cent of children who have been exposed to a range of traumatic events are likely to meet criteria for PTSD (Giaconia *et al.* 1995; Copeland *et al.* 2007).

> The incidence of PTSD varies depending on the type of trauma.

Of those who develop PTSD in the initial months post trauma, a proportion will recover without treatment. For example, when assessed a fortnight after attending hospital, almost 25 per cent of young people (aged 10 to 18) who had been assaulted or involved in traffic accidents met criteria for PTSD (except the one-month duration criterion). Six months later, although none of the young people had received treatment, this figure had halved to 12 per cent (Meiser-Stedman *et al.* 2005). These findings mirror those from studies of adults exposed to trauma, with the most substantial natural recovery occurring in the first six months.

Although many young people will recover spontaneously, PTSD can last for many years in a significant minority of children, if left untreated. Yule and colleagues (2000) assessed a group of over 200 teenagers who had been involved in a shipping accident (the sinking of the cruise ship *Jupiter*) at between five and eight years post trauma. Around half of the teenagers developed PTSD. Five years on, a third of those who had developed the disorder continued to meet diagnostic criteria. A very long-term 33-year follow-up of child survivors of the Aberfan disaster (in which a coal heap collapsed on to a primary school, killing 116 children) showed that PTSD can persist for decades, into adulthood, for a significant minority of trauma-exposed children (Morgan *et al.* 2003).

Cognitive models of PTSD

A number of cognitive models have been proposed to explain the clinical characteristics of PTSD, and to account for why some individuals develop chronic problems while others appear resilient. These include models based on: network theory (e.g. Foa *et al.* 1989); schema theory (e.g. Janoff-Bulman 1985; Horowitz 1997); dual representation theory (Brewin *et al.* 1996;

Brewin 2001); and appraisal processes and theories of memory (Ehlers and Clark 2000). Although developed to explain PTSD in adults, some of these models have been adapted for use with children (discussed in Meiser-Stedman 2002; Salmon and Bryant 2002).

The treatment described in this book is based on Ehlers and Clark's (2000) cognitive model of PTSD and treatment programme (e.g. Clark and Ehlers 2004; Ehlers *et al.* 2005), adapted for use with children and young people. This model seeks to explain how a sense of serious current threat persists in people with PTSD, despite the traumatic event having happened in the past. Two factors are proposed. The first concerns individual differences in the nature of the trauma memory representation. The second concerns individual differences in appraisal processes relating to the traumatic event and its sequelae. While these factors serve to generate a sense of current threat, the use of unhelpful coping strategies – often characterised by behavioural and cognitive avoidance – have the unintended consequence of maintaining PTSD. This model is illustrated in Figure 2.1 and explained in more detail below.

Nature of the trauma memory

A striking feature in PTSD is the frequent *involuntary* re-experiencing of intrusive memories, alongside poor *intentional* recall of the trauma which is characterised by disjointedness, missing details and a muddled temporal sequence. Ehlers and Clark (2000) propose that trauma memories in individuals with persistent PTSD are poorly elaborated and inadequately integrated into an autobiographical memory knowledge base. That is, trauma memories lack contextual (time, place, subsequent and previous information) and abstracted (event type, personal time period, related autobiographical themes) information. Furthermore, trauma memories in PTSD are heavily laden with sensory detail, and characterised by strong stimulus–stimulus and stimulus–response links (i.e. strong associative learning), with strong perceptual priming (i.e. a reduced perceptual threshold) for trauma-related stimuli. This poor elaboration of trauma memories helps to explain the poor intentional recall of traumatic material, the weak inhibition of cue-driven retrieval, and the sense of 'nowness' accompanying such unwanted memories. Strong associative learning and a reduced perceptual threshold further help to explain the easy triggering of unwanted memories by physically similar or temporally associated cues. The implication for treatment is that the trauma memory needs to be better elaborated and the matching sensory cues better discriminated if intrusions are to be reduced (Ehlers *et al.* 2003).

Persistent PTSD is associated with a poorly elaborated and integrated trauma memory, and a reduced perceptual threshold for trauma-related stimuli.

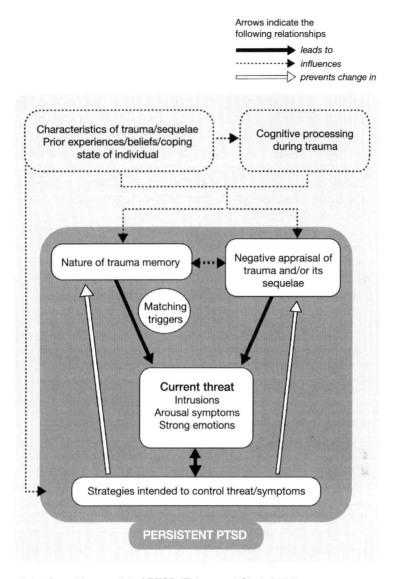

Figure 2.1 Cognitive model of PTSD (Ehlers and Clark 2000)

Idiosyncratic appraisals

Central to Ehlers and Clark's (2000) cognitive model of PTSD is the role of idiosyncratic appraisals (regarding the trauma and/or its sequelae) in generating a sense of serious current threat. First, in relation to the trauma itself, misappraisals may take the form of over-generalisation of danger (e.g. an overestimate of the likely reoccurrence of a similar traumatic event, and/or an appraisal of normal activities as being more dangerous than they are). Mistaken beliefs about the causes of the trauma may lead to a sense of inflated responsibility and excessive guilt. Individuals may negatively evaluate the way they reacted during the trauma, leading to negative beliefs about their competence and feelings of shame. Second, in relation to trauma sequelae, it is common for individuals with persistent PTSD to misappraise the meaning of PTSD symptoms. For example, individuals may believe the presence of distressing symptoms indicates that they are going crazy, that they cannot cope, that they are weak or that they have been permanently damaged. If there are physical effects of the trauma such as scarring, then individuals may believe that other people notice the scars and judge them negatively as a consequence. Survivors may negatively appraise other people's reactions in the aftermath of the trauma – for example, evaluating the perceived uncaring manner of emergency medical staff as evidence that one is worthless.

The disjointed nature of intentional recall in PTSD can mean that it is difficult for individuals to access these problematic meanings associated with the worst parts of the trauma by just talking about it. Likewise, the disrupted temporal sequence in intentional recall can also contribute to misappraisals such as over-inflated responsibility.

> Appraisals regarding the trauma and its sequelae (such as trauma-related symptoms and people's reactions) contribute to the maintenance of a sense of current threat.

Unhelpful coping strategies

Frequent PTSD symptoms and idiosyncratic misappraisals contribute to generating a sense of serious current threat, which motivates a range of coping strategies. Typical coping strategies in individuals with persistent PTSD tend to be characterised by behavioural and cognitive avoidance. This may take a number of forms: pushing thoughts and memories out of mind, trying not to think about the event and staying away from trauma reminders. Other common efforts at coping include repeatedly scanning for danger in the environment (hypervigilance), safety behaviours such as taking excessive precautions, and ruminating about the event and its consequences. Ehlers and Clark (2000) note that such strategies may be either intentional or habitual; that they make sense to the individual (i.e. they are meaningfully linked to appraisals and beliefs); and that they may provide short-term symptom relief. Importantly, however, they have a number of unintended consequences which can maintain PTSD: they directly produce PTSD symptoms; they prevent changes to problematic appraisals; and they prevent changes to the nature of the trauma memory. For example, a trauma survivor who believes that his vivid intrusive recollections mean that he is going crazy may attempt to suppress the intrusions. This has the unintended effect of increasing the frequency of intrusions, which in turn reinforces his belief that he must be going crazy, leading to further attempts at suppression, and so on.

> Unhelpful coping strategies include behavioural and cognitive avoidance which prevent cognitive processing of the traumatic event.

Cognitive models and children

There is now good evidence to support Ehlers and Clark's (2000) cognitive model in explaining the variety of reactions to exposure to trauma among adults, and more recently with children and young people. Meiser-Stedman (2002) and Salmon and Bryant (2002) have discussed in detail how the application of adult cognitive models to children must take into account developmental factors (such as language abilities, memory encoding and retrieval, and emotion regulation) and family factors (such as parental symptomatology and coping style).

There is some evidence that trauma severity (e.g. Pynoos *et al.* 1993; Giannopolou *et al.* 2006), trauma type (Copeland *et al.* 2007), pre-trauma history (Udwin *et al.* 2000) and gender (Copeland *et al.* 2007) are associated with risk of developing chronic PTSD in children. However, these personal vulnerability factors and objective trauma severity indicators explain only a modest proportion of the variability in children's reactions after trauma. In other words, knowledge of these factors would only go so far in helping to predict which individuals go on to develop chronic PTSD (see Ozer *et al.* 2003). Even if these factors are (modestly) helpful in screening for risk of developing PTSD, more important from a treatment point of view is to identify maintaining factors that may be modified or reversed.

More recent work has therefore attempted to test whether theoretically derived cognitive factors play a role in maintaining children's PTSD. Broadly, this work has examined whether the three factors specified by the adult cognitive model (memory quality, negative appraisals and unhelpful coping strategies), as well as the family factors highlighted by Salmon and Bryant (2002), predict chronic PTSD in children and young people.

First, there is emerging evidence that trauma memory quality is related to PTSD symptoms in children. In a prospective study of 93 children (aged 10 to 16 years) who had attended hospital accident and emergency departments following assaults or road traffic accidents, Meiser-Stedman *et al.* (2007) found that, as predicted by the cognitive model, the presence of more sensory-based memories was related both to symptoms of acute stress disorder (ASD) at two to four weeks post trauma and to the severity of later PTSD symptoms at six months post trauma. The nature of the child's trauma memory in these studies was assessed via a new questionnaire, the Trauma Memory Quality Questionnaire (TMQQ, Meiser-Stedman *et al.*

2007), which contains items referring to visual quality, a variety of non-visual sensory qualities (e.g. auditory, olfactory, proprioceptive sensations), temporal context, and the extent to which the memory is in a verbally accessible format. This work requires replication (e.g. see Stallard and Smith 2007 for negative findings) and extension to younger samples, but appears promising.

Second, there is now a growing body of work from a number of research groups that shows that idiosyncratic misappraisals of the sort specified by cognitive models do indeed play an important role in the maintenance of PTSD in children. For example, Salmon *et al.* (2007) found that misappraisals measured by the Child Post Traumatic Cognitions Inventory (CPTCI, Meiser-Stedman *et al.* 2009) accounted for 44 per cent of the variance in ASD symptoms among 7 to 13-year-old children who had been hospitalised after traumatic injury. When this group of children was followed up at six months post trauma, the majority of the variance in PTSD symptom severity was accounted for by negative appraisals about future harm (Bryant *et al.* 2007). Similarly, Stallard and Smith (2007) found that in young (7–18 years old) survivors of traffic accidents assessed at eight months post accident, misappraisals relating to subjective threat and negative interpretation of symptoms accounted for 60 per cent of the variance in symptom severity. Consistent findings have also been reported by Ehlers *et al.* (2003) and Meiser-Stedman *et al.* (2007) in two prospective studies. The extent to which these kinds of misappraisals play a role in children younger than about seven years is not known, but it is now clear that among 7 to 18-year-olds, misappraisals are highly significant in the maintenance of PTSD symptoms. Importantly for theory-driven treatment, Smith *et al.* (2007) found that changes to these cognitive misappraisals during CT for childhood PTSD mediated the effect of treatment.

Third, with regard to unhelpful coping strategies, there is evidence from retrospective (Udwin *et al.* 2000) and prospective studies of children (Stallard 2003; Meiser-Stedman *et al.* 2009) that cognitive and behavioural avoidance and thought control strategies such as rumination and thought suppression serve to maintain PTSD symptoms.

Fourth, family factors in childhood PTSD have received relatively little attention to date. Available evidence suggests that maternal symptoms of PTSD and depression are related to child PTSD symptoms across a variety of settings and populations (e.g. Wolmer *et al.* 2000; Smith *et al.* 2001; Meiser-Stedman *et al.* 2006). General family functioning and atmosphere (characterised by 'irritable distress') has also been found to relate to children's PTSD symptoms (McFarlane 1987), but this finding requires replication. The mechanisms by which PTSD is maintained within a family are not well understood. One possibility is that children and carers negatively reinforce each other for avoiding discussion of or exposure to reminders of the trauma. That is, parents and children may get locked into cycles of avoidance, each maintaining the other's maladaptive coping. Meiser-Stedman and colleagues (2006) found that parental endorsement of worry as a helpful strategy appeared to mediate the relationship between maternal depression and child PTSD. Further research is needed, but evidence to date implies that psychopathology and cognitive styles within the family play a significant role in maintaining children's PTSD.

> There is growing evidence for the important role of cognitive variables in PTSD in children.

Treatment targets

Ehlers and Clark's (2000) cognitive model of PTSD, adapted for young people, provides clear treatment targets. CT for PTSD focuses on these targets, which will differ from case to case, but are likely to include one or more of the following:

- to reduce memory disjointedness and help the child to build a coherent narrative of the traumatic event
- to identify and modify unhelpful misappraisals of the trauma and reactions to it
- to identify and change maladaptive cognitive and behavioural avoidance and other unhelpful coping strategies
- to recruit carers as co-therapists and to alter counterproductive patterns of interactions between child and carer about the event.

Treatment overview

The treatment programme described later in this book is based on Ehlers and colleagues' cognitive therapy programme for adults with PTSD (Ehlers and Clark 2000; Ehlers *et al.* 2003a, 2003b, 2005, in press; Clark and Ehlers 2004), suitably adapted for children and teenagers.

The current treatment shares many intervention components with other forms of trauma-focused CBT for children (e.g. Cohen *et al.* 2002, 2006; Scheeringa *et al.* 2007), which have been evaluated in rigorous controlled trials (e.g. Stein *et al.* 2003; Cohen *et al.* 2004). Overlapping components contained in most approaches include:

- psycho-education and normalisation of PTSD symptoms and treatment
- some form of behavioural activation in the early stages of treatment
- imaginal and in vivo exposure to the trauma memory and reminders
- working with parents and carers
- relapse prevention work.

Following Ehlers' treatment programme (see Ehlers *et al.* in press for an up-to-date and comprehensive description of her trauma-focused cognitive therapy for adults with PTSD), the current treatment places relatively more emphasis on:

- identifying and changing unhelpful trauma-related cognitions
- updating trauma memories through close integration of cognitive work with imaginal reliving/narrative writing
- stimulus discrimination techniques for working with traumatic reminders and intrusions
- dropping unhelpful behavioural and cognitive 'coping strategies'
- revisiting the site of the trauma to help update the trauma memory and to help discriminate between 'then' and 'now'.

The approach described here also places relatively less emphasis on general anxiety management techniques such as relaxation training, certainly for older children and adolescents. Nevertheless, this particular form of CT for PTSD builds on previous work and has more similarities than differences with other forms of CBT for PTSD.

3

Assessment

As should be clear from the preceding chapter, post traumatic stress disorder (PTSD) is not the only outcome of exposure to trauma in children and adolescents. Nevertheless, there is ample evidence that the three symptom clusters of intrusion, avoidance and hyperarousal are the most common reaction in children and adolescents, regardless of trauma type, severity or duration (Perrin *et al.* 2004). Further evidence in support of a careful PTSD post-trauma assessment comes from two important findings. First, the presence of PTSD significantly increases the risk of additional disorders over time, but these additional disorders tend to remit as the PTSD resolves (Bolton *et al.* 2004). Second, in controlled trials of cognitive behaviour therapy (CBT) targeted at PTSD, co-morbid symptoms of anxiety and depression also improve even though such symptoms are not targeted directly (Smith *et al.* 2007; see also Stallard 2006). This is not to say that clinicians should ignore the assessment or treatment of co-morbid conditions. However, it suggests that detailed assessment and treatment of PTSD symptoms is likely to have significant beneficial effects beyond PTSD itself. Issues relating to the timing of assessment and treatment are discussed later in Chapter 8. As an overview, the initial assessment will involve:

- a joint parent and child meeting to describe the interview process
- completion of standardised, self-report measures
- separate parent and child interviews
- a joint parent and child meeting to feedback and arrange for further assessment if necessary.

The aims of this first assessment are:

- to establish rapport and an empathic environment
- to gain an understanding of the child's pre-trauma functioning

- to gather child and parent accounts of the traumatic event(s) and the immediate aftermath
- to carry out a detailed assessment of PTSD symptoms over the past week
- to begin to normalise the child's and parents' reactions to the trauma.

Tools for assessing PTSD and related reactions

Structured diagnostic interviews for PTSD

Most practice guidelines recommend using a structured interview as part of the assessment as they improve accuracy at both the symptom and diagnostic level. These interviews take symptoms from *DSM-IV* (American Psychiatric Association 1994), and less often *ICD-10* (World Health Organization 1992) and place them in the form of questions to be asked by a clinician trained in the use of the interview. Most interviews include screening questions that allow the interviewer to move on to another disorder if the child or parent does not report affirmatively to the screen. The benefits of using such interviews need to be weighed against purchase costs, training requirements and the additional time they take to administer. For reviews of the various structured diagnostic interviews and self-report measures that cover childhood PTSD, see McNally (1991), Nader (1995) or March (1998).

Anxiety Disorders Interview Schedule (Silverman and Albano 1996)

The Anxiety Disorders Interview Schedule (ADIS-C/P, Silverman and Albano 1996) includes parent and child report modules for each *DSM-IV* anxiety disorder, plus modules for other internalising and externalising disorders. The PTSD modules take about half an hour each to complete. If the child or parent reports symptoms of another disorder (e.g. depression), the relevant module in the ADIS-C/P can be used to assess that condition. It is often unnecessary to go through the whole ADIS-C/P; more typical is the assessment of two or three disorders including PTSD. The aim is to establish the presence of symptoms/disorders that are currently causing marked impairment in functioning.

PTSD Semi-structured Interview for Infants and Young Children (Scheeringa et al. 1995)

For children aged four and younger, the Post Traumatic Stress Disorder Semi-structured Interview and Observational Record for Infants and Young Children (0–48 Months) (Scheeringa *et al.* 1995) can be used. This clinician-administered interview assesses both the *DSM-IV* criteria for PTSD and the alternative criteria developed by Scheeringa *et al.* (1995), described in detail in Chapter 2. In the main, assessment will be carried out via interviews with the parents. In respect of the intrusion criteria that are additional to the

DSM-IV, assessment will focus on the child's play. This includes: post traumatic play which represents part of the trauma, is repetitive, less imaginative and elaborate than regular play, and which fails to relieve anxiety; and play re-enactment which represents part of the trauma. In addition, Scheeringa *et al.* (1995) suggest assessment of: constriction of regular play; social withdrawal; loss of acquired developmental skills (especially language regression and toilet training); night terrors; difficulty going to sleep (which is not related to being afraid of having nightmares or a fear of the dark); night waking (not related to nightmares or night terrors); new aggression; new separation anxiety; and new fears of stimuli not obviously related to the trauma.

With a few questionnaires and a firm grasp of the *DSM-IV*, *ICD-10* and Scheeringa criteria for young children, clinicians may be able to assess PTSD accurately without a diagnostic interview schedule. However, it is recommended that the *DSM*, *ICD* or Scheeringa diagnostic criteria are kept close to hand, and that both parents and child are asked about each and every symptom. Clinicians may also find it helpful to keep a copy of the symptom criteria for conditions that often present alongside PTSD, including separation anxiety disorder, major depression and traumatic grief.

> Structured interviews are available for diagnostic assessment of PTSD.

Self-report measures

There are numerous well-validated self-report measures available for assessing post traumatic reactions in children and adults. It is beyond the scope of this book to discuss them all here (see Nader *et al.* 1994), but a selection is described below.

A fairly brief battery of self-report questionnaires for parents and children is recommended. For children with a reading age of about eight years and above, we administer either the Children's Revised Impact of Event Scale (CRIES-13, Children and War Foundation 1999) or the Child PTSD Symptom Scale (CPSS, Foa *et al.* 2001); the Spence Children's Anxiety Scale (SCAS, Spence 1997); and the Depression Self-Rating Scale (DSRS, Birleson 1981). For children younger than eight years old, we ask the parents to complete the Paediatric Emotional Distress Scale (PEDS, Saylor *et al.* 1999). Parents are given a very similar battery of questionnaires to complete about themselves, including the adult versions of the CPSS (see Foa *et al.* 1993) and the Hospital Anxiety and Depression Scale (HADS, Zigmund and Snaith 1983).

Child PTSD Symptoms Scale (CPSS, Foa et al. 2001)

The CPSS was specifically designed to assess each of the 17 PTSD symptoms described in *DSM-IV*. It is made up of 23 items, the first 17 items assessing PTSD and the last six addressing impairment arising from the symptoms (see Appendix A). For the first 17 items, the child is asked to rate how frequently the symptom occurred over the past week on a four-point scale (0, 1, 2, 3). For the impairment items, the child is simply asked to circle a Yes or No for six areas of potential disruption: pleasurable activities; relationships with peers and family; school; chores; and general happiness.

The CPSS is very easy to score. None of the items is reversed. The total score is the sum of 1–17 items, ranging from 0 to 51. A total score of 12 or more suggests PTSD symptoms in the clinical range (Foa *et al.* 2001). The six impairment items are not scored as such, but are used to help the clinician gauge the degree of impairment over the previous week.

The CPSS may be administered to children of around eight years old through to 18. Whatever the young person's age, it is recommended that clinicians test out children's understanding by having them read one or two items aloud and ticking the appropriate box. The CPSS takes a few minutes to complete and can be readministered throughout treatment at the beginning of each session.

Children's Revised Impact of Event Scale (CRIES, Perrin et al. 2005)

The CRIES-13 was derived from the 15-item Impact of Event Scale (IES, Horowitz *et al.* 1979). The IES was developed for use with adults prior to the introduction of the PTSD criteria into *DSM*. It was never designed to map specifically on to the *DSM* criteria. Nevertheless, the IES measures the core symptoms of intrusion and avoidance and is perhaps the most widely used self-report measure of PTSD in the world.

Yule (1998) modified the language and content of the original IES to make it easier to use with children. The 15 items were reduced to eight items covering intrusion and avoidance. An additional five items on hyper-arousal were added so that the measure overlaps more with the diagnostic criteria (Smith *et al.* 2003). Additional information on the development and validation of the measure is available in Perrin *et al.* (2005) and via the Children and War Foundation website (www.childrenandwar.org).

On the CRIES-13, the child is asked to rate the frequency of 13 symptoms during the past week on a four-point scale (0, 1, 3, 5). No items are reversed. The total score is obtained by summing all 13 items (range 0–65). In general, higher total scores indicate a higher frequency of PTSD symptoms (and distress) during the past week. Unlike the CPSS, however, subscale scores are important to interpreting the measure. A score ⩾17 on the eight items of the Intrusion and Arousal Subscales combined indicates a greater than 80 per cent chance that the child would meet criteria for a PTSD diagnosis if so interviewed (Perrin *et al.* 2005).

The CRIES-13 can be used with children from about eight years old through to 18 and takes only a few minutes to complete. Again, it is recommended that the child reads one or two items aloud and ticks the appropriate box to check that they understand the measure.

- The Child PTSD Symptom Scale (CPSS) assesses each of the PTSD symptoms described in *DSM-IV*.
- The Children's Revised Impact of Event Scale (CRIES-13) is a child version of the widely used Impact of Event Scale (IES).

Paediatric Emotional Distress Scale (PEDS, Saylor et al. 1999)

For children under eight years of age, the PEDS (Saylor *et al.* 1999) can be administered to parents. The PEDS is a 21-item parent-report rating scale. It includes 17 general behaviour items and four trauma-specific items. The PEDS has been shown to distinguish children exposed to a traumatic event from non-exposed controls. The parent is asked to rate the frequency of 21 symptoms on a four-point scale. Higher scores indicate greater behavioural problems and distress, with a total score of >27 indicating problems in the clinical range (Saylor *et al.* 1999).

Self-report measures for parents

Finally, it is important to recognise that parents of traumatised children are very often experiencing post-traumatic reactions of their own. Their reactions may be of sufficient severity to warrant separate treatment, and may influence the nature and timing of the child's treatment. It is recommended that self-report measures of PTSD, trauma-related cognitions and depression are completed by parents. There are numerous adult measures available for assessing PTSD and depression, including the PTSD Symptom Scale (PDS, Foa *et al.* 1993) and the Hospital Anxiety and Depression Scale (HADS, Zigmund and Snaith 1983).

Assessment process

The assessment of PTSD can be an anxiety-provoking experience and needs to be conducted with sensitivity and respect for the child and family, both in terms of the family's current emotional state and the developmental/verbal abilities of the child. Prior to the first appointment, the family may be contacted by phone to inform them about the nature of the assessment. It is helpful to enquire about any medical, police or school records that may provide details of the event, injuries sustained or school functioning and ask parents to bring these to the assessment.

Separate interviews of the child and parents are advisable because parents and children will sometimes try to 'protect' each other from painful, shameful or embarrassing material. The child may be reluctant to disclose the full extent of their symptoms in order to appear brave in front of the parents. Likewise the parent may be reluctant to disclose all symptoms in front of their child so as not to embarrass them. Sometimes during joint interviews, parents send subtle (and not so subtle) signals that the information the child is providing is factually incorrect, embarrassing or simply too upsetting for them. These cues can sometimes inhibit the child from giving full and accurate responses.

> Children and carers should be interviewed separately.

It is reasonable to assume that both the child and the parents arrive for the assessment with a good deal of anticipatory anxiety or negative beliefs about the assessment process itself. For example, children sometimes report after the interview that they were surprised because they thought they were going to be told they were crazy or were going to be forced to talk about the trauma. Occasionally children will be harbouring the belief that they might have to remain at the hospital after the assessment or will be subjected to a physical examination. Anticipatory anxiety and beliefs about the assessment will depend to some extent on age, previous experiences with health professionals and whatever the parents have told them. Regardless of the child's age, the clinician should assume that anticipatory anxiety and misconceptions about the assessment process are present and deal with them in a straightforward manner at the start of the assessment.

It is worth mentioning what form anticipatory anxiety can take for parents. Again, when asked, parents will sometimes report that they thought the interview would involve them being blamed for their child's reaction or that they would be told they needed to 'move on' from the trauma, leaving them feeling embarrassed or ashamed. It is not uncommon for parents to worry that they are wasting clinicians' time with their concerns – time that could have been given to families with more serious difficulties. Perhaps the most common fear that parents express is that the assessment will confirm something is profoundly wrong with their child.

With these issues in mind, initially it is helpful to meet the family together in order to reduce anxiety about the assessment process itself. First, it can be explained what the interview is (and is not) about, and what it will involve. It can be made explicit that although the child is being seen in a hospital clinic, no injections or physical examinations will be carried out. It is made clear that the assessment will only involve talking – and that children can talk as much or as little as they want to. It is explained that the trauma need not be described in great detail and that the child will go home with their parents after the interview.

Second, it is made explicit that the people seen at the clinic are not 'crazy'. Children and families are told that people who come to the clinic have had something very scary happen and as a result may find it hard to do things they used to enjoy:

'We see kids here every day that had something really scary happen to them. It could be a road traffic accident, a fire in their home, a mugging, or maybe they saw someone get really hurt. All of these kids find it hard to talk about these things and all of them tell us they feel a bit anxious or sad. There is nothing crazy about that. Everybody feels scared when something really scary happens to them.'

At this point, it can be helpful to give a very brief example of what another child has been through and what they said bothered them afterwards. This can model disclosure for both the parents and child and give them an idea about what is to follow.

Third, the clinician explains that they would like to interview the parents and child separately and then meet together again at the end. The child can be offered the choice of going first or second. Whoever is not being interviewed completes questionnaires while they sit in the waiting room. If the child will separate but appears apprehensive about doing so, the clinician can explain that it is perfectly understandable if they need to check up on their mum or dad at any point during the assessment. If the child is too scared or too young to sit in the waiting room on their own, then one of the parents can wait with them and help them with their questionnaires (if necessary). If the child is accompanied by only one parent or will not separate, both parent and child can be seen together. In such cases, the child may be asked to fill out questionnaires while background information is obtained from the parent.

- At the start of the meeting, the clinician should say what will happen, and whom they will talk to.
- Common misconceptions that children or parents may have about the assessment can be dispelled.

If the child is willing to separate and has no preference for order of interview, then it is generally helpful to interview the parents first. In such cases, it is helpful to go through a few items on the child questionnaires to check the child's comprehension, before escorting them to the waiting room.

The parents are then interviewed about family and developmental history, the trauma and its immediate aftermath, and any current difficulties. Using the Anxiety Disorders Interview Schedule or Scheeringa Interview (see above), this is followed by a more structured set of queries about their child in respect of the PTSD symptoms or symptoms of any other condition that might be present from the parents' description of the child's current functioning (e.g. separation anxiety disorder, obsessive compulsive disorder, phobias, depression, etc.). Having formally assessed the parents' view of the child's current symptoms, this is a good time to ask how the parents are doing. Diagnostic assessment of the parent is not required at this stage, but it is recommended that a brief screen for PTSD and depression is completed. This may precipitate a conversation about whether the parents want a separate referral for treatment. It is not unusual for the parents to say that they want to focus on their child for the present. When necessary the clinician may recommend a referral be made because of the time it will take for them to be seen, indicating that they can always decline the offer of an appointment later. Parents are then asked to complete questionnaires in the waiting room while the child is seen alone.

> If the child expresses no preference, it is advisable to interview parents first.

Once the child has returned to the interview room, the clinician briefly re-explains why the child is here, checks how the child got on with the questionnaires and helps them to complete any missed items. It is then helpful to start with some general warm-up questions about school, interests and favourite activities.

Once some rapport has been established, the child can be asked about the trauma itself. In a calm and supportive way, ask the child if they are now ready to tell you what happened, from the beginning until the end, giving as much or as little detail as they want to. For younger children, it is helpful to have paper, pens and crayons to hand and ask them to draw what happened. Many children are often quite relieved to be able to tell what happened in this way, and the clinician can give plenty of praise and encouragement. This is usually a suitable moment to inquire about symptoms of PTSD, using the Anxiety Disorders Interview Schedule (see above).

For children who are reluctant to talk, the clinician might enquire about their fears of what would happen if they did talk about it right now. It can help to try to normalise these fears by giving an example of another child's experiences of talking about the trauma with a stranger for the first time. Alternatively, the child can be asked to listen to the clinician's account of the trauma and contribute further details or correct any mistakes. If the child is insistent about not talking about the trauma, then move on. This type of avoidance is symptomatic of PTSD and can be addressed after the treatment itself has been explained in a later session.

After completing the interview with the child, the parents will be brought back for feedback and discussion. It is important to check with the child how much of what they have reported may be disclosed to parents. On occasion, children may prefer not to be present at this feedback meeting.

> During the interview with the child, try to gain a general understanding of the trauma.

At the end of the assessment with all family members present (if possible), ask the family about their experience of the assessment. It is not uncommon for families to report that they feel a bit better already having talked about what happened. The clinician can then comment on how helpful and brave the child has been in talking about such difficult issues. Parents can be reassured that bringing their child to the clinic is an indication of just how much they care about their child. The symptoms reported are then briefly summarised, and if appropriate labelled as PTSD – a common, well-understood and treatable reaction to having been involved in a traumatic event. For example, the family may be told that the reactions they are experiencing are similar to those of other trauma-exposed families.

When carried out along these lines, an initial interview in which the trauma is discussed in a clear, direct, sensitive and empathic manner can be enormously helpful for parents and children alike as a first step towards overcoming their difficulties.

- The initial assessment interview ends by praising the child and their family's attendance and contributions.
- The clinician remains supportive and optimistic and identifies any symptoms as understandable and treatable.

Making the PTSD diagnosis

The information gathered from the child and parent interviews and any questionnaires administered is combined to arrive at a best-guess estimate of the child's current symptom profile. In general it is easier to reach the criteria for PTSD under the *ICD-10* criteria than it is under *DSM-IV*. The *ICD-10* criteria (see Chapter 2) describe the occurrence of similar symptom clusters (intrusions, avoidance and hyperarousal), but do not require the same number of symptoms to be present as in *DSM-IV*. For a PTSD diagnosis to be made under *DSM-IV*, the trauma must be followed by the development of six or more symptoms that have been present for at least one month. Of the six *DSM-IV* PTSD symptoms required, at least one must come from the re-experiencing category (Criterion B), three from the avoidance/numbing category (Criterion C), and two from the persistent hyperarousal category (Criterion D).

Unsurprisingly, parents are often quite unaware of intrusion symptoms, unless their child is having overtly disturbing nightmares. Children, on the other hand, are readily able to describe intrusions and nightmares – but will rarely do so unprompted. Questions such as 'Do you think about [the event] when you don't want to?' or 'Do you have upsetting pictures about [the event] pop into your mind?' will be readily understood by children. It is helpful to listen for language that indicates the presence of intrusive recollections which have a 'here and now' quality. For example, some children will report that they 'see' the event in front of their eyes, or 'hear' the sounds associated with it. When asking about the content of intrusions, remember that intrusions are often associated with worst moments or hotspots. A fine-grained analysis of the content and quality of intrusive recollections can help in distinguishing them from depressive ruminations or anxious worries – although, of course, both are often present.

> Intrusive recollections are rarely volunteered and should be directly asked about by the clinician.

If intrusions are present, then cognitive avoidance (efforts at suppressing thoughts and images) is very likely. However, children and parents will sometimes downplay behavioural avoidance of external reminders of the trauma. This might be because the family insists on talking about the trauma, or the parents do not permit the child to avoid (e.g. they are not allowed to avoid cars after a road traffic accident), or because avoidance seems impossible (e.g. the trauma happened in or very near the home). Most PTSD experts would agree that a child's wishes or efforts to avoid traumatic reminders, even if they are not permitted or able to do so, is evidence of avoidance. It is also suggested that the clinician query the child and parents about the use of 'safety-seeking behaviours' in trauma-related situations the child is not permitted to avoid, such as holding on tightly to the parent's hand when walking near the scene of the trauma.

> The child's desire to avoid trauma reminders should be assessed.

Children and parents are also able to respond to questions about marked decreases in interest or participation in significant enquiries (e.g. 'After a really scary thing happens, some kids will say that they don't feel like going to school, playing or spending time with friends. Is that true for you? Are you playing and spending time with friends as much as before? Why not?'), although of course it is a normal part of development for children and adolescents to drop what had seemed to be favourite activities. On an everyday basis the disruption or contraction of behaviour may translate into the child no longer sleeping, reading, playing, or going out of the house on their own, or no longer sleeping at friends' houses or going on school trips. Some children will continue to remain as active as before the trauma but may do so only with a good deal of encouragement and without their normal sense of enthusiasm.

However, the remaining avoidance and numbing symptoms listed under *DSM-IV* Criterion C can be very difficult to detect in children because they are developmentally less appropriate. For example, the child (and clinician) usually has no way of knowing whether the child is unable to recall important aspects of the trauma; they simply have their recollections of the event. There is rarely a separate, definitive account of the trauma available against which the clinician can judge the child's recollections. Teenagers may feel misunderstood by adults and peers, but it can be helpful to ask questions along the lines of 'After a really scary thing happens, some kids will say that everybody treats them different. Some will say that nobody really understands them anymore. Is this true for you? Can you give me some examples of how things have changed between you and your friends or family?'

Children and teenagers often have no idea about what they will do later in life, so assessing a sense of a foreshortened future is difficult. It can therefore be helpful to ask questions such as 'After a really scary thing happens, some kids will say that when they think of the future, they can only imagine bad things happening or they draw a complete blank. What do you think about when you think about the future? How far ahead do you look? Can you tell me what bad things you think might happen? How was it before the trauma?'

Emotional numbing (termed 'restricted range of affect' in *DSM-IV*) is apparent in some teenagers, but rare in children. It is helpful to ask 'After a really scary thing happens, some kids will say that they feel scared [angry, sad] all of the time. It's like there is no room for any other feelings. Is this true for you?'

> Concrete questions are helpful to assess symptoms of avoidance and emotional numbing.

In contrast to avoidance symptoms, it is not difficult to gather evidence of persistent hyperarousal as outlined in Criterion D. Children and parents can usually report whether the child is having sleep or concentration difficulties, or is more irritable or hypervigilant since the trauma. Exaggerated startle is the exception. If you ask any parent or child, almost all of them will say that they 'jump' when they hear a loud or unexpected noise. Such startle reactions are completely normal. Exaggerated startle is about the quality and duration of the startle response. Ask the child and parent if it feels like the child has become more reactive to loud or sudden noises since the trauma. Ask if the child finds it more difficult to calm down after being startled than before the trauma. Most people without PTSD will say that they calm down within seconds of having been startled. For a person with PTSD, that startle response can last several minutes and in extreme cases they may say that being startled 'ruined' their whole day.

When it comes to very young children (i.e. four years or younger), relying solely upon the *DSM* or *ICD* criteria for PTSD as the basis for diagnosis may mean that clinically significant post-traumatic reactions worthy of treatment are missed (Scheeringa *et al.* 1995). The Scheeringa PTSD criteria require only four symptoms in addition to the experience of a traumatic event, whereas *DSM-IV* requires at least six symptoms plus distress at the time of the trauma and evidence of impairment. The four symptoms required under the Scheeringa criteria include the alternative symptoms mentioned above, whereas the requirement for impairment in social, occupational or other important areas of functioning is dropped.

If assessing the child within one month of the trauma and they report several symptoms of PTSD, then the appropriate *DSM-IV* diagnoses to consider are either acute stress disorder or an adjustment disorder. The symptom criteria for acute stress disorder overlap with those of PTSD but also include symptoms of dissociation (see Chapter 2).

Core areas to cover in interviews with children and carers

Developmental history

Diagnostic decisions based on detailed and structured symptomatic assessment as above are made in the context of a thorough developmental, personal and social history. In addition to pre-trauma problems that might influence the course of treatment (such as physical, learning, behavioural or social difficulties), it is helpful to ask about the range of activities that are particular to this child (sports, reading, playing alone or with friends, going out, school attainment, etc.). That is, an assessment of pre-trauma functioning is necessary to gauge the extent of impact of trauma exposure.

Account of the traumatic event

When getting an account of the trauma, it is important to try to ascertain the events leading up to and immediately following the trauma. It is helpful to try to get as detailed an account possible of the whole story – that is, the family's recollections of what happened in the hours before the trauma, during the event and the days afterwards. Secondary exposure to traumas or severe stressors is not uncommon. For example, frightening experiences when trying to leave the scene of the trauma, the reactions of bystanders, riding in an ambulance or police car, physical examinations and police interviews, hospital stays, telling extended family members what happened and the first night at home after the trauma are all important to assess. It is not unusual for clinicians to wonder whether getting an account of the details of the trauma in the first assessment is necessary at all as it elicits strong affect. Clearly, one needs to be guided by clinical judgement. However, it is important to realise that reviewing details of the traumatic event often helps to identify key meanings (associated with memory 'hotspots') that would not otherwise be evident. Accessing such meanings can greatly facilitate treatment planning.

Common co-morbidity

In addition to a thorough developmental history, an account of the traumatic event and detailed assessment of PTSD symptoms, it is also advisable to screen both the child and the parents for depression, bereavement reactions and other anxiety disorders.

Anxiety reactions

Additional anxiety difficulties may present as non-trauma-related worries about harm. When worries about a range of normal everyday issues (school, health, family finances) are experienced as frequent or difficult to control and accompanied by physiological symptoms, then assessment for generalised anxiety disorder may be warranted. Alternatively, the worries may be more narrowly defined, of extremely low probability or of an unusual nature. For example, the child may worry about kidnappings, home invasions, fires in the home, terrorist attacks, or the parents dying or abandoning the child. Such worries might suggest the presence of separation anxiety disorder. In some cases, the child may develop obsessional worries about severe harm or death arising from extremely unlikely situations (e.g. deadly contamination from everyday objects; causing the death of a loved one with thoughts, simple mistakes or not doing things in the proper order). Compulsive rituals meant to prevent negative outcomes may accompany such worries and as such a diagnosis of obsessive compulsive disorder needs to be considered. Perhaps most common are specific, situationally dependent, excessive fears (e.g. the dark, public transportation or lifts, animals or medical procedures). Such specific phobias are common in the general population but can sometimes be exacerbated or triggered by a traumatic event. If the fear is about a situation unrelated to the trauma and is causing significant impairment, a separate diagnosis of specific phobia may be warranted.

Bereavement reactions

When traumatic events involve the loss of a loved one, the child may develop both PTSD and a traumatic or complicated bereavement reaction. When there has been a loss, it is important to ask both child and parent about how the loss was initially dealt with and how it continues to affect the child now. Ask about the funeral, final arrangements (burial/cremation), whether pictures of the deceased are still on display, visiting the cemetery, and whether it is all right to talk about the deceased. It is not unusual for children (and parents) to say that they are 'visited' by the deceased and to find such visitations disturbing. If asked, some children (and parents) will admit that they are deeply afraid of forgetting the deceased. This fear can drive the child to avoid potentially pleasant activities because feeling happy is equivocated with forgetting or not loving the deceased anymore. Some children (and parents) will view their normal grief reaction as evidence that they will never be able to be happy again, or indeed are losing control of their mind. Evidence that the child has difficulty expressing their grief, or shows misappraisals about what their grief reaction says about them, or feels excessively guilty, may indicate the presence of a complicated bereavement reaction. Dealing with complicated bereavement reactions will be addressed in a later chapter.

Depression

There are considerable similarities between the *DSM-IV* criteria for PTSD and those for major depression. It is beyond the scope of this chapter to disentangle the biological, psychological and methodological reasons why there is so much co-morbidity between PTSD and major depression (see Chapter 9). Nevertheless, it is unlikely that the high rate of co-morbidity between PTSD and depression is due solely to symptom overlap. One possible explanation for the co-morbidity is that the PTSD symptoms cause a constriction in the child's behaviours, and thus a significant loss of individual and social sources of enjoyment and support. This behavioural constriction can take the form of active avoidance of traumatic reminders, devoting all of one's attention to identifying dangers or suppressing traumatic images, or ruminating excessively about the effects of the trauma. It is also possible that depression arises from deeply held negative beliefs which developed in the aftermath of the trauma (e.g. 'the trauma was my fault . . . everything I do has been negatively affected by the trauma . . . I will never be the same again'). The clinician should anticipate there being some depressive aspect to the presentation of a child with PTSD.

> The presence of co-morbid conditions such as anxiety disorders,
> complex bereavement reactions and depression needs
> to be assessed.

Potential hurdles to undertaking a good assessment

If assessments are well planned and conducted with sufficient time, then they usually go smoothly. However, some hurdles to undertaking a good assessment can be anticipated.

1   If the child is reluctant to separate – reassure them that this happens sometimes and that you are comfortable with proceeding together with the parents present. Ask the child to complete the questionnaire while you chat first to the parents. Sensitivity is needed as you can be certain the child is listening in even if they are filling out questionnaires. You

need not be dissuaded from asking the parents to describe the trauma while the child is in the room. This will provide you with an opportunity to directly observe the child's and parents' anxiety while the parents try to describe the trauma. If the child is reluctant to answer questions, ask them if they can whisper the answers in their parent's ear or just point to a piece of paper where you have written in large black letters 'Yes', 'No', 'Sometimes', 'I don't know'. Do have them fill out any questionnaires and try to review their responses – even if by a head nod. In certain cases you may simply have to abandon the child portion of the interview and try again in another session.

> If children are reluctant to separate, continue the assessment with the parents present.

2 Sometimes parents will make statements of a critical or catastrophic nature about their child in their presence; for example, 'He's just not the same anymore. It's like he's brain damaged. He just can't do anything anymore except drive me crazy.' There is no way to predict when these statements will be made, or to guard against them. Whether the child is present or not, it is not suggested that such statements are tackled directly during the assessment. Parents will already be feeling bad about not having protected their child from the trauma, or not having helped their child to cope in the aftermath of the event. A useful way of dealing with these statements is to quickly reframe them in a sensitive but non-judgemental way: 'That's just what many parents tell us when we first see them. They really notice big changes in their child and they worry these changes are permanent. As hard as it is to believe right now, these changes are part of a normal stress reaction, and your child will get back to where they were with a bit of help from you and us.'

> Positively reframe carers' negative or catastrophic comments.

3 Sometimes during an assessment where both the child and parent are present, either the parents or the child will become extremely upset. On the one hand, the clinician needs to demonstrate to the family their confidence in dealing with intense emotional reactions and their ability to look after the upset individual. On the other hand, they need to be careful about further probing because extreme parental reactions may be upsetting for the child. In general, when either the child or parent becomes extremely upset, try to normalise their reactions (e.g. 'I think you really needed a good cry there. Most people we see do. It helps to get

feelings out in the open. It is really a sign of recovery for you to express your feelings that way.').

Very rarely, either the child or the parents might continue to cry inconsolably. Under such circumstances, it may help to have a quick break. Try to have a quick chat with the upset individual separately and see how they would like to proceed. Often the break gives the parent or child enough time to collect themselves and you can proceed with the interview as planned. Try not to let the family leave the assessment in a high state of upset and without having had some time to reflect on the normality of their response and their existing coping strategies.

> **Normalise distress as an understandable reaction.**

4 Sometimes the discussion of the trauma is so upsetting for parents that it can feel as if the assessment is parent-focused rather than child-focused. That's okay. Assessments do not have to be completed in the initial meeting. If the parents are really upset and bring their own symptoms to the fore, screen for PTSD and depression in a formal but supportive way. Normalise their reactions and discuss with them the possibility of a separate referral for assessment and treatment. Let carers know that it is helpful to focus on their needs for now, and that the child's functioning may be fully assessed in a later session.

While it may be apparent that a parent is suffering from PTSD or related problems, parents may not want treatment for themselves because they prefer to focus on their child's needs. Clinicians sometimes find it difficult to know what to do in such circumstances, believing that the child cannot get better as long as the parent is suffering the same condition. In fact it is possible to help a child overcome anxiety, PTSD and depression through individual CBT even when the parent has similar conditions that are untreated and do not change during the child's treatment. Some parents may experience a reduction in their own symptoms as a function of their child's improvement in individual CBT. Understanding their child's treatment and seeing them get better may be a powerful prompt to use similar coping strategies, and it may destigmatise the whole process of seeking help themselves.

> **Parents' or carers' psychological problems need to be noted and appropriate guidance and help suggested.**

Summary

By the end of the assessment, the clinician will have a list of all the child's current symptoms (PTSD and otherwise) and their frequency over the past week. The same information about parents may have been obtained. As will be seen in the next chapter, the symptoms experienced by the child (and to some extent by the parents) will be used to start developing the formulation and plan intervention.

It is important to note that the decision to treat the child is not based solely on whether they meet the minimum symptom requirement in *ICD-10*, *DSM-IV* or under the Scheeringa alternative criteria: the presence of sub-diagnostic threshold symptoms can be sufficiently debilitating to warrant treatment.

A significant percentage of children with PTSD will have one or both parents with either the same condition or another mental health disorder, but the decision to treat the child should not be based on whether the parent(s) are getting help for PTSD or another condition.

When carried out thoroughly and skilfully, the assessment process – while perhaps daunting initially for many children and families – can be a very powerful means of engaging families and explaining and normalising their reactions. Assessment is itself therapeutic for many and sets the scene for the treatment that follows.

4

Case formulation and treatment planning

Having established that post traumatic stress disorder (PTSD) is the primary disorder in need of treatment, the next step is to carry out further detailed assessment in order to help to plan treatment. This is essentially a cognitive conceptualisation or formulation. Whereas the first assessment session, as described in Chapter 3, concerned symptoms and functioning (leading, when appropriate, to diagnosis), this session focuses on assessment of maintaining factors, leading to a treatment rationale and plan. The cognitive model described in Chapter 2 specified four potential maintaining factors in childhood PTSD:

- a disjointed trauma memory with lowered sensory threshold for triggering of intrusions
- unhelpful appraisals of the trauma and subsequent symptoms
- dysfunctional avoidant coping strategies
- parental reactions.

A key task of this session is to begin to discover which of those factors are operating for this particular young person. This will point towards appropriate individualised treatment targets. Once idiosyncratic maintaining factors are specified in detail, then a customised course of treatment which aims to reverse them can be implemented.

Case formulation is at the heart of cognitive behaviour therapy (CBT) approaches for adults (Dudley and Kuyken 2006) and children alike (Friedberg and McClure 2002). It is the bridge between general theory and individualised treatment. In the context of CT for PTSD with young people, formulation is a way of making sense of this particular young person's problems, within the overarching cognitive theoretical framework described earlier. While it is important to gather as much information as possible in this initial session, formulation is inevitably a process that will continue throughout therapy. For example, as the clinician monitors the effect of therapeutic interventions, they may need to revise their hypotheses about what is keeping the problem going and implement alternative or additional techniques accordingly. Equally, the nature of PTSD in young people is such that some key maintaining factors – peri-traumatic appraisals, for example – may not be recognised until the young person has fully accessed his or her trauma memory in subsequent sessions. Formulation is an ongoing process that blends into the active treatment components described later.

It is useful to spend at least a full initial session on detailed cognitive assessment, leading to a provisional formulation and treatment plan. This in turn can help the process of socialising the young person (and carers) to the cognitive model and provide a treatment rationale. Traumatic stress reactions can be normalised and clear goals set for treatment. These tasks are described in detail below and illustrated with a case example.

> Case formulations provide a way of conceptualising the child's problems within a cognitive framework.

Formulation

Narrative account of the trauma

Obtaining an account of the traumatic event from the young person will help in gauging two possible maintaining factors: the disjointed nature of the memory; and peri-traumatic misappraisals, usually associated with emotional hotspots in the trauma memory. The clinician may recently have heard the child's account of what happened if they carried out the diagnostic assessment. Alternatively, the initial diagnostic assessment may have been carried out by a colleague, or some time may have passed since first assessment. Whichever is the case, it will still help to ask the young person to tell again what happened, perhaps with more detail than was given initially. Bear in mind that the purpose is to obtain an overview of what happened while beginning to assess thoughts and feelings at the time. This is not intended as an 'imaginal reliving' (described in Chapter 5), so the account is provided in the past tense. At this stage, the clinician does not want to raise the emotional temperature too quickly because this may be counterproductive for young people who have yet to be socialised into the model. In this early session, attention to developing rapport and ensuring that the child feels safe must take precedence.

After checking in with the young person that they know why they have come to see the clinician again today, it will help to enquire how they have been since the previous assessment, and to give them some time to warm up by discussing non-trauma-related topics such as friends, family and school.

Next, the clinician might remind and praise the young person for having talked about the trauma previously, and say that they would like to hear about it again so that they can understand it better. The young person can choose to tell the clinician as much or as little as they want to. The stance taken is to be clear and straightforward, but at the same time expressing obvious empathy. Depending on how willing the child is, they may need more or less prompting or encouragement.

Some children will give quite detailed accounts. This may allow the clinician to judge the degree of disjointedness in the trauma memory: listen carefully for skipped or hurried parts, or for events that appear out of sequence. A useful rule of thumb is that if the clinician finds the account muddled or confusing, then there is likely to be some disjointedness to the memory. Equally, some children may spontaneously mention what they were thinking at the time (such as 'I thought I was . . . going to die . . . never walk again . . . see my mum again . . . to blame for what happened'). For those who do not, the clinician can prompt for appraisals by asking children if they remember what they were thinking at the time, or what was going through their mind. If possible (bearing in mind the caveats about rapport and engagement taking precedence over assessment), ask what the worst part of the event was – and then probe sensitively for associated thoughts and feelings.

> The aim is to begin to 'map out' the young person's trauma memory, including details of emotional hotspots, associated appraisals and degree of disjointedness.

Symptom review

Although assessment for diagnosis will already have been completed, the clinician may not have carried out a detailed assessment of symptoms. The aim here is to assess the nature of the most troubling symptoms, their triggers, associated cognitions and affect, and how the young person copes with them. This enables further assessment of possible maintaining factors such as the sensory-based nature of the trauma of the memory, and the appraisals associated with intrusions. It also orients the young person towards attending to and working on cardinal symptoms (rather than automatically avoiding them).

It may help to review the Child PTSD Symptom Scale (CPSS, see Chapter 3), which the young person will complete before each session. The clinician can ask directly about PTSD symptoms, particularly intrusions:

- What is the worst problem?
- Can the young person describe the image in detail?
- When does it occur?

- How often?
- What triggers the intrusive memories?
- What thoughts and feelings accompany intrusions?

The clinician may need to spend some time helping the young person to slow down in order to reflect in detail on his or her symptoms. This process can help to build a therapeutic alliance, along the lines of the collaborative scientific teamwork approach mentioned earlier. As the young person reveals further details of current distressing symptoms, the clinician can begin to label and normalise them (see below).

> At the end of this section, the clinician will have a detailed account of triggers, the content and quality of intrusive memories, and associated peri-traumatic appraisals

Beliefs and appraisals

Following from the symptom review, it is important to begin to assess beliefs – both about the meaning of these distressing symptoms (e.g. 'Something is wrong with me, I am weak.'), and about the trauma itself (e.g. 'It was my fault. Something bad is going to happen.'). For children of eight years and older, the Child Post Traumatic Cognitions Inventory (CPTCI, Meiser-Stedman *et al.* 2009; see Appendix A) is helpful. This is an adaptation of the Post Traumatic Cognitions Inventory for adults (Foa *et al.* 1999). It measures the level of agreement with 25 trauma and symptom-related appraisals. For each item the child is asked to rate their level of agreement on a four-point scale: *Don't agree at all* = 0; *Don't agree a bit* = 1; *Agree a bit* = 2; *Agree a lot* = 3. The scores for the 25 items are summed, with higher scores indicating unhelpful beliefs about permanent negative change and about being a fragile person in a scary world. The young person may be asked to complete the CPTCI beforehand and to review it in the session; or it can be completed in the session. The aim is to assess in detail the sorts of beliefs or appraisals about symptoms and the traumatic event that are likely to be maintaining symptoms, and thus become a target for change.

Children who are too young to complete standardised measures such as the CPTCI may be able to report key cognitions if interviewed sensitively. Young children's misappraisals often tend to concern harm to self and others (including an over-generalised sense that caregivers might get hurt), and perceived blame from others ('Dad was angry, Mum told me off', etc.). It is important to elicit such thoughts early on. Sometimes, such muddles might be clarified quite simply and quickly by carers of young children. If this is not possible, then misappraisals are likely to become a focus of treatment later on.

> Beliefs and appraisals about the trauma and symptoms
> should be elicited.

Current coping

Following again from the symptom review, it is important to know how the child has tried to cope with such symptoms. Have they worked out ways of dealing with intrusive images for example? What do they do to relax? To whom do they talk? Is there someone whom they can trust and confide in? The clinician will want to ensure that any avoidance or any other strategies that may be maintaining the problem are identified here. To identify the widest range of avoidance and safety behaviours, it will help to refer to the list of triggers that were discussed in the symptom review. Simply go through the list asking what (and how) the child does to avoid these triggers – or what they would do if they suddenly encountered one of them. Be certain to ask about a wide range of physical, sensory and situational cues including:

- the scene of the trauma
- being around people involved in the trauma
- being around people talking about similar events
- seeing people arguing, shouting or crying
- watching news or hospital programmes on television
- seeing ambulances, police cars, hospitals or cemeteries
- hearing sirens or other loud noises
- encountering strong or distinctive smells such as petrol or smoke
- being in the dark, alone or separated from loved ones
- seeing injured people
- seeing scars on their body
- having painful, unusual or unpleasant physical sensations.

The child's response to how they cope with any triggers might simply be to say, 'I stay away from it.' In such situations, the clinician can help the child to be as specific as possible. Provide examples of what other children with PTSD sometimes do to cope with symptoms, such as:

- taking a different route to avoid going near the scene of the trauma
- only sitting in certain seats of the car, bus or train after a crash
- continuously scanning the road for danger
- focusing on schoolwork, watching television or talking about other things to distract from trauma memories
- checking up on friends and family members to see if they're okay
- staying close to parents or friends while outside the house
- seeking reassurance from friends and parents.

Identifying low-level sensory triggers may need some careful detective work. Equally, avoidance and safety behaviours may be quite subtle and ingrained and will also require careful detailed assessment.

> Identify maintaining factors such as dysfunctional cognitive strategies or behavioural avoidance.

Normalising reactions

During this individual interview, be alert for opportunities to normalise the child's reactions. This might be best done when any misinterpretations of symptoms are revealed. In the first instance, normalising is about information provision. For example, the clinician might teach the child what anxiety involves (in terms of bodily reactions, thoughts and behaviours), and how it can be helpful because it protects us (the flight-or-fight response). With older children, the clinician might discuss how evolution has prepared us to attend and respond to threats. The aim is to communicate to the child that they are having a normal anxiety response, which is the way bodies are 'designed' to respond, and which is usually functional because it protects us from harm. However, in the child's case, the anxiety response has gone too far because they are now 'highly tuned' to potential threats (the radar is always turned on full, the child is on constant red alert).

A second part of the normalisation process is to explain to the child that PTSD is a very common reaction after a trauma. Everyone, adults as well as other children, has PTSD symptoms similar to the child's soon after the trauma. In many adults and children, these symptoms persist. The clinician could talk about older children, or people like firefighters and police officers having PTSD. The point to get across is that lots of very competent and able people develop PTSD after a trauma and it is nothing to be ashamed of. It is also important to emphasise that lots of people get better after treatment, and so it might be helpful to give a brief example of another child who had similar problems and was successfully treated.

In educating children and their carers about the nature of PTSD and its treatment, it is helpful to provide written information. The handouts in Appendix B can be given out at the end of this first session. Children are asked to read them carefully, to discuss them with parents if they choose to, to mark any sections which apply to them and to bring them back to the following session to discuss with the clinician. The process of educating and normalising reactions continues in the following session when you review this homework (see Chapter 5).

> Provide information that normalises the child's reaction.

Socialisation to the treatment model

It is important that from the beginning of therapy young people understand the rationale for treatment, particularly the reasons for carrying out reliving and exposure to reminders. The core message in this initial session is that the sort of avoidance that has been identified, although entirely understandable, has the unwanted effect of 'keeping the problem going'. There are various ways of conveying this message, depending on the age and abilities of the child.

In many cases, developing a shared treatment rationale will follow quite naturally from the cognitive assessment described above. When asked, many young people will describe how they have been trying to cope using various forms of avoidance and distraction. Further questioning will usually reveal that while this sometimes works in the short term, it does not work over the long term: intrusions return later in the day, or in the form of nightmares. The futility of attempting to push images and memories out of mind can be demonstrated in a lively behavioural experiment using thought suppression (Wenzlaff and Wegner 2000). Here, the young person is asked to try hard not to think of something (e.g. pink elephants, their favourite sportsperson or musician, or a red London bus) for several minutes. To their surprise, children find that the harder they try to push such images away, the more likely images are to come back. Children are often intrigued by this finding and have described it in various ways:

> It's like throwing a tennis ball against a wall – the harder you throw it, the harder it comes back.

> It's like a boomerang – the harder you try to get rid of it, the stronger it comes back.

The explicit link to the young person's prominent intrusions is then made: the more effort they put into pushing images away, the more likely it is that the image will 'bounce back'. Some young people will spontaneously conclude that instead of pushing memories away, it will help to face up to them. For other children, the clinician may need to explain that because pushing images away keeps memories coming back, the young person will be helped to stop pushing the memory away so that it does not keep bouncing back into their mind. Instead of pushing unwanted thoughts and memories away, the clinician will help them to talk, write and draw what has happened in order to help put the memory back in the past, where it belongs.

Use of behavioural experiments in this way can be combined with metaphor. Ehlers and Clark (2000) provide an excellent clothing cupboard metaphor for socialising adults to the cognitive model of disorder and treatment. Alternatively, a jigsaw puzzle metaphor can be used. Metaphors such as these are helpful because they can convey key points:

- Treatment involves deliberately 'looking at' aspects of the memory – i.e. one has to closely examine the jigsaw pieces or articles in the cupboard if one is to sort them out.
- It is helpful to reorder and restructure the memory – i.e. to stop things falling out of the cupboard, it is necessary to put them away in their right place.
- the aim of therapy is not to forget or 'wipe clean' the memory but to choose when to remember. That is, we are not emptying the cupboard or throwing away the jigsaw puzzle, but putting items away neatly so that the young person can choose when to open the door and have a look; and equally, choose when to close the door so that the memory is 'filed away'.

For younger children, simpler analogy may be used. Most children of eight years and older will readily grasp a fear avoidance (i.e. phobia) analogy. It can be helpful to choose a simple phobia that does not apply to the child and ask what advice they would give to a friend who had such a fear. With gentle encouragement and careful questioning, most replies will contain elements highly relevant to a cognitive model of anxiety such as exposure and cognitive reappraisal. For example, children might say something along the lines of 'I would find a friendly dog and get my friend to go up and stroke it and find out it is not fierce.' Use of a height phobia analogy might emphasise gradual exposure in the form of going up a ladder rung by rung. Again, the explicit link is made to the young person's trauma memory: in order to stop the memory coming back and making the child afraid, he or she will need to face up to the memory. Some young children have described this as 'getting used to remembering', similar to the way that others might 'get used to' high places or dogs.

It is crucial to establish a solid rationale for treatment in early sessions and to return to it in subsequent sessions. Unless a good rationale is set up properly early on, it is hard for young people to engage fully in treatment. Establishing a firm shared rationale early on can help if young people become 'stuck' in later sessions.

It is also important for parents to have a full understanding of the rationale and procedures in CT for PTSD if they are not to discourage, impede or actively undermine the therapeutic process. Similar techniques to those above in arriving at a shared understanding of the treatment model can be used with parents.

Provide a clear rationale for CT for PTSD to children and carers:

- Avoidance doesn't work (it keeps intrusions going).
- Avoidance is actively counterproductive (it exacerbates intrusions).
- The aim of therapy is therefore to stop avoiding and instead to deliberately recall what happened so that it can be processed to a point where it is no longer troublesome.

Treatment goals

Having carried out a detailed assessment of potential maintaining factors, started the process of psycho-education and normalisation, and begun to develop a shared treatment rationale, it helps to conclude this initial session by assisting the young person to set some treatment goals.

It is helpful to ask about what the trauma and its aftermath have stopped the child from doing. Enquire about school (including academic work and concentration), sports and physical activity (especially if there is any physical injury), and friendships (especially if mood is low, if there is visible scarring). Ask about family life, especially rows or upsets with parents and siblings, free time and travel (particularly if the trauma was a transport-related accident).

This conversation about general impairment should lead to discussion about meaningful and measurable treatment goals. The child can be asked about what they would like to be different. Goals should be both meaningful to the child and measurable (e.g. *I wish I could spend more time with my friends and not be so scared to leave the house. I wish I could go to bed at night and not have nightmares.*). These goals will be reviewed and agreed with the parents later (where appropriate).

> Clear and measurable treatment goals should be agreed.

Interviewing parents or carers

After seeing the child alone, parents or carers are interviewed alone. With the child's permission, let the parents know what was discussed with their son or daughter. An important aspect of this review will be to point out triggers and avoidance/coping behaviours that the child uses. Ask the parent if there are other triggers or coping responses that the child may have missed. It is common for children not to report behaviour which they find embarrassing (e.g. being clingy, asking for reassurance or to be near the parents all the time). Discussion of triggers and avoidance can lead to a helpful discussion with parents about the nature of PTSD – especially the key role of avoidance in keeping the problem going. Parents will find it helpful to read the handout (Appendix B) between sessions and to discuss it with the clinician in the following session.

Even if the parents were not directly involved in the trauma, the event will have been highly stressful and potentially traumatising for them. Ask about their reactions to the trauma, and whether they are seeking or getting help for themselves. Also ask about parents' reactions to their child's problems. Be particularly alert to the presence of unhelpful beliefs:

- My child has gone crazy or is permanently damaged.
- It is my fault they are feeling this way.
- I should have prevented the trauma.

Ask parents about how they cope with their own symptoms (if present) and how they cope with their child's symptoms:

- Do they encourage the child to talk about the trauma (or their thoughts and feelings), or is this too upsetting?
- Do they see the world as a more dangerous place since the trauma?
- Are they more protective of their child now?

When there is overprotectiveness (or separation anxiety), it can be pointed out how treatment will help both child and parent to get back to the types of activities they did before the trauma (e.g. the child and the parents being able to do more things independently of each other, and do more fun things together).

The decision to refer the parents for separate treatment or to treat them for PTSD alongside their child will depend in part on a variety of factors. Parents with PTSD or other post-traumatic reactions sometimes find that their symptoms improve without treatment provided their child experiences an improvement in treatment. This is often true where the parents' traumatic exposure is limited to knowing that their child was involved in a trauma (i.e. they were not directly exposed). In such instances, the child's improvement may help to undermine any parental beliefs about their child being permanently damaged and/or the need for overprotective behaviours. It is also true that some parents mimic the more functional coping behaviours taught to the child in treatment (e.g. elaborating the memory of the trauma, confronting feared situations).

Let the parents know what the child's treatment goals were. Ask what the parents' goals are for themselves and for the child. Explain the treatment rationale and procedures, emphasising early on that they will be included to help their child with homework assignments which are designed to help them feel more confident. Use appropriate metaphors (as above) to explain the model of PTSD and its treatment to the parent.

The interview with parents should help to:

- assess parental factors that may be maintaining the child's problems (e.g. parental symptoms, parents' avoidant coping style)
- engage parents
- normalise the child's reactions
- give a rationale and overview for treatment.

At the end of this session, the clinician should bring the family together again to summarise, jointly agree the treatment goals and to timetable future sessions. It is very important in this part of the session to be upbeat and to provide praise for the child (in front of the parents) for talking so openly, being brave and deciding to change things. Again, at the end of the session give the family the chance to ask any questions.

Henry (age 10) and his mother were involved in a road traffic accident six months prior to assessment. While waiting at traffic lights, they were hit from behind, causing the rear of the car to crumple. Both suffered minor bruising from their seatbelts, and mother had a minor whiplash injury. Neither Henry nor his mother had any prior history of trauma or mental health difficulties.

Initial diagnostic assessment
At the initial assessment, Henry said that after the accident he simply could not get the thoughts and pictures of the accident out of his head. The intrusions and nightmares both contained images of his mother holding her neck or being in a neck brace. Sometimes in his nightmares he dreamt that his mother actually died – when he woke up, he would have to run and check on her. That led him to start staying in his mother's bed every night. He then started to worry that something bad would happen to his mother when he was at school, and particularly if she was driving without him. He wanted to stay with her all the time. Nothing helped him to feel better except to be near his mother or to have her tell him she was okay. At school or home, he pushed all scary thoughts out of his head and either tried to distract himself or sought reassurance from his mother. The overall impact of Henry's symptoms was a severe constriction in his behaviour. While he still attended school and football practice, he did not want to go out to play with friends on his own any longer. He would not sleep over at friends' or relatives' houses. He would not get in a car with anyone but his mother. The effect of all of this avoidance was that Henry was spending less time in activities that he enjoyed prior to the accident.

His mother reported that she was now jumpy and hypervigilant in a car – often triggered by Henry's requests to slow down and be careful. She felt that her confidence as a parent had been shaken by her inability to help Henry settle after the accident. She felt particularly bad that she was not able to get Henry back into his own bed. She tended to down-play how well she had done to keep Henry in school and to get him back in cars. She often worried whether Henry had been permanently damaged by the accident and tended to blame herself. Her primary coping response was to tell herself to 'get a grip'.

Henry met diagnostic criteria for both PTSD and separation anxiety disorder. His mother was diagnosis free, although it was clear that she worried a good deal about Henry and questioned her abilities as a mum.

Cognitive assessment and formulation

In the subsequent session a week later, after giving Henry some time to settle, he was asked to describe again what had happened in the accident.

'We were driving and there was a really loud bang! A van ran into the back of us and we couldn't drive anymore because our car was wrecked. My mum's neck was really hurt and they put a brace on her neck. I thought she was going to die. She was arguing with the other driver and then the police came. We went to the hospital and I was really scared.'

Henry was asked to elaborate a little further. From this still rather brief account, it appeared that there were two fairly clear hotspots. The first was seeing his mum sitting in the front seat rubbing her neck. At this point, he thought that her neck was broken and she might die. The second was seeing his mum sitting in the ambulance with a neck brace on, looking really upset. At this point, he didn't believe it when they told him that mum was okay. He thought that they put this neck brace on her because she was really hurt; he thought that she might die.

Nature of the trauma memory

Henry's memory is poorly elaborated and primarily an account of the worst moments or hotspots. Indeed, it is the intrusive image of his mother rubbing her neck or being in the ambulance that comes back to Henry most often. Henry's account of the accident also included information that is not entirely accurate and slightly out of sequence. Finally, his memory is primarily defined by sensory and emotional data (i.e. loud bang, pain, seeing his mother in a neck brace, and fear). When the memory is activated, these intense sensory and emotional data give Henry the sense that the accident is recurring in the present and that there is an imminent risk of harm to him and his mother.

As Henry's memory of the accident is poorly elaborated, disjointed and predominantly made up of sensory/emotional data, it is much more likely to be activated when he encounters either external (e.g. loud sounds, tyres screeching, cars coming close to theirs, his mother looking upset) or internal reminders (fear, arousal, thoughts about accidents or some other calamity separating him from his mother). Thus an initial focus of treatment will be helping Henry to fully elaborate this memory and place it into a coherent and linear structure through the process of reliving. In addition, factual information about actual outcomes will be integrated through the process of reliving with restructuring (e.g. 'I am thinking my mother's neck was really hurt but now I know she just had a bit of whiplash.'). Both interventions should lead to a significant reduction in intrusions and nightmares and co-morbid symptoms of separation anxiety disorder.

Idiosyncratic appraisals

Henry identified a range of trauma- and symptom-related appraisals at interview and on the Child Post Traumatic Cognitions Inventory (CPTCI):

'Something bad happened to my mum because I didn't warn her. She could have been killed by the whiplash. Emergency professionals don't always tell you the truth.' Such appraisals are activated with his intrusions or on their own by contact with other traumatic reminders. They cause Henry to feel more vulnerable and distressed and to believe that his mother is at increased risk of harm now when she is not with him. They motivate him to remain ever vigilant and to seek reassurance from and proximity to his mother.

Imaginal reliving may help to update such appraisals – but standard cognitive techniques will probably be used to help Henry identify appraisals and their links to his beliefs about the risk of future harm. He would be helped to modify his misappraisals by seeking out more factual information, and when necessary incorporate this information into his trauma memory.

Unhelpful coping behaviours

Henry has developed a range of unhelpful coping behaviours aimed at reducing intrusions, distress and preventing further harm. He tries to suppress traumatic intrusions as soon as they occur by distracting himself or seeking proximity to his mother. With the exception of cars, he avoids any discussion of the accident or his mother's actual injuries. He avoids separation situations whenever possible. He constantly scans the environment for signs of danger in cars and signs that his mother is unwell. These behaviours have the unintended effect of increasing his contact with traumatic reminders, activating intrusions and maintaining his fears. They also prevent him fully elaborating the trauma memory, confronting traumatic reminders and modifying his idiosyncratic appraisals.

Thus a major focus of treatment will be helping Henry to identify and test out the unintended and unhelpful consequences of avoidance and safety behaviours. In the first instance, this will be achieved by helping Henry overcome his avoidance by intentionally activating and elaborating his memory of the trauma via reliving. Later in treatment, in vivo exposure to physical reminders (e.g. sitting in the back of the car) and behavioural experiments (e.g. thinking about the accident and not checking up on his mother) would be used to help him drop his avoidance/safety behaviours and challenge his misappraisals.

Parental post-traumatic reactions

During interview and on the Post Traumatic Cognitions Inventory (PTCI) for adults, Henry's mother identified characteristic appraisals that had arisen directly from the accident (I have to be on guard all the time; the accident was my fault; the world is a dangerous place). These appraisals may be contributing to her general worries about Henry, and maintaining her hypervigilance while driving. While she has done well to keep Henry travelling in the car and going to school, mother has tended to comply with his constant requests for reassurance and proximity (for example, by not setting firm rules about staying in bed at night). She also complies with requests to sit up front in the car, to avoid the scene of the accident, and to avoid any discussion of it. As such she does not encourage or model more active and helpful coping behaviours. In addition, her ongoing anxiety (particularly in the car) serves as a frequent reminder to Henry that she is 'not quite right' since the accident and may be more vulnerable to harm.

It is likely that individual interventions aimed at reducing Henry's PTSD and SAD symptoms will be effective, and that his mother's anxiety will diminish as well. However, interventions targeted at mother's anxiety, trauma-related beliefs and overprotective responses toward Henry may be needed. This might include a review and update of her trauma memory with a particular focus on causality, to help challenge her belief that she was responsible. Standard cognitive therapy techniques would be used to help her identify triggers for her anxiety and to drop her own safety behaviours (e.g. not immediately complying with Henry's requests for reassurances; not checking up on Henry as often) – particularly those that appear to be maintaining Henry's difficulties.

Prioritising symptoms

Henry rated his intrusions and nightmares as his most distressing symptoms. In general, a decision is needed whether to treat these symptoms or other co-morbid aspects (discussed in Chapter 9). At this stage it is helpful to remember that for children and adolescents with a primary diagnosis of PTSD, but with co-morbid symptoms of anxiety and depression, treatment of the PTSD often leads to improvement in the anxiety and depression. In Henry's case it was assumed that targeting the PTSD would improve his SAD as these conditions were thematically linked (he worried he would lose his mum during the accident and after). Furthermore, it made sense that his mother would be better able to encourage Henry to be more independent (less clingy) and to sleep on his own if intrusions and nightmares could be reduced.

Goal setting and treatment planning

Following from the initial symptomatic assessment, the subsequent detailed cognitive assessment with Henry and his mother highlighted likely maintaining factors that will become targets for treatment change. These include:

- reducing the disjointed, out of sequence nature of Henry's trauma memory
- updating his peri-traumatic appraisals about the extent of his mother's injury
- modifying his beliefs about the risk of future harm
- reducing his wide range of unhelpful coping behaviours
- modifying mother's beliefs about responsibility
- encouraging his mother to model more active and helpful coping behaviours.

This formulation was shared with Henry and his mother in different ways. For example, Henry found the jigsaw puzzle metaphor appealing as a way of understanding how to 'put his memory back together so that pieces didn't fall out'. A thought suppression experiment was used to help him understand that his avoidant coping actually meant that the memory kept 'bouncing back'.

In a separate discussion with mother, she was readily able to see the link between her anxiety and Henry's reactions, and was highly motivated to learn new ways of dealing with her anxiety as a means to help her son.

Finally, clear treatment goals were agreed. This was done first with Henry and his mother separately, and then reviewed jointly. Goals included both symptom reduction (e.g. for Henry to have fewer intrusive memories and to be able to travel in the back of a car), but also goals aimed at increasing rewarding activities – described in more detail in the Chapter 5 (under Reclaiming Life).

The aims of this first treatment session are to:

- carry out a detailed cognitive assessment, leading to an individual formulation
- discuss symptoms in detail and to normalise the child's reactions
- discuss unhelpful coping, leading to a developmentally appropriate treatment rationale
- set clear goals
- agree a plan for the remainder of the treatment sessions.

5

Cognitive therapy for PTSD

The intervention is not presented as a highly structured session-by-session protocol. This is because, under the broad rubric of post traumatic stress disorder (PTSD), children show diverse reactions to trauma and will require individually tailored treatment packages. Instead of session-by-session prescriptions, the treatment techniques are described in some detail, in the rough order that they might be implemented over a two to three month course of therapy. Individual children may spend relatively more or less time on the various treatment components. The pace and content of cognitive therapy (CT) for PTSD will vary from child to child, determined by the case formulation (and reformulation as treatment progresses), clinical judgement, and the extent to which young people are engaged and motivated at various stages in therapy.

Generally, sessions are offered on a weekly basis for 10 to 12 weeks. Many young people will show substantial improvement after weekly treatment for about three months, but some will require further sessions. Most young people prefer a time-limited rather than an open-ended approach, so it helps to specify an initial contract of up to 12 sessions, with a planned review at the end to see whether additional sessions might be useful. While maintaining a pace that is comfortable for the young person, it is helpful to build up some momentum in therapy. Young people are invited to attend on a weekly basis; sessions are missed it can help to double-up sessions in the following week.

> The initial treatment contract is for up to 12 weekly sessions.

Session structure is likely to differ from week to week, depending on the sorts of intervention carried out. However, children are generally seen for longer than the usual therapeutic hour, especially in sessions when reliving or memory work is being carried out. Sometimes, parents might not be involved at all, for example, when working with older adolescents. Alternatively, they may be closely involved in all aspects of therapy, for example, when working with pre-school children. As a general rule, the young person is seen alone for the bulk of many sessions, but parents and carers are always invited to check in at the end of each session.

> The initial extent of parental involvement will vary during the intervention.

In the second half of a 12-week course of CT for PTSD, session structure is likely to differ as the young person is accompanied by the clinician outside the therapy room to carry out behavioural experiments or to revisit the site of the trauma. Behavioural experiments play a central role during CT for PTSD. These are planned exercises designed to gather information to test out the validity of the young person's cognitions, and/or to demonstrate the adverse effects of a maladaptive coping strategy. From a theoretical point of view, behavioural experiments stand in contrast to exposure techniques used in behaviour therapy. In exposure therapy, the presumed mechanism of change is habituation as a result of repeated exposure to the feared stimulus. In behavioural experiments, it is assumed that the key mechanism is belief change. As a consequence, the experiment is set up in a way that is intended to maximise belief change. Specific examples are provided in later sections. An excellent up-to-date guide to using behavioural experiments in cognitive therapy across a range of disorders among adults (Bennett-Levy *et al.* 2004) is a helpful starting point for using behavioural experiments with children and young people.

> Behavioural experiments are an important means of testing out unhelpful beliefs.

The therapeutic stance is crucial throughout the course of therapy. It is important that therapists are comfortable with listening to detailed first-hand descriptions of traumatic events. Indeed, it is sometimes the task of the therapist to probe for a level of detail that would, in non-therapeutic circumstances, naturally be avoided. Expression of affect may be intense at times, particularly in the early sessions, and therapists must be able to tolerate and manage these strong feelings. Maintaining high levels of empathy is important throughout, but especially at the beginning of a course of therapy, and when challenging misappraisals later on. Therapists should be aware of how they demonstrate empathy, both explicitly and non-verbally, and how they might adapt this for individual young people with differing needs.

Appropriate levels of empathy, care and sensitivity are needed to help and support the young person in turning their attention towards the worst moments in the trauma. It is equally important not to become overwhelmed by the level of detail or intense affect: the stance taken is one of being matter-of-fact, supportive and encouraging. Clinicians should be attuned to their own reactions to the young person's history and trauma narrative, and ensure they do not inadvertently reinforce avoidant responses. The message from the outset, conveyed directly and implicitly in the structured, focused work, is that trauma memories are to be attended to and worked on, in a supportive and collaborative way.

> The traumatic event needs to be directly discussed in a supportive and empathic manner.

Because this form of treatment can be demanding – even upsetting – for the clinician, it is helpful to set up regular supervision. This will serve a number of functions. It will provide a space to reflect on and receive advice about treatment strategies, but also to debrief some of the intense emotional material that may arise. Informal supervision, peer support and teamwork are just as valuable in this regard.

Overview

A course of CT for PTSD with young people usually comprises up to 12 weekly 90-minute sessions. Detailed descriptions of the various CT for PTSD procedures and their variations follow in the sections below. Not all techniques will be used in every case, and it is up to the clinician to decide which techniques to use and when to implement them, depending on individual case formulation. The list of components is ordered according to a rough sequence as shown in Figure 5.1. Techniques that tend to be used early in therapy are listed first, although it is not intended that these are worked through in order from beginning to end. Homework is set and work with parents and carers carried out as needed throughout a course of treatment.

Psycho-education and normalisation

Common to all CBT approaches for PTSD is the early dissemination of information about the nature and treatment of PTSD. The aims are to

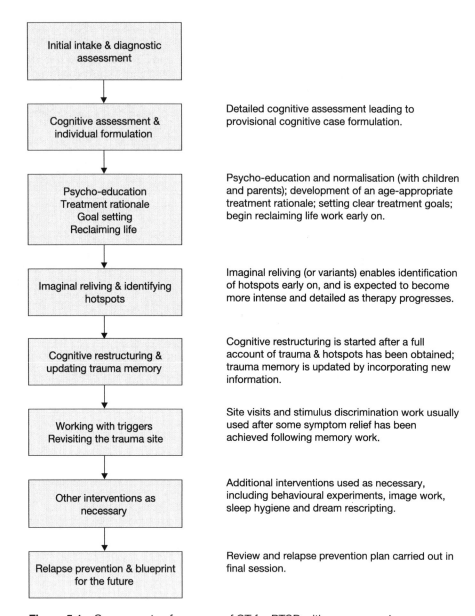

Initial intake & diagnostic assessment	
Cognitive assessment & individual formulation	Detailed cognitive assessment leading to provisional cognitive case formulation.
Psycho-education Treatment rationale Goal setting Reclaiming life	Psycho-education and normalisation (with children and parents); development of an age-appropriate treatment rationale; setting clear treatment goals; begin reclaiming life work early on.
Imaginal reliving & identifying hotspots	Imaginal reliving (or variants) enables identification of hotspots early on, and is expected to become more intense and detailed as therapy progresses.
Cognitive restructuring & updating trauma memory	Cognitive restructuring is started after a full account of trauma & hotspots has been obtained; trauma memory is updated by incorporating new information.
Working with triggers Revisiting the trauma site	Site visits and stimulus discrimination work usually used after some symptom relief has been achieved following memory work.
Other interventions as necessary	Additional interventions used as necessary, including behavioural experiments, image work, sleep hygiene and dream rescripting.
Relapse prevention & blueprint for the future	Review and relapse prevention plan carried out in final session.

Figure 5.1 Components of a course of CT for PTSD with young people

increase children's and parents' knowledge about PTSD and its treatment, and to begin to change unhelpful beliefs about PTSD. Providing written information in the form of handouts for children and carers can be helpful (see Appendix B), as discussed in Chapter 4. Handouts are provided at the first session and closely reviewed and personalised with the child in the second session. Children and parents often express surprise and relief that their symptoms are clearly described and labelled in the handouts. The Child

Post Traumatic Cognitions Inventory (CPTCI, see Appendix A) can be used to detect and address any obvious misappraisals about symptoms. Parents may express surprise that what was previously viewed as a permanent character change is instead a symptom of a treatable condition. It is emphasised that PTSD is normal in that it is common in both children and adults. This is an opportunity for children and carers to ask any questions they have about the nature of PTSD and its treatment. In addition to countering misappraisals of PTSD symptoms, the process of normalising PTSD as a common treatable condition is important in developing the client–therapist relationship, in instilling hope and in bolstering motivation to change.

> Information about the nature of PTSD can help children to understand their symptoms.

Socialisation to the treatment model

It is crucial to establish a solid rationale for treatment. Unless a good rationale is set up properly early on, it is hard for young people to engage fully in treatment. Establishing a firm shared rationale early on can help if young people become 'stuck' in later sessions. It is equally important for parents to have a full understanding of the rationale and procedures in CT for PTSD if they are not to discourage, impede or actively undermine the therapeutic process. The key message at this early stage is that: avoidance doesn't work (it keeps intrusions going); avoidance is actively counterproductive (it exacerbates intrusions); and the aim of therapy is therefore to stop avoiding and instead to deliberately recall what happened. Conveying this message is not a one-off process. It is helpful to continue check and bolster children's understanding of the treatment rationale, using experiments and metaphor, as described in Chapter 4.

Reclaiming your life

Young people with PTSD often seem as though they are mentally stuck in time around the point of the trauma. As a consequence of this preoccupation, they may give up many of the activities they previously enjoyed and which gave them a sense of meaning and social connectedness. One way of overcoming this problem is to identify the things that they have stopped doing and encourage them to take them up again. This is termed 'reclaiming your life'. By connecting the pre-trauma past to the post-trauma future one can help young people to move on from being stuck in time around the trauma so that they can regain a sense of having a future to look forward to. Additionally, children may show a reduced level of activity compared to pre-trauma levels because:

- they are avoidant of traumatic reminders or have developed an over-generalised sense of danger
- they have low mood with an accompanying reduction in interest in activities (not necessarily in those activities related to the traumatic event)
- parents or carers have developed an increased sense of danger since the trauma and are overprotective of the child.

Countering reduced levels of activity early on in therapy can therefore be useful to lift the child's mood, reduce overprotectiveness on the part of parents or carers, and to give the whole family a sense that normal life is progressing and that things are moving forward. It also encourages the child to access memories of themselves from before the trauma. Care must be taken that scheduled activities are normal enjoyable activities for the child. That is, this treatment component is not concerned with confronting traumatic reminders (see section below on working with triggers).

Depending on the age of the child, scheduling enjoyable activities will probably need to be done with parents. The procedure will differ according to whether the reduction in activities is due to the young person's lack of interest, his or her trauma-related avoidance, or overprotectiveness on the part of the parents. The clinician might ask child and parents the following questions:

- How does he or she spends his or her free time?
- How does this compare with pre-trauma activities?
- What things are missing from their schedule now?
- What have they given up or stopped doing?
- What would they like to be doing?
- What do they wish they could do?

When parents are overprotective, children are often quite clear about what they would prefer to be doing. However, they may accept parents' overprotectiveness for fear of upsetting them. The aim in this case is to encourage parents to be less protective. Discuss with parents (alone) what they fear may happen if the child is given more independence:

- How realistic are these fears?
- What are the advantages and disadvantages for the child (and family) in restricting activities?
- What do other children of his or her age do?
- What would their child be doing now if they had not been involved in the trauma?

It is important to emphasise that increasing activities is an important part of treatment which will give the child a sense of moving on from the trauma, and allow him or her to get back on a normal developmental track. In the context of what the child has said about preferred activities, the clinician can begin to plan with the parent how to schedule more activities into the child's week. This may need to be done in a graded way if parents are anxious (gradually increasing the amount of time the child is away from the parents), or it may be a matter of joining after-school or other activities. With the child and parent together, these activities can be agreed and written down. An activity diary can be used, or younger children might design and decorate their own diary (see Appendix C).

When children show a lack of interest in previous activities, be careful to distinguish those that are avoided because they are traumatic reminders, and those that have been dropped from the child's repertoire for other reasons, such as low mood. Try to brainstorm with the child about activities that they could do. These might include resuming previous activities, or building new age-appropriate activities into their schedule. It helps to start with realistic achievable activities which can be gradually increased. Again, it helps to plan this in a concrete way with parents, making a list or a diary for the child to keep if appropriate.

Activity scheduling can be done in an upbeat and positive way with the family early on in treatment, emphasising that normal life can be resumed. When graded tasks are introduced early on, these can be reviewed each week and increased as therapy progresses.

> Increasing enjoyable activities helps to improve mood, creates hope and gives the whole family a sense that normal life is now progressing.

Imaginal reliving

Activation of the trauma memory via imaginal reliving is a core treatment component, first developed in the treatment of adults with PTSD (Keane *et al.* 1989; Foa *et al.* 1991), and subsequently adapted and evaluated in treating children (e.g. Saigh 1992; Cohen *et al.* 2004; Scheeringa *et al.* 2007). It is a powerful technique that can address several of the treatment targets (maintaining factors) derived from the cognitive model (see Chapter 2). That is, imaginal reliving enables emotional processing and semantic elaboration of the trauma memory so that it can be better integrated into autobiographical memory. Accessing problematic meanings of the trauma can be difficult by interview alone (because of the disjointed nature of intentional recall), but identification of hotspots during reliving allows any associated misappraisals to be identified (and later modified). The process of carrying out reliving is also a powerful demonstration to the child that they can think about the trauma without going crazy or losing control.

> Imaginal reliving enables emotional processing and semantic elaboration of the trauma memory.

Rationale for reliving

Most children recognise that sooner or later they will have to face up to what has happened to them, but imaginal reliving must be preceded by a careful age-appropriate explanation of the rationale for doing it. This can be linked to discussion of cognitive avoidance. Many children will report trying to push intrusive thoughts or images away, or report trying to distract themselves from intrusive memories. Through careful questioning, children can recognise that while such avoidance may work in the short term, it is not helpful in the long term because intrusive memories return in the form of nightmares or daytime intrusions. It may be useful to review the procedures on general treatment rationale – including thought suppression experiments – which are detailed in Chapter 4. It may also be helpful to set up reliving as a behavioural experiment to test the child's beliefs about the consequences of remembering. In this case, it will be necessary to elicit specific testable predictions from the child, such as 'I will get so angry that I will lose control'; or 'I will get so upset that I will never recover.' However, care must be taken not to increase anticipatory anxiety through prolonged discussion before reliving.

Preparation for reliving

Before starting reliving, tell the child that it might be hard to do, that it is okay to get upset or scared, but that this will get better the more they do reliving. It is important that children are able to fully access the trauma memory, including thoughts and feelings associated with worst moments. Clinicians should not convey the message that the aim of reliving is to control or suppress thoughts and feelings while reliving, but instead should be ready to hear the details of worst moments, and be able to tolerate expression of high affect. The clinician may comment to the child that their decision to talk about the trauma in detail is a sign of bravery and courage, and shows their readiness to begin to change things.

At certain points during and after a reliving, it is useful to ask the child to rate their degree of upset or fear, using a simple 0–10 numerical scale (referred to below as Subjective Units of Discomfort Scale, or SUDS ratings). It therefore helps to prepare the young person by writing down a scale, with anchors and descriptors, and practise using it with some imaginary examples. For teenagers, a simple line with numbers will be enough. For younger children, spend some time explaining the procedure in detail, drawing out a 'feelings thermometer', perhaps using colours (green, orange and red zones) and numbers (see Appendix C). This scale may be reviewed prior to reliving, and the child reminded that they may be asked for ratings as they are talking through the trauma.

Initially, it will help to demonstrate the reliving procedure by using an example of a non-traumatic event – such as walking to the shops or travelling to school. When doing this, be certain to talk in the present tense and to include lots of sensory detail, thoughts and feelings. Children will be asked to talk about their traumatic event in a similar manner, from the beginning until the point where they felt safe again – so it is important to identify the safe end point before beginning reliving. The clinician can explain that they would like the child to really imagine that they are back in the trauma, and so they will ask the child to talk as if it is happening now (a little like a sports commentator on television), saying out loud all the things that they can see, smell and hear, as well as what they are thinking and feeling. This is an unusual way of talking, so it can be hard for some younger children to grasp. Children may tend to rush through quickly at first, so ask them to take it slowly, or be prepared for the first reliving to be quite quick and then repeat it more slowly.

> Reliving is done in the present tense and includes lots of sensory detail.

Begin by asking the child to sit comfortably and allow themselves to relax. When they are ready, they can close their eyes if they feel comfortable doing so. Ask the young person to begin telling what happened, in the first person, present tense, paying attention to sensory detail and thoughts and feelings, as above. The first reliving may be brief, but it is usually best to let the child run through the event without prompts. Afterwards, be sure to allow enough time to hear what it was like for the child:

- Was it as you expected it to be?
- Did anything new come up?
- How did it make you feel?
- How do you feel now that you have done it?

This is a good time to give plenty of praise for taking an important step in facing up to the trauma.

In the second and subsequent relivings, the clinician can help and prompt where necessary. Use judgement as to whether the child will be disrupted and 'come out' of the reliving if you prompt. Gently rephrase if the child uses past tense. Ask 'What happens next?' to keep the child going. Stay in the present tense when prompting: 'What can you see now? What are you thinking?' Prompt for what the child can see, hear, smell, feel in their body and for what they are thinking. Asking about different sensory memories is useful at hotspots or points where the child seems to miss parts out or rush through. Hotspots are parts of the trauma memory that are associated with particularly strong distress. At hotspots, clinicians may also use a 'rewind and hold' analogy. Ask the child to 'stop the tape' and describe what they can see, feel and think. A lot of the work, especially at the beginning, is in encouraging the child to slow down so that the event can be remembered in detail – particularly at hotspots. You might ask for SUDS ratings periodically. Continue in the reliving until the previously agreed point at which they felt safe again.

> Guide the child through the reliving, paying particular attention to emotional hotspots.

After reliving

After the reliving, ask for SUDS ratings. Continue to do so periodically and use the decline in self-reported SUDS to demonstrate the natural decline of anxiety. In this way, reliving is a powerful demonstration that the child can tolerate the memories, and that anxiety associated with remembering will decline quite quickly – without any active efforts at control or suppression. Review any predictions about the consequences of reliving. It helps to make the results of the behavioural experiment explicit and clear (e.g. 'Now I know I can remember without going crazy.'). After the reliving, remember to praise the child for having done it despite it being hard. Allow time for anxiety levels to return to normal – longer therapy sessions may be needed for this. By enquiring about what it was like to do, and what the worst part of the event was, the clinician can encourage a supportive discussion of the event in a non-reliving style: this discussion of the reliving can lead on to cognitive restructuring work, described below. If possible, relivings can be audio-taped, the tapes clearly labelled, and the child asked to listen to the tape for homework.

Variations on reliving

Drawing

Some children find it hard to do a full imaginal reliving. Drawing can be used instead, and this may be especially helpful with younger children. Ask the child to draw what happened. The drawing does not have to be good but can be used as a basis to talk about what happened. Ask the child to tell about the drawing. As with imaginal reliving, the therapist's task is to encourage recall of detail – especially thoughts, feelings and sensory impressions. For some young children, constructing a narrative with the sequence of events in a coherent order can be achieved by using 'cartoon strip' drawings or 'storyboards', rather than one-off sketches (see section below on working with young children). Clinicians can ask similar questions to those in imaginal reliving: what did the young person see, hear and smell; what were they thinking and feeling; what were the worst parts? As usual, give lots of praise for being courageous in talking about the trauma. Drawing may also be useful in conjunction with conventional imaginal reliving to clarify events. For example, children might draw a sketch of the accident site. They may be invited to describe or explain what happened using model cars or people alongside their sketch map.

Writing

The use of writing techniques within sessions can be a powerful alternative to the classic imaginal reliving; writing may also be easily combined with imaginal reliving. Children can be asked to dictate a trauma narrative to the clinician, who will write down verbatim what they say on a whiteboard so that it can be constructed and worked on together. A written account of the event, in the first person, present tense, and with lots of detail, including all sensory modalities and thoughts and feelings, is then produced for the child to keep and read over (and add to) as homework. Writing seems especially helpful for young people with very chronic PTSD and/or excessively patchy and disjointed trauma memories. Because it generally results in less intense arousal and affect, writing is also useful for highly avoidant young people who may refuse to engage in classic imaginal reliving. A written narrative is helpful in identifying hotspots and associated appraisals, and is also very useful when integrating the results of cognitive restructuring into the trauma memory. Written and imaginal reliving may easily be combined. In practice, it is helpful to carry out at least one full imaginal reliving early on in a course of CT for PTSD, followed by several sessions of written narrative work (including restructuring), completed with at least one full imaginal reliving which incorporates new information and modified appraisals.

> Alternative methods such as drawing or writing a narrative about the trauma can be useful.

New perspective

In order to discover or integrate new information into the trauma memory, it can be helpful to ask the young person to relive from a perspective other than their own. They can relive a car accident, for example, from a bird's-eye view or from their parent's point of view if they were separated from their parents during the event. This technique can be hard to grasp for young children but may be very useful for teenagers, especially as a means of integrating the results of cognitive restructuring into the trauma memory.

Cognitive restructuring

Children may show maladaptive cognitions about the trauma itself and/or about symptoms of PTSD. Misappraisals of symptoms are commonly to do with going crazy or losing control. Misappraisals about the trauma may be to do with:

- responsibility ('I caused the accident')
- guilt ('I should have been able to save my mother')
- shame ('I wet myself')
- others' reaction ('Nobody cares about me')
- magical thinking or omen formation ('I just knew something bad would happen that day')
- heightened sense of danger ('I will have another crash if I go in a car').

Misappraisals of this sort may change spontaneously through the application of standard reliving techniques as above. However, spontaneous shift in key cognitions does not always result from standard imaginal reliving, and in this case direct modification of cognition is indicated. Furthermore, while shifts in cognition may occur on an intellectual level, there is commonly a failure to integrate this new meaning/information/perspective into the trauma memory (for example, teenagers might say something along the lines of 'I now know that X is true, but when I recall the event/have an intrusion, it feels as if Y is true'). In this case, direct efforts are needed to closely integrate cognitive restructuring with reliving in order to update the trauma memory.

Eliciting key cognitions

Peri-traumatic cognitions (thoughts at the time of the trauma), commonly to do with threat appraisal, are often associated with hotspots in the trauma memory (Grey *et al.* 2002). Hotspots are key moments in the trauma memory which generate intense affect. As a first step in eliciting key cognitions, it is therefore helpful to identify trauma memory hotspots. This may have already been started during the first session by enquiring about the worst moments. In subsequent sessions, additional hotspots may emerge during a reliving. These can be identified by asking for SUDS ratings during reliving. Clinicians can also identify hotspots by being alert during a reliving to: changes in observable affect or anxiety; pauses and silences; skipped or hurried sections; switches between past and present tense. After a reliving, ask the young person what the worst moments were. There are usually several hotspots within a trauma memory. Further hotspots are often identified following reliving because the young person has begun to access hitherto avoided memories. In identifying hotspots, it can be helpful to remember that they are often associated with intrusive recollections.

Having identified trauma memory hotspots, the next step is to elicit associated 'hot' cognitions. This may be done during a reliving. For example, while the young person is carrying out reliving, the clinician can ask 'What are you thinking now, what's going through your mind, what do you think is about to happen?' The 'rewind and hold' technique described above may be used in order to focus on the hotspot and elicit associated appraisals. After a reliving, the clinician might ask 'What did you think when [hotspot], what did you say to yourself when [hotspot], what did that mean to you (say about you)?' Many of the hot cognitions are likely to be about appraisals related to injury or death. Because these sorts of appraisals appear to be particularly important in the onset and maintenance of PTSD, enquire directly about them if open questions do not reveal them. For example, you might ask something along the lines of 'Did you think at the time that you [your mother, friend] were going to die?' Because intrusive recollections and memory hotspots are often closely related, the clinician could also enquire about peri-traumatic misappraisals by asking the young person about the thoughts that may arise when they experience an intrusion.

In addition to focusing on memory hotspots and intrusions to identify peri-traumatic appraisals, a more general supportive discussion of the event and aftermath may also reveal key misappraisals concerned with guilt, responsibility, omen formation, shame, danger and self-devaluation based on symptom misappraisals. The CPTCI can also be very useful in the beginning stages of therapy to help identify key misappraisals and cognitive themes: reviewing a completed CPTCI with the young person can be productive as a means of exploring key misappraisals.

> Maladaptive cognitions about the trauma or symptoms need to be identified.

Care must be taken in modifying misappraisals. First, it is important to allow sufficient time to identify and explore misappraisals. At times, key cognitions will be obvious. At other times, young people may not initially be aware of them, may have trouble articulating them, or may be reluctant to disclose them for a variety of reasons. One of the clinician's tasks in early sessions is to help and support the young person in turning their attention towards the worst moments in the trauma. As noted above, full access to thoughts and feelings associated with the trauma including the details of the worst moments is needed. Therapists should be aware of timing issues and not rush in too soon to modify what appear to be important cognitions. Second, in common with all cognitive therapy approaches, cognitive restructuring must be a genuinely collaborative exercise, with the clinician guiding and helping the child towards a new shared understanding, rather than telling the child what they should think. Cognitive restructuring must be handled with care and sensitivity while maintaining high levels of empathy.

Peri-traumatic appraisals and hotspots

Peri-traumatic misappraisals are often to do with imminent threat (Hackman *et al.* 2004), for example:

- A child trapped in a car after a head-on collision thought at the time 'I'm going to lose my legs.'
- A boy involved in a train derailment thought at the time 'Dad must be dead.'
- A girl lying on the road after having been hit by a car thought 'That bus is going to run me over.'
- A teenager who had been badly assaulted thought at the time 'This will go on until they kill me, I'll get brain damage.'

It is crucial to maintain high levels of empathy when helping young people to update these threat appraisals. For example, the clinician may say that it is entirely understandable that the young person had that thought at the time, that it is reasonable to have thought such a thing, that other young people and adults in the same situation would surely have thought something similar. It can be useful to explain that, just like trauma images, thoughts can also 'get stuck', and that the young person will be helped to update the thought. To help update peri-traumatic misappraisals, useful questions include:

- What do you know now that you couldn't have known at the time?
- What actually happened in the end?
- How did you (or your mum or friend) survive?

The aim is to help the child to discover new information that can update the hotspot appraisal. New information to update the appraisal is sometimes present in the memory itself, but will need further detailed unpacking to elicit. In the example above, the girl who had been run down while crossing the road did see a bus, but during a detailed reliving she recalled that she had also seen passengers getting on and off the bus. She realised that the bus must have been stationary and would not have run her over. This previously forgotten detail was used to update the 'hot thought'.

New information may also be obtained from friends, family or witnesses. In the example above, the teenager who thought that the assault would 'go on forever' was able to estimate the actual time by talking to friends who were present. New information may also be obtained from medical records and hospital staff. In the same example above, the assaulted teenager was invited back to the hospital emergency department to talk to medical staff about head anatomy (learning that his brain is very well protected in a thick skull), and to review his medical records from the time, which showed that he had been thoroughly assessed and given the all clear.

At times, new information emerges following a site visit (see below), and can be used to update hotspot misappraisals. In most cases, it is productive to help young people to incorporate a sense of self-agency when re-evaluating how they survived: for example, it is often the case that attributes of the young person (their strength), or their attitude (quick thinking), or actions they took at the time (running, shouting, etc.) were instrumental in surviving. It can be enormously helpful for children to know that they have 'good instincts' which helped them to survive previously, and which they can rely on to help them in the future. It is helpful to give clear structure to these sessions, summarising results of the 'detective work' for new information in a written format on whiteboards. For example:

> **Situation**
> *I'm lying on the ground being punched and kicked, he's stamping on my face.*
>
> **What I thought at the time**
> *This is going on forever.*
>
> **What I know now**
> *Now I know that it did not go on forever. It stopped after less than a couple of minutes. The man driving past saw what was happening, stopped his car, and rushed over to help. My friends ran over to help when they heard me shouting. The boys ran off as soon as other people came. Although it felt like ages at the time, I did everything I could to protect myself, and the assault stopped after a minute because I shouted out for help.*

Alternatively, you may wish to complete forms with the young person, such as shown in Figure 5.2.

Note that in the example shown in Figure 5.2, the 'New information/ What I know now' is a summary of the results of restructuring, in the young person's own words, arrived at after at least a session of supportive and collaborative work around two cognitions from the same hotspot including: discovering new information about the event (from the reliving itself); talking to friends (set for homework); education about anatomy of the head; diary-keeping for headache triggers; a visit to hospital, and so on. It is helpful to begin cognitive restructuring to update peri-traumatic misappraisals in early sessions because of the following:

- It can give a clear agenda and structure to early sessions.
- It conveys a clear message that trauma memories and narratives are to be attended to and worked on, in a particular way, rather than avoided.
- It often results in a decline in associated anxiety and arousal (from the young person's point of view, it starts to 'take the heat out of the memory').
- It increases engagement in therapy.

Situation	Thought at the time	Feeling	New information – what I know now	Feeling
Lying on the ground being punched and kicked, he's stamping on my face.	He's going to give me brain damage.	Scared 9/10	Now I know I don't have brain damage. The brain is very well protected in a special sort of liquid inside a thick skull. They did all the right tests at hospital and afterwards, and there was nothing wrong. Any headaches I get now always come when I am tired or nervous, and they are not a sign of brain damage.	Relief

Figure 5.2   Cognitive restructuring to update peri-traumatic misappraisals

The process is completed by integrating the results of restructuring into the trauma memory, described in detail below at the end of this section.

> The young person is helped to identify new information which helps to change their maladaptive cognitions.

Before describing some of the techniques for integrating restructuring with reliving, some of the broader cognitive themes that are often apparent in young trauma survivors are summarised below, alongside suggestions on how they might be tackled. This is neither an exhaustive list of cognitive themes in paediatric PTSD, nor of techniques to address them. While CT for childhood PTSD is firmly based on the cognitive model of the disorder, intervention draws on a broad array of cognitive therapy techniques, including specific techniques borrowed from interventions for other disorders.

Guilt

Younger children can easily become muddled about the causes of traumatic events, often blaming themselves, or perceiving blame from parents. Sometimes, this may be helped by giving information. An eight-year-old boy assumed that he was responsible for a car crash. After some preparation with mother alone, she told him in a joint session that although he had been talking to her just before they crashed, he did not cause the accident by distracting her, and she did not blame him for it. To help the boy have a more accurate understanding of the accident, mother and son were encouraged to list other reasons for the crash, such as the poor weather and the other inexperienced driver.

In considering other factors and explanations, it can be useful to draw out a circle to fill in as a pie chart, with each segment representing a causal/contributing factor (bigger slices of pie for more important factors). This is a helpful way for children to see graphically their own minor role relative to other important factors. If the child begins to fill in the pie with other factors, there is often little room left for the child's contribution.

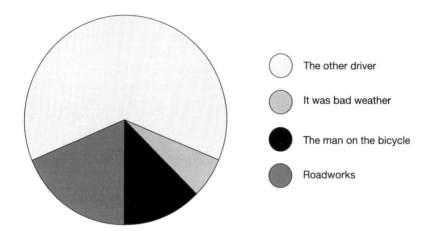

Figure 5.3 Pie chart with each segment representing a causal/contributing factor

Older children's guilt often appears to be based on:

- hindsight reasoning (evaluating their actions based on what happened later rather than what they knew at the time)
- discounting other factors or explanations
- unreasonably high standards ('I should have known what was coming, been able to run faster, react more quickly, fight back').

Addressing older children's guilt may draw on traditional cognitive therapy techniques, including Socratic questioning to consider the evidence. Useful questions include:

- What other factors were there?
- What else could you have done at the time?
- What would someone else or your best friend have done?
- How could you have known what was going to happen?
- What helpful things did you do at the time?

> Actions or failures to act in the midst of a trauma are usually understandable and entirely reasonable, based on what the young person believed at the time.

Magical or superstitious thinking

Closely related to guilt, teenagers' hindsight reasoning can lead to problematic coping behaviour. An adolescent reported that on the morning of the day he had been assaulted, he 'just knew' that something bad was going to happen. Since he 'had a feeling' on the day that something bad would happen, and it did indeed happen, he believed that he should remain highly attuned to his felt sense of current danger in order to protect himself. Consequently, he was markedly hypervigilant. This sort of problem is best tackled through behavioural experiments to test out the consequences of dropping safety behaviours, as described later.

In some young people, this reasoning goes one step further. They may believe that their thoughts caused the traumatic event to occur. Consequently, such children may spend a great deal of time monitoring the content of their own thoughts in order to ensure that they do not think of the trauma (in case they make it happen again) or any other 'bad things' (that they may make come true). Behavioural experiments drawn from the obsessive compulsive disorder (OCD) literature can help here. The child is asked to make a prediction about the consequences of having a thought, and this is tested out. It helps to start with a non-threatening thought, such as thinking really hard about a computer game or box of money. The child is asked to think as hard as they can, visualising the computer game or money, and then look to see if it has appeared. Children will engage readily with this sort of experiment or game, even if they know that they cannot actually make objects appear by mere thinking. The child is then asked to repeat the experiment with increasingly 'dangerous' thoughts, and to test out their predictions. For example, children are asked to deliberately think hard about their assailant to test out the prediction that this will make him appear; or to think about a car crash to test the prediction that such thoughts can cause accidents.

> Behavioural experiments can be a powerful way to demonstrate that the child's thoughts did not cause the traumatic event to occur.

Shame

Shame is closely related to guilt. Some of the techniques described above for guilt may help in cases in which shame is prominent. For young people who feel ashamed about the way they acted or failed to act at the time of the trauma, exploring in detail the possible or likely outcomes of alternative ways of acting may be helpful.

For adolescents in particular, shame and embarrassment may arise as a consequence of visible scarring from injuries sustained in accidents or assaults. Sometimes, this is accompanied by marked avoidance, as in the case of a teenager who had not looked directly at scarring to her leg for more than a year. This can result in a striking failure to update the initial image of the injury. It can be helpful in this case to encourage teenagers to make specific predictions about the appearance of scars (in terms of their size, shape and colour), and then to examine their scar in order to test the prediction. Having discovered that scar tissue had in reality healed a good deal since the time of the accident, the teenager is then encouraged to reveal the scar to family and friends in order to test out predictions about others' likely responses.

Where scarring is visible, adolescents are often concerned that others will notice the scar and think badly of them because of it. In this case, techniques borrowed from the social anxiety literature (e.g. Clark 2005) can help in designing behavioural experiments. Young people are asked to make specific predictions about whether someone will notice the scar, what they will notice, and what they will think when they notice the scar. The young person then has a brief conversation in the therapy room with someone (usually a colleague unconnected to the clinic) who is naive as to the patient's reason for attending. After the conversation, the colleague is asked to write down replies to a series of questions such as:

- Did you find X to be a friendly person?
- Did you have an interesting conversation?
- Did you notice anything unusual about X?
- Did you notice anything unusual about their face?
- Did you notice a scar?
- If you did notice a scar, what colour was it?
- If you noticed a scar, what did it make you think about X?

Young people are often surprised and relieved to learn that others do not usually notice scars; if others do notice, then this does not lead them to negatively evaluate the young person. The experiment can then be repeated with a variety of other people if necessary. When there are safety behaviours to cover up the scars (high collars, hats, make up), we would encourage the young person to drop these if appropriate and repeat the experiment.

Similar experiments combined with video feedback may be carried out for young people who present with high shame because of a belief that others think they are weird, bad, ugly or anxious as a result of the trauma.

> Behavioural experiments provide a way of testing appraisals related to shame.

Others' reactions

In addition to shame-based misappraisals outlined above, more general misappraisal of other people's reactions is common in many young people with persistent PTSD. Sometimes, these may relate to others' reactions at the time of the trauma. For example, a boy who was knocked off his bicycle by a car recalled hearing the screams of bystanders at the time, and interpreted this as meaning that he was going to die; a girl who had been assaulted recalled the horrified look on a policeman's face, which she interpreted as meaning that she 'must look like a monster'. Adolescents who attend hospital often interpret the delays in being assessed and the business-like nature of clinical staff as meaning that no one cares about them, or that they are 'not worth anything'. Similarly, in the months after a trauma, friends at school may avoid discussing the trauma. This may be because they care a lot and do not want to upset the survivor, whom they think has suffered enough; or because they feel they do not know how to mention the trauma in a constructive way. However, avoidance of discussion by peers is often misinterpreted by the survivor as meaning that no one cares or is interested, or that others believe the trauma was actually the survivor's fault.

A number of techniques can be used. Socratic questioning can help the adolescent to identify alternative appraisals. In the example above, the boy realised through discussion that the screams of bystanders were natural instinctive reactions, or may have been intended to alert him or the car driver. Similarly, a visit to a hospital accident and emergency department can be used to gather information about triage procedures and waiting times to modify the appraisal of delays as meaning that no one cares. In cases when others' current reactions are misinterpreted (such as friends' or family members' continued avoidance of discussion of the event as meaning that no one cares), then it can be helpful for the young person to discuss this with the people involved. For example, in a joint session, the clinician might facilitate a discussion between the child and parent, so that the child can hear directly from his mother that she was concerned about him, wanted to talk about the event, but thought that it would be too upsetting for him. When children appear to be misinterpreting peers' ongoing reactions, then they can be encouraged to ask their friends about it. Usually, this is best done with one or two trusted friends first, and may require some planning and practice using role play within session beforehand.

For older children and adolescents, gathering information from others in order to update misappraisals is sometimes done via surveys with friends or family. Systematic surveys are used to gather information relevant to the young person's idiosyncratic belief. For example, a teenager who had been assaulted while out with a group of friends carried out a survey among them to test his belief that they thought he was a coward (for an example, see the end of therapy letter, Appendix D). Surveys may also be useful in work with parents. For example, a young mother who felt guilty about leaving her son unsupervised carried out a survey among her friends to test her belief that they thought she was a bad mother (see the example of Simon in Chapter 7, p. 126).

> Carrying out systematic surveys with friends and family can be a useful means of updating misappraisals.

Danger

An exaggerated and over-generalised sense of danger is common in childhood PTSD. Since this can be due to triggering of the trauma memory in situations reminiscent of the trauma, or when confronted with reminders of it, exaggerated threat appraisals often diminish once processing of the memory has progressed.

In parallel with work aimed at processing and elaborating the memory, additional techniques may be helpful. Initially, standard cognitive therapy methods aimed at examining the evidence and estimating the likely recurrence of another trauma can help. For example, a child who has been involved in a car accident can be helped to gather information about the number of car accidents as a proportion of the number of journeys taken. Creative and graphic ways of illustrating small probabilities can be helpful. For some children, detailed calculation of probabilities taking account of base rates appears to be helpful, but for others it can be harder to understand. For many, a discrepancy between a rational thought and a felt sense remains. Young people might say 'It's good to know that the chances of another accident are only X per cent, but when I'm back in the car, I really feel like another accident is going to happen again.'

In this case, supportive questioning can help many adolescents to recognise that although the world now feels more dangerous, it has not in reality become more dangerous since the trauma. Young people can find it helpful to realise that anxious thoughts and feelings in safe situations are 'just the memory talking'. The task is to bring felt sense and rational knowledge in line, and for this behavioural experiments and in vivo exposure tasks are usually indicated. In essence, such experiments involve the child going back into situations which are safe (such as walking down the street, going in a car), while dropping any safety behaviours (hypervigilance in the street, holding on in a car) in order to test out the prediction that another trauma will happen.

> Children need to test and challenge appraisals that the world is more dangerous following the traumatic event.

Rumination

Rumination, usually comprising repeated 'what if' and 'why' questions, is common in traumatised adolescents, particularly in those with low mood. It may act as a trigger to intrusive memories, or may itself be a consequence of experiencing intrusions. Functionally, rumination appears to be a form of avoidance – thinking about the causes and consequences of the trauma instead of thinking directly of the trauma itself. From the young person's point of view, rumination is often a deliberate attempt to reappraise the trauma, driven by a belief such as 'If I can just sort out what happened, then I can move on and put the memory to rest.'

Since rumination is so closely linked to intrusions and mood, it may diminish once memory processing has progressed or mood has lifted. In cases where rumination persists, usually in older adolescents, the following may be helpful. Begin with a detailed discussion of the process of rumination including: triggers, frequency, duration, content, and effects on intrusions and mood. Discussion of this sort can lead to a formulation which helps the adolescent to realise that although they may have asked themselves 'why?/what if . . .?' questions many hundreds of times since the trauma, they have yet to come up with an answer. In this way, young people may conclude that rumination has been unproductive in the past and is likely to remain so in the future. In addition to being unproductive in that it fails to provide answers to 'why?' questions, a shared functional analysis with the young person may lead them to the realisation that rumination actually increases intrusions and prevents processing of the memory. The task is then to help the young person find ways to switch out of ruminating. One of the most effective ways is for young people to switch from a 'why?' to a 'how?' mode of processing. That is, when the child asks themselves again why the trauma happened, instead of persisting with rumination they ask themselves how it happened – what were the facts and sequence of events in the trauma, how did it start and how did it end? That is, ruminative processing is nipped in the bud and replaced with direct memory processing (as in imaginal reliving or 'reviewing the tape'). This can be practised in session before being set for homework.

> Rumination should be discouraged and young people helped to switch to direct memory processing instead.

Last, for young people who ruminate a good deal with 'what if . . .?' questions, it is sometimes helpful to explore the consequences of the imagined alternatives in detail. For example, an older teenager who had been assaulted by a gang of youths repeatedly asked herself why she had not fought back. Detailed discussion and imagery work led her to the conclusion that the outcome would almost certainly have been worse if she had done so.

Updating trauma memories

One of the most striking issues in PTSD is a failure to spontaneously update the trauma memory, despite cognitive reappraisal. This is apparent when children say things like:

- 'I know I didn't really break my leg, but when I'm back in the memory or have a picture pop into mind, it feels as if my leg's broken.'
- 'Although I know mum's OK now, I feel like I've lost her when I let myself remember the crash.'

When there is a failure to update trauma memories, then direct integration of the results of restructuring with reliving is indicated. That is, the trauma memory needs to be activated and new information or meaning inserted. A number of techniques can be used to achieve this:

1 It may be carried out as part of imaginal reliving. At the hotspot, the child says out loud her original 'hot cognition', followed by the results of the cognitive restructuring. This can be done during a full reliving of the whole event, or during a reliving of the hotspot alone. The purpose is to have the trauma memory activated and 'online' while accessing and integrating new meaning and information.
2 It may be done as part of written rescripting. Here, the child is helped to develop the written narrative. The original misappraisals and hot cognitions are included and the results of the restructuring are inserted in the relevant place, so that the trauma script is updated. It can help for new information to be written in a different colour to make it more salient.

In both imaginal and written format, the process is repeated for various cognitions at different hotspots. It may be helpful to combine written and imaginal methods with at least one full imaginal reliving incorporating new information when possible.

3 New information may be incorporated in imaginal reliving by taking a different visual perspective while reliving. For example, a boy who believed that he was about to get run over was able to view the scene from above while reliving in order to help insert newly discovered information that no traffic was approaching him. In another example, a

passenger who had been in the front seat of a car which was shunted from behind into a brick pillar experienced intrusive images of the pillar rushing towards her, stopping within inches of her face. However, discussion revealed that the pillar had in fact been several feet away from her face at the time of the accident. To help her improve the reality of the intrusion (i.e. 'It is a distorted image, not an accurate memory'), she imagined that the brick pillars were items on a computer screen saver: her anxiety reduced and the intrusions quickly ceased.

4　Incorporation of new information which is incompatible with the old belief is helpful. This has proved especially useful when there are 'frozen' beliefs about bodily injury. For example, a boy who was trapped in a vehicle after a car crash could not move his limbs because he was physically boxed in. He had interpreted this at the time as meaning that he was paralysed. Although he knew currently that he was not paralysed (he was in reality fit and well), he reported having a strong sensation that he was paralysed when he remembered the crash. He was asked to carry out a reliving (to 'go back into the memory') and to articulate the original 'hot' thought that he was paralysed. Then, in addition to articulating out loud the new information ('Now I know I am not paralysed, my legs were boxed in at the time, now I can walk, run and play football'), he was asked to touch, feel and move his legs and to stand up while in a reliving. This proved to be a powerful non-verbal means of updating his frozen peri-traumatic misappraisal and 'body memory'.

> New cognitions can be inserted into the trauma memory during imaginal reliving.

The following is an example of a written narrative completed by an 11-year-old boy who witnessed his friend's death. As therapy progressed, he was helped to update the narrative with new information, after sessions focused on guilt and some joint work with his mother.

It is just after four o'clock, and I am leaving the house to go and see my mate Charlie. It's a sunny day, and I'm feeling quite happy. I am walking down our street and I can see Charlie running after a football. The ball is rolling out into the street and Charlie is still chasing it. I can see a car coming and I am thinking, 'What is Charlie doing?' It's all going in slow motion. My heart is pounding, I'm so scared, and I want to scream, 'Charlie, look out!' but I don't. I wish I'd shouted, but now I know that I didn't even have a chance to make the words come out because the accident happened so fast. I hear brakes screeching and see Charlie flying through the air. He is spinning like a rag doll. What's happening? I am shouting, 'Oh My God!' I am running to where Charlie is lying in the street. I see blood coming from his mouth, nose, ears and eyes. The blood is really thick and red. I feel sick in my stomach. Charlie's eyes are open and he is looking at me. His mouth is moving and I am thinking, 'What is he trying to say?' Now I know that he could not really feel, see or say anything; these were just reflexes. I want to turn away because I am going to be sick. I am thinking, 'This is my fault. I should have told him to stop.' Now I know that it was not my fault – it was the driver's fault because he was talking on his phone and driving really fast. My legs are feeling wobbly and I sit down near Charlie. I can hear my mum running up behind me and shouting, 'Call an ambulance!' I can't move. My mum goes right for Charlie and starts feeling his chest. She starts saying, 'No! No! No!' She won't look at me and I think she is angry at me. Now I know that she was not angry at me, she was just trying to revive Charlie. She felt really sorry for me losing my best friend. Somebody comes and pulls my mum away. My mum and I watch Charlie as people crowd around. I can hear a siren and an ambulance stops. People jump out of it and look at Charlie. His mouth keeps moving like he is trying to speak but no sound comes out – only more blood. The ambulance men put Charlie on a bed and take him away. My mum takes my hand and walks me home. She is not saying anything. She is so quiet that I think she must blame me for what just happened. Now I know that my mum was quiet because she was sad and in shock. We sit in the kitchen and my mum starts calling people. I go to my bedroom and I keep seeing Charlie's face in my mind. I wonder if there is something wrong with me. Now I know that this is normal when somebody just dies in front of you – and it doesn't mean it there is anything wrong with me. My mum comes in my room sometime later and tells me Charlie is dead. She gives me a hug and we stay up all night crying together and talking about him.

In vivo exposure

Children with PTSD will often actively avoid the site of the trauma or physical reminders of it. Under the cognitive model, such avoidance is maintained in part by beliefs about the likelihood of current harm or upset if the child is exposed to reminders. Avoidance and escape behaviours help to maintain PTSD because they prevent the young person from semantically elaborating the trauma memory and from having experiences that disconfirm their beliefs about the need for continued vigilance or the likelihood of harm in the present. In vivo exposure to the site of the trauma and reminders allow the child to break the link between harmless triggers and the trauma memory by distinguishing between 'then and now'; that is, it helps children to discriminate current harmless triggers and their context from stimuli encountered during the traumatic event.

Site visit

Many children show marked avoidance of the site of the trauma. In some cases, this may have generalised to wide areas surrounding the trauma site. In other cases, avoidance is very specific. For example, a boy who was assaulted on a pavement would cross the road to walk along the opposite pavement for several yards before recrossing to continue his route. Many children will ask at the beginning of therapy if they will have to go back to the scene – an implicit recognition that it will help to 'face the fear'. Site visits to the scene of the trauma are usually conducted in the second half of the course of treatment, after some work on the trauma memory has been carried out.

A site visit may be set up as a behavioural experiment to test predictions about the consequences of exposure. It helps to obtain concrete, specific, testable predictions, such as 'It will make me go crazy, I will collapse, I'll run away, another trauma will happen.' Site visits can be set up as a demonstration that the young person is fighting back against the trauma, progressing in therapy and 'winning back' lost activities or places. In relation to previously carried out memory work, one purpose of a site visit is to help gather information to update 'frozen' or disjointed memories.

During a site visit, it helps for young people to retrace their steps, starting from before the traumatic event, and progressing through until the point where it finished. Children are asked to be detectives for changes. That is, they are asked to allow the memory to come to mind (it invariably will in the context of so many reminders) and to make a deliberate effort to compare the memory to current reality; to move backwards and forwards between the memory and current reality, contrasting differences, and noting all the things that have changed. For some children, there is often a great deal of positive surprise that current reality is not identical to their memory of the site. For children whose PTSD is especially chronic, site visits may become confusing initially because of the wide discrepancy between memory and reality. In this case, longer site visits may be needed to help reconstruct the memory – work that may be continued in later sessions via reliving and narrative work. Some children may not notice differences initially and will need encouragement to pay attention to contextual details.

Site visits provide ideal opportunities to correct distortions in trauma memories. For example, a young man who had been assaulted on a local train remembered getting off the train after the assault. He also remembered walking into a police station later. However, he had no memory of how he managed to get to the police station, which he knew to be about a 30-minute walk from where he had disembarked from the train. He was distressed by this 'missing 30 minutes' in his memory of the event, wondering if something too painful to remember had happened. During a site visit, he and his therapist retraced the train journey, hoping to be able to reconstruct the 30 minutes for which he appeared to be amnesic. However, by retracing the journey he quickly discovered that he had not disembarked at the stop which was 30 minutes from the police station, but at the next stop, which was very close to the police station. He was relieved to find out that he was not suffering from amnesia and that there was no missing period of time in which further trauma could have occurred. His anxiety and intrusions reduced accordingly.

During site visits, the stance taken is one of collaborative enquiry and discovery. Ask children to describe the traumatic event, pointing out where and how things happened. Allowing memories and associated feelings to arise, rather than making efforts to suppress them, is crucial: memories are then contrasted with current reality and changes to the scene. When specific predictions about the emotional or behavioural responses have been made, it will help to make their disconfirmation explicit. It is also helpful to point out and praise children's tolerance of intrusive recollections (also see Current Coping below). It can be useful to take a camera so that photos of the visit may be kept by children afterwards. These photos can serve as reminders of the child's bravery in facing up to the trauma, and of the ways that the site has altered since the trauma. As with in-session reliving, leave sufficient time so that arousal has decreased before leaving the scene: this usually happens quite quickly with these procedures. Last, it is helpful to set aside time in a subsequent session to 'debrief' the site visit, reflecting on what was learned and how it could be built on, and to set up further site visits as homework.

> Site visits provide an opportunity to compare trauma memories with current reality.

Working with triggers (stimulus discrimination)

In contrast to site visits, many young people are often unaware initially that exposure to triggers might be helpful. The first task here is to identify triggers. For children whose intrusions seem to arise out of the blue, listing triggers in this way can be therapeutic because it reduces a sense of being out of control and at the mercy of intrusive recollections. Detective work for triggers may involve detailed discussion in session of the context that intrusions tend to occur in. Trigger detection may also be set for homework, with the use of diaries. Note also that this procedure itself, akin to symptom monitoring, may have direct therapeutic benefit (perhaps because it reduces automatic avoidance of intrusions by encouraging the young person to pay attention deliberately to intrusions and their associated context and triggers). In carrying out this detective work for triggers, it will help to remember that triggers may not bear any meaningful relationship to the trauma, but may be sensory-based, such as particular shades of colour. For example, a child was assaulted by a man wearing a blue football shirt and it was noticed that the child seemed very anxious in geography lessons. Detective work revealed that the notebooks in the geography class had covers that were the same shade of blue as the assailant's shirt. This example reveals two key points. First, the trigger for the intrusion can be just a physical similarity. Second, sometimes the intrusion itself is the fear or terror which was experienced at the time of the trauma, without any conscious recollection of the context.

The second task in stimulus discrimination is to give a rationale for working with triggers. The message to convey is that harmless things (such as cars, the colour blue, the sound of breaking glass) have become triggers because they were present at the time of the trauma. They are not in themselves dangerous, but they now signal danger and trigger intrusions because they were linked with the trauma in the past. The task is to help the young person to 'break the link' between the harmless trigger and the trauma memory, which will in turn reduce intrusions.

The procedure is similar to that for site visits as described above. The young person is helped to deliberately expose themselves to a previously avoided trigger; to allow the intrusion and associated thoughts and feelings to arise; and to contrast the current context with the events of the past. For example, a teenage boy who had been assaulted and kicked in the head experienced a distressing intrusion when he encountered trainers of the sort that his assailant had worn. A pair of identical trainers was brought into the session. Looking at the trainer immediately triggered a strong intrusion. He was asked to allow the intrusion to come to mind, but then to look around the therapy room, noting what he could see and hear, and telling himself out loud where and when he was. This was repeated several times with triggers that progressively resembled the original more closely – for example, the sole of the trainer; then the sole of the trainer approaching his face. Each time he deliberately exposed himself to a trigger, he allowed feelings and memories to arise and then reoriented himself to the current context in order to 'break the link' between the trigger and the trauma. As with site visits, he was asked to look out for the differences between the harmless trigger in its current context and in the original traumatic context.

Stimulus discrimination techniques of this sort can be carried out with any identified triggers. Sound recordings are helpful for children who have been involved in traffic accidents and for whom the sound of emergency vehicle sirens or breaking glass are strong triggers. The sound can be played in the session, using the 'breaking the link' rationale and procedures of contrasting then versus now. Having carried this out in session, the young person can then be accompanied for in vivo trigger exposure (such as listening to real ambulances near a hospital) using the same procedures. Self-exposure to triggers might also be set for between-session homework.

Triggers may be subtle and specific. An assault victim who had been attacked from behind realised after detailed discussion that intrusions were triggered by quick movements in his far right visual field. The 'then versus now' stimulus discrimination procedures were carried out by having a colleague approach the teenager from the side to create the same movement in his visual field. Attention to the current safe context in the presence of this specific trigger allowed him to break the link between the trigger and the trauma memory.

For stimulus discrimination to be beneficial, safety behaviours need to be dropped. A girl who had been involved in a traffic accident experienced intrusions when she travelled by car. She was helped to deliberately expose herself to being in a car, to allow intrusions to arise, and to contrast 'then versus now' in order to break the link between the trigger and the trauma memory. This set of procedures began to show therapeutic effect only after a range of safety behaviours (such as holding on to the seat, keeping her hand near the emergency brake, scanning for danger) had been identified and dropped.

Finally, for both site visits and trigger work, it is important that the child is not dependent upon the therapist or the parent to confront avoided reminders. In vivo work at the site or with triggers for the intrusions may be set up for homework, to be done in conjunction with parents, but also alone as the young person grows in confidence.

> Stimulus discrimination can help to break the link between
> the harmless triggers and trauma recollections.

Current ways of responding

Behavioural and cognitive avoidance maintain symptoms of PTSD. In order for the memory to be adequately processed, avoidance needs to be dropped from the child's repertoire. Avoidance is tackled directly via imaginal reliving and in vivo exposure as above. Nevertheless, children may continue to avoid reminders in their day-to-day life, or to suppress thoughts and images when spontaneous intrusions occur. These unhelpful ways of responding need to be clearly identified and changed. Note that dysfunctional coping strategies on the part of the child may be maintained within the family via:

- the provision of instructions (parents may say something along the lines of 'don't talk about it now as it only upsets you')
- modelling of avoidance and fear (parents may not let their child go out alone anymore; parents may say that the neighbouring streets are too dangerous to walk at night)
- acceding to the child's efforts to avoid (parents may readily allow children to avoid cars)
- parents becoming angry or upset when the child attempts to talk about what happened or when they exhibit fearful behaviour.

To begin to help the child change their current way of responding to symptoms, it will help to review the model of PTSD and rationale for treatment that was agreed at the first session. Recap how avoidance, although it may provide temporary relief, does not work in the long term. Use metaphors as appropriate and behavioural experiments such as thought suppression to show how avoidance is unhelpful. Remind the child how well they are doing in changing avoidance through reliving and in vivo exposure. If possible, make the link between reductions in avoidance so far and improvement in intrusion symptoms. Some initial increase in anxiety is expected if the child drops his or her avoidant coping. Make sure the child understands this and also understands that it is a temporary increase: by minimising avoidance, memories will through time cease to intrude.

Next, ask what intrusions have occurred during the week (refer to the Child PTSD Symptom Scale, CPSS, if necessary), and how the child usually responds to such intrusions. Ask specifically about avoidance such as 'pushing thoughts away' or 'thinking of something nice instead', or about distraction. Ensure the child has understood that this sort of avoidance is unhelpful because it keeps the intrusions coming back. A variety of ways for alternative responding to intrusions can be explored. It is usually helpful to practise these in session before asking the young person to carry them out for homework.

> Help young people to identify and change avoidant coping.

Letting intrusions come and go naturally

In later sessions, having worked on the trauma memory and reinforced the model of PTSD, some older teenagers may be able to discuss the remaining intrusive memories as 'events in the mind' that cannot harm them and are not signals of imminent danger. They may be able to become observers of these events in their mind. That is, rather than automatically and habitually responding by attempting to push the intrusions out of mind, teenagers may experiment with taking a step back and 'just watching' the intrusions in their mind. They may watch the intrusion as it enters and watch it as it leaves naturally. A metaphor of watching the intrusion as if on a cinema or television screen can be introduced. Alternatively, the intrusion may be seen like a train coming into a station: rather than suppressing (i.e. trying to hold up the train), the young person is encouraged to 'step aside' and just watch the train from the platform as it passes through. Contrasting the effect of pushing intrusions away with just watching them come and go can be set up as a behavioural experiment, either in session or for homework.

Grab the image and hold it

To help the child switch out of habitual cognitive avoidance, ask him or her to imagine that the distressing image is like a picture floating in front of their face. Instead of pushing it away, children are asked to try to grab it deliberately and hold it at arm's length. Children can be asked to slowly bring the image closer to their face and then push it back out again. They may try zooming in and out, or try to turn it from colour to black and white, or try to make the image larger or smaller.

Deliberately play the full memory

This may be used with 'grab and hold' as above. When an intrusion occurs, children are instructed to 'freeze frame' it. They then press 'rewind' to play back to a few minutes before the intrusion. Next, children are asked to pause it, press play and watch the memory unfold until the end (the identified point when they felt safe). Integrating the intrusive image with events that occurred immediately before and afterwards in this way may also help to reduce disjointedness in the memory.

Self-talk

For younger children, it can help to ask them to remind themselves when an intrusion occurs that they are having a memory (i.e. it is just a memory, even though it feels real, but things are different now). For younger children, this may be helpful as an 'add on' to stimulus discrimination techniques. You may choose to set these alternative strategies for homework, and then review them in the following session. Not all techniques will work for everyone and children will probably need to try out several of them to see which works best.

> Children can learn to observe intrusive images come and go.

Dropping unhelpful coping strategies

In addition to identifying and changing avoidance, as described above, other unhelpful ways of coping should be identified so that the child can learn to change them. First, subtle forms of safety-seeking behaviours may prevent the young person from truly testing out problematic beliefs. For example, as described above, a girl who had been involved in a traffic accident was able to relearn that car travel remained safe only after she had identified and dropped her safety behaviours (such as holding on to the seat and keeping her hand near the emergency brake) while travelling by car.

Second, hypervigilance is common in young people with PTSD, especially those who have been assaulted, usually driven by beliefs such as 'Unless I am on guard all the time, I will be attacked again.' For example, a teenager who had been assaulted on a train reported that he felt safer if he made sure that he was always the last to board a train because this allowed him to check who else was boarding. After discussion in session, an alternative account was that although this strategy made him feel temporarily less anxious, it did not in reality make him any safer. It maintained his anxiety over the longer term because it prevented change in his belief that he was in grave danger unless he checked thoroughly. With his clinician initially, and then on his own for homework, he contrasted the effect of boarding trains with and without excessive checking. He discovered that although dropping his hypervigilance resulted in a temporary increase in anxious feelings, these soon declined. Importantly, he was not assaulted again, as he had predicted: he had learned that he was safe even if he 'dropped his guard'.

Third, rumination about the causes and consequences of the traumatic event is common to young people with PTSD. From the young person's point of view, rumination is often an attempt to 'sort out' what happened. However, it is unhelpful because it prevents direct memory processing. It rehearses and strengthens (rather than changes) unhelpful guilt- and shame-based appraisals and it lowers mood. It is therefore important to identify and change rumination. Suggestions as to how rumination might be tackled are given above and illustrated in the case example of Joshua in Chapter 6 (p. 108).

Image techniques

Children's intrusive images, usually of hotspots, may have a 'frozen' quality. The same image keeps intruding and it is extremely vivid and accompanied by a feeling of 'now-ness'. Children often report that these qualities change following reliving in that the image becomes less vivid, less frozen and less 'now', and more like other regular autobiographical memories. For some children, this change does not occur through reliving alone. Such changes may therefore need to be kick-started through direct attempts to change the image. This approach has the advantage that it can reduce avoidance by asking children deliberately to hold on to an intrusive image before manipulating it. It can also reduce the sense of uncontrollability that children report when experiencing intrusive images. A variety of techniques can be used. Not all techniques will work for all children so they will need to try them out to find out which works best for them.

Start by asking the child to deliberately recall their intrusive image, 'project it on to a wall' and stare at it. Children are invited to frame it like a picture or imagine that it is a picture on a television screen. Ask the young person to describe the image in some detail. Is it in black and white or colour? Is it still, or moving like a film? Ask the child to hold on to the image and move it around the wall, sliding it from corner to corner. Imagine taking a remote control and slowly turning the brightness control or the colour. If there are sounds associated with it, imagine turning down the volume. Imagine the picture becoming blurry or fuzzy as if the reception is bad. Imagine the picture fading away. Some children choose to imagine their intrusions as pictures on a computer screen. They imagine manipulating the image by using digital graphics and art software which can shrink, flip or distort the image; or combine and overlay with other images; or change the colours (see Dyregrov 1997a, 1997b for further examples).

It helps to explore different techniques to play around with the image and the child can be asked how they would like to manipulate it. This can have a marked effect on the child's sense of being out of control and helpless. Practise these techniques in session and set them for homework. Take care that the child is encouraged to engage with the traumatic image, rather than avoiding it. This is best achieved by doing the exercises slowly. Some children report that with repeated practice images will fade if they just hold on to them without doing much to alter them. If this happens, praise and encourage the child for obtaining this result.

Sleep hygiene

Children's sleep may be disrupted because of nightmares, and they may have trouble getting off to sleep if they are over-aroused. This can result in irritability, poor concentration and fatigue, which quickly have a knock-on effect on the whole family. Poor sleep and nightmares are best tackled early on in therapy. Advice and planning good routines to promote better sleep are usually carried out with parents, especially for younger children, whereas interventions for nightmares can be done with children alone. Advice for parents and children together may include emphasis on the importance of a regular routine before, with a wind down period or quiet time in the lead-up to bed. If necessary, children can practise some form of relaxation technique before bed. Once in bed, children may like to hear stories read to them, or like to read to themselves. They may like to listen to music to help them drop off to sleep. Children and adolescents should stay away from drinks that are high in sugar or contain caffeine in general, but particularly before bed.

When nightmares are a distressing symptom, two main techniques can be used to deal with them. As usual, bad dreams should be normalised as common reactions to trauma among young people and adults alike. This can be helpful for older children who may feel that nightmares are embarrassing and immature. For younger children, acknowledge that dreams are frightening and seem real at the time, but that they cannot come true or really hurt you.

Rehearsal relief of nightmares

Ask the child to tell you about their dream in detail from beginning to end. Younger children may like to draw some part of the dream. Older children can be asked to write it down in detail and from beginning to end for homework. As with reliving, it will help to engage all senses and include as much detail as possible. Children should then be asked to read their description of their nightmare until it becomes boring rather than frightening. Homework is to talk about their nightmare to parents or older siblings during the day (but not at night or just before bed!).

Changing endings of nightmares

Rehearsal alone may result in a decrease in nightmare frequency. When this does not happen, children can be helped to directly change the content of their nightmare. Ask the child to imagine a positive ending to their nightmare. Be creative, for example, by encouraging younger children to think about imaginary helpers or superheroes who might help in their dream. Older children may like to imagine a friend helping. Start rehearsing the dream as usual. Introduce the imaginary helper or change the ending to a positive one. This positive ending should be imagined in as much detail as the real dream. Ask children to say out loud the dream with a positive ending, from beginning to end. As above, ask them to draw or write the new dream for homework and to rehearse the new ending to it before bed.

> Encourage good sleep hygiene and reduce the emotional distress associated with nightmares.

Parent and carer work

All parents will be involved to some degree with their child's treatment. The extent to which they are involved will depend on their own reaction to the trauma and how well they are coping with their child's PTSD. Separate parent sessions, with minimal involvement in joint sessions initially, might be considered if the parent has repeated difficulty in inhibiting themselves from making catastrophic or blaming statements in front of the child:

- 'He is never going to walk normally again.'
- 'We were all almost killed.'
- 'It was the worst thing that could ever have happened to us.'
- 'It is his own fault for not looking before he crossed the street.'

For carers who have been affected by the trauma, the process over the course of CT for PTSD often involves separate sessions initially to reduce parental anxiety, before bringing child and parent together for joint sessions later. However, most parents will be encouraged to help their child with homework and, when necessary, to modify the way they cope with their child's distress. Some parents may be more closely involved in therapy from the outset, with a number of joint parent–child sessions. With very young children, separation anxiety is a frequent co-morbid condition and some might refuse to be seen alone. As treatment progresses and the child experiences some relief from PTSD symptoms, the parent can be faded out of the treatment room.

With most children, parents will always be asked to join at the very end of the session so that the therapist and child can explain what has been done in that session and to discuss the homework assignment for the coming week. In some cases, this joint child–parent meeting should be followed by a brief meeting with the parent to discuss difficulties the child may be under-reporting (e.g. bedwetting, clinginess, aggression). Joint sessions with the parent and child may be needed to help challenge any misappraisals on the part of the child, or for the parent to model talking and expressing feelings in the clinic environment.

Education for parents about PTSD and rationale for treatment

At the end of the first session, give parents or carers the handout about children's PTSD to take home and read (see Appendix B). Let the parents know that their child's current difficulty is a very common reaction to traumatic events, for which effective treatment is available. When appropriate, emphasise how their child's reaction is a classic example of PTSD with the hallmark symptoms of the disorder. It helps at this early stage to show how avoidance and intrusions are related as part of the rationale for treatment. Use the thought suppression experiment and metaphor with the parents to demonstrate this. Whenever possible, draw out any similarities between the child's and parents' reaction and their ways of coping to help parents understand their child's reaction and the rationale for treatment. This is an opportunity to describe treatment and the parents' likely involvement, and for parents to ask questions about the nature of PTSD and its treatment.

> Psycho-education provides parents with information about PTSD and the rationale for treatment.

Involving parents and carers in reclaiming the child's life

It will help to explain in detail the importance of children beginning to re-engage in normal activities as a means of moving on from the trauma. Plan activities for the week with the parent and child jointly and schedule these using diaries when appropriate. A separate discussion with parents might be needed beforehand to address any concerns about current threats and to tackle overprotectiveness if it is impeding resumption of normal activities.

> Parental overprotection needs to be identified and addressed.

Facilitating talking about the trauma within the family

It is especially important to assess early on carers' views on talking about the trauma because many carers will hold firm views that talking about the trauma is unhelpful, or even harmful. Parents may not want to talk about the trauma and their child's reaction to it with the child because they underestimate their child's difficulties, because they believe talking will further upset the child, or because they believe that talking will result in further parental upset. In separate sessions with parents, it is therefore helpful to begin to elicit and change any maladaptive beliefs about the value of talking.

1   If parents minimise their child's difficulties, it is important to let them know – with the child's permission – what the child has told you about their current state.
2   For parents who have difficulty empathising with their child, it can help to relate the child's difficulties to the parents' own when appropriate. Consider asking the parents to join the end of future sessions: in such a joint meeting the child can be encouraged to tell the parents directly about their difficulties, especially symptoms such as daytime intrusions which parents can easily overlook. Later, if appropriate and with the child's permission, consider having parents listen to the child's reliving tape.
3   If parents feel strongly that talking about the trauma in the family will further upset the child, again consider asking the parents to join in at the end of a session and model talking about the event. Facilitate and encourage the child and parents to talk to each another about the event. Some parents may benefit from quite specific advice about how and when to talk with the child, and may want to practise this with you in a role play before joining for a family session. The general advice is for parents to let the child know that they can talk when they want to and to answer questions honestly but in a way that the child can understand. The child should not be 'forced' to talk things through with parents, but should feel able to approach parents when they want to.
4   If parents feel that talking will be too upsetting for them (rather than for their child), this needs to be addressed. This is most likely to happen if parents themselves have been involved in the trauma and have developed PTSD symptoms. Here, joint sessions in which the trauma is talked about in detail are not advisable without first having had individual sessions with the parents. Consider referring the parents on to adult services if appropriate.

Joint sessions such as these in which memory work is carried out are usually preceded by some separate sessions with the adults. In family meetings, the therapist's skilful use of questions and probes can help to regulate the emotional temperature and facilitate memory processing.

> Identify parents' problems and address unhelpful parental appraisals about the trauma.

Cognitive restructuring with parents as co-therapists

Children's hotspots and misappraisals may be to do with parents. For example, children may have thought that their parents or siblings were going to die during the trauma. They may be concerned that the parent blames them for the accident; that awful things happened to the parent while they were separated; or that the parent is now at risk of dying because they had to go to hospital in the aftermath of the trauma. Often, parents are unaware of such issues and so it can be very helpful for the child to tell their parent about their worst fears. Depending on the nature of the trauma, when children tell parents that they thought that mum or dad was going to die, most parents will respond with great warmth and care. This can have the effect of freeing the child and parents to talk to each another outside the session about the trauma.

Again, misappraisals can often be corrected simply by having the therapist or the parents provide the child with more factual information. Having had a separate session with the parent alone if necessary, invite the parent in for a joint session. Have the child tell the parent what they thought at the time and ask the parent to respond. Parents can help to clarify the facts of the trauma and clear up any misunderstandings. Where the child and parent were separated, it can be very helpful for children to hear about the trauma and its aftermath (such as the parent going to hospital) from the parent's point of view, but take care that parents are able to do this without becoming overwhelmed or upset.

> Parents' account of the trauma can provide new information to help update the child's trauma memory.

Over-generalised fear within the family

Some parents may become overprotective following a trauma. This is particularly likely if the parents were themselves involved in the event or its aftermath and will usually require individual sessions with the parent. This will be an adjunct to (not a substitute for) weekly individual sessions with the child. It helps to address any parental separation anxiety of this sort through advice about graded separation. If possible, enlist the help of the other parent or carer. It will help to tie this work on graded separation into the notion of the parent reclaiming their life from the trauma – just as their child is doing.

Sessions with parents alone

For some children, it will be appropriate to have a session or two alone with parents. This may be done mid-treatment and can be set up as a progress review. Parent-alone sessions are indicated when one or both parents are anxious themselves and need advice on managing their own traumatic memories or their child's responses. Such sessions are particularly helpful when the child is aggressive or has behaviour problems and advice and planning of behavioural management can be given.

> Plan one or two parent-only sessions into the intervention.

Parents and carers with PTSD

Parents and carers may have developed significant symptoms of PTSD through being involved in the same event as their child, hearing about the event or via an unrelated trauma. It is not uncommon for a current trauma which is affecting the child to remind parents of their own previous traumatic events. At times, this may reactivate painful memories and in some parents may amount to a full, delayed-onset PTSD. Presentation can be complex in such cases because parents' intrusion symptoms might relate to both the recent and the earlier traumatic event, while cognitive themes (helplessness, worthlessness, incompetence) may link the two events. Significant symptoms of depression may also be present.

It is therefore helpful to screen routinely for PTSD and depression in parents as part of the initial intake procedure. When there have been minor or transient symptoms relating to the current trauma, it may be worthwhile discussing with parents the links between their symptoms and those of their child. This can help some parents to gain insight into what is troubling their offspring. When symptoms are more persistent or troubling for parents, it can be helpful to have a longer session with parents alone. Initially, the aim will be to provide information about PTSD in adults and to explain the principles and rationale for treatment. For milder symptoms, some advice on self-care and guided self-help can easily be given, perhaps linked to feedback about their child's treatment. While some parents may be reluctant to discuss their own reactions, they will readily talk about their children – and this can be a way for therapists to begin discussing whether treatment is indicated for parents and what the options are for treatment.

Some parents will be quite clear that they do not want to pursue treatment for themselves. Our clinical experience and recent published reports (Scheeringa *et al.* 2007) suggest that while treatment for parents is usually beneficial for children, it is not necessary for parental PTSD to be treated in order for children to improve. However, it may be that an underlying avoidant response style in parents (rather than PTSD symptoms per se) may impede children's recovery. This may be seen, for example, when parents who have been co-traumatised in a road traffic accident refuse to drive their offspring along the same stretch of road, or when parents refuse to talk about the trauma with their child. Clinical judgement will be needed to decide whether to pursue such interventions. It will be unhelpful for children to talk about the trauma to parents if they are not yet ready to do so and likely to show a very strong emotional reaction, or if they might terminate a discussion midway through. Similarly, it would not be helpful for children to carry out exposure-based homework with parents if they are likely to become overwhelmed with emotion, panic or want to escape. Ultimately, this may place some limits on what you are able to achieve for children.

Some parents who seem reluctant to pursue treatment for themselves initially may change their minds later. This sometimes occurs as a result of having had positive experiences of discussing the trauma and their reactions with their child's therapist, or as a result of seeing the beneficial effects of treatment on their child. Some parents may decide that, although they are reluctant to pursue treatment for themselves, they will do so in order to help their children. When parents want to pursue treatment, this could be provided by the child's clinician, or referral could be made to adult services. If specialist services with short waiting lists are available, then the latter option is often preferable. Close contact between child and adult services is helpful. Referral to adult services may be the preferred option if parents are presenting with complex PTSD or significant co-morbid depression. If parental symptoms are uncomplicated and treatment is to be provided by the child's clinician, then it will help to separate this from the young person's treatment, with sessions offered for parents on a different day. Although this may present practical problems, it is advisable because parents' individual treatment may at times be demanding and exhausting and they may not be in an optimal state of mind to care for their child immediately after an intensive session.

> **Assess parents' treatment needs and consider their implications on the child's treatment.**

Relapse prevention

Relapse appears to be very rare in successfully treated children. However, some symptoms may return, particularly around the anniversary of the trauma, or if the child is exposed to another traumatic event, or experiences stressful life events such as bullying, illness or bereavement. The main procedure in preventing relapse is to assist the child in identifying what they discovered in treatment that helped them to get better. This can take the form of a written 'Blueprint for the Future', usually completed in the final session. Using a whiteboard or simple paper and pencil, the child is talked through a number of questions – suitably adapted for age and ability – and their summary answers are written down for them to keep and refer to in the future if needed:

1   Start by asking the young person to look back and recall what problems were present at the start of treatment and how they developed. This can help children to realise just how far they have come in a short course of therapy.
2   Ask what was previously keeping the problem going: this is a good opportunity to help the child recall the unhelpful maintaining factors that were operating for them.
3   The next key question concerns what children learned in therapy that was useful.
4   This might be followed up with more specific prompts about any unhelpful beliefs that they used to hold, or maladaptive coping strategies that they previously used – and the alternative more helpful ways of thinking or behaving that they have learned in sessions.
5   Young people can be asked to write down what they would do if symptoms were to return, or if they were to be involved in another scary event.
6   Similarly, it is often helpful for children to think about what help and advice they would give to another child who was involved in a frightening event.

Finally, younger children can be provided with a personalised diploma or certificate. The diploma will note their bravery in overcoming the effects of the trauma and their having successfully learned a lot of skills for dealing with anxiety-provoking events. For older children and adolescents, we sometimes provide them with a letter setting out the specific skills they learnt in treatment and how they used them, and thanking them for their efforts and willingness to share. A copy of something very similar is given to the parents of both younger and older children. Examples of a diploma and letter are given in Appendix D.

Working with younger children

The components above can be characterised as 'evidence based' for children and young people of around eight years of age and older. That is, there is evidence that the cognitive model from which treatment components are derived is applicable and that this treatment is effective for this age group. The same is not true for children younger than eight years old, especially pre-school children. First, PTSD presents differently in younger children, as described in detail in Chapter 2. Second, the degree to which cognitive models of the disorder apply to younger children is less clear. Third, there are fewer treatment outcome studies of pre-school children on which to base firm conclusions.

Nevertheless, the available evidence suggests that the broad principles of intervention described above are applicable to much younger children. Younger children's memories may be disjointed and out of sequence. They may be muddled about the causes and consequences of the event. They may show clear behavioural avoidance and parental reactions (at the time and subsequently) appear to be highly relevant to young children's adjustment. In that case, the clinician's task is to use these first principles in helping to formulate the young child's problems, and then to adapt the sorts of techniques described above so that they are appropriate for young children and their carers. Examples of the ways in which some of these treatment components can be adapted when working with young children from about four to seven years old are described below (see also Scheeringa *et al.* 2007).

Context and process in working with younger children

The assessment process can follow a similar structure to that for older children, but it is important to have two professionals involved so that the young child is not left alone while the parent is being seen. The family is seen together initially, and some drawing material can be provided for the young child. The aim here is for the child to observe the therapists and parents interacting, discussing non-traumatic material (such as home life, the child's school and teachers), and then talking gently about the facts of the trauma. The clinician can say to the parents that they would like to talk to the child about the trauma too, and ask parents to agree in front of the child. In this way, parents 'give permission' for the child to talk about what has happened, and the child sees that the strange new adults are trusted by the parents. At a suitable point, the clinician will suggest that the child continues to play while the parent goes outside to talk alone to one of the clinicians. Children will usually want to see where their parents are going to be, but having satisfied themselves that they are nearby can readily be encouraged to continue to draw or play with the second therapist. From time to time, it is expected that the child may want to pop out to check in on their parents.

When separation issues are handled in such a way, with the child being given time to warm up and get used to the therapist, being allowed to check in on the parent, and with shorter sessions than for older children, then separation issues rarely present a problem. It is important that parent and child can separate so that the parent can give feedback on the child's current state and be given advice about management, and for the child to be able to recall scary experiences without being influenced by or concerned about parental reactions. Depending on the age of the child, his or her level of separation anxiety, and the parents' level of anxiety and beliefs about treatment, you may need to manage separation in a similar way in subsequent sessions – at least in early sessions.

> Carefully plan any separations of young children from their parents.

Affect regulation and relaxation training for younger children

A distinctive feature of the CT protocol for PTSD described above for older children is that it does not routinely require anxiety management skills such as relaxation training. Under Ehlers and Clark's (2000) cognitive model of PTSD, there are two competing considerations with regard to relaxation training. First, an optimal level of engagement with the trauma memory is required. Excessively high levels of arousal (as in dissociation) can interfere with this. Some sort of grounding or other arousal reduction techniques may therefore be required. Second, it is important that intentional efforts to reduce arousal do not become safety behaviours which prevent disconfirmation of inaccurate beliefs. With these two considerations in mind, relaxation training can have a value, but it is not assumed to be routinely required (as it is in some other CBT programmes).

Older children and teenagers can often tolerate high levels of anxiety within a therapeutic environment, and so are able to learn that anxiogenic cognitions are inaccurate by exposing themselves to the feared situation while dropping efforts at control such as safety behaviours or relaxation. There are reasons to proceed cautiously before dropping routine relaxation training for younger children. First, it is not clear that young children have the skills necessary to tolerate high levels of fear and anxiety. Second, it is not clear that they have the cognitive capacity to understand the rationale for allowing themselves to become anxious. For these reasons, brief relaxation training, in combination with other techniques, may be helpful for children of about seven years or younger.

Brief relaxation training may take a number of forms. Progressive muscle relaxation is a method of tensing and then relaxing major muscle groups sequentially; children can be taught a shortened form involving fewer muscle groups. Diaphragmatic breathing (or 'belly breathing') is included in many yoga practices and can be taught to children in a simplified form to counter hyperventilation. Safe place techniques utilise children's imagination to help visualise calming scenes, and can be combined with breathing and body exercises. Variants of these procedures are common in many treatment approaches for paediatric anxiety and have been described in detail elsewhere (e.g. see Bernstein *et al.* 2000).

In combination with relaxation training, young children can be taught how to rate and report degrees of feeling scared or upset by using feelings thermometers (see Appendix C). These can be drawn out with the young child, using a scale appropriate to their level of numeracy, or using simple labels, colours or stickers. It can be enormously helpful for young children to learn to monitor and regulate their level of anxiety and upset. It is also of course useful for the therapist to be able to check in quickly with the child to enquire how they are feeling, and to ensure that they do not leave the session in a state of high arousal.

> Relaxation techniques and feelings thermometers can be helpful with young children.

Imaginal reliving with younger children

As with adults and older children, some form of exposure to the trauma memory is needed for therapeutic effect. Young children may not have the cognitive capacity to engage in a classic imaginal reliving, nor be able to sustain concentration for long enough to gain benefit from such a procedure. For young children with only elementary literacy skills, narrative exposure through writing is also ruled out. Other creative ways of helping young children to access the trauma memory must be found. Drawing and playing are obvious choices. Pynoos and Eth (1986) describe the use of drawing in the initial assessment of traumatised children. The child is asked to draw a picture, 'something that you can tell a story about', as a means to begin discussion of the trauma itself. Most children love to draw and so one-off pictures of the trauma can be a useful starting point in beginning to talk about what has happened.

While one-off drawings can be a useful starting point, more structured procedures are useful in later sessions. Young children often appear confused about the sequence of events and so, in line with the cognitive model, it is helpful to construct a pictorial narrative with a beginning, middle and end. Over several sessions, young children are helped to construct a coherent narrative in cartoon strip or storyboard form. A booklet can be provided, with empty frames to be filled in sequentially, perhaps just one or two frames per page. Children can be helped to personalise them with their name and stickers. The narrative is worked on week by week, with perhaps one or two drawings completed per session. As the child draws, they are encouraged to verbalise as much as they can about what happened. Children may be able to give Selective Units of Discomfort Scale (SUDS) ratings from their feelings thermometer. Others may want to write some words next to each cartoon. In helping the child to reconstruct the narrative in this way, the clinician may be able to identify hotspots and associated misappraisals. Young children may be able to tell what their thoughts and feelings were at the time – and in this way muddles and confusions can be identified and altered.

It is helpful to give a very clear structure to sessions, with immediate rewards contingent on trying to work on the 'memory book'. For example, the clinician may wish to let children choose a story and agree that it will be read together at the end of the session for five minutes. Other children may prefer to play or to make some other drawings. It is important that this does not interfere with the focused work of the session, but is instead planned for the end of the session not only as a concrete reward for effort, but also as a means to allow the young child's arousal levels to decrease before ending the session. Planning treats also makes the sessions enjoyable and helps with engagement. Having carried out relaxation training before embarking on construction of the cartoon-strip narrative, the clinician may wish to check on the child's feelings thermometer, and guide him or her through some brief relaxation at the end if appropriate.

It is helpful for the child to leave their memory book at the clinic. This means the book is always there to work on from session to session. At the end of the session, the child is able to shut the book and leave it with you: as with older children, the message is that one can learn to choose when to remember and when not to remember.

> Non-verbal means can be used to facilitate imaginal reliving with younger children.

Parents and carers of younger children

In early sessions, parents will generally be seen alone while the child is being seen separately. The focus of these early sessions is likely to be on psycho-education about the effects of trauma on children and parents; identifying and changing unhelpful beliefs about the avoidant coping strategies; and continuing assessment and specific advice regarding helping the child with separation issues or bedtime battles.

Parents are updated in detail about the content of sessions with their child and the child's progress. In this way, the value of addressing the trauma (rather than avoiding it) is demonstrated to the parent from the beginning. An important goal when working with young children is for the parent and child to be able to talk through the trauma together. Before doing this, it is helpful to gauge the parent's ability to talk through the trauma, and to identify parental misappraisals such as guilt and begin to address these. The clinician might ask the parent to tell them about the trauma from the child's point of view, and enquire about any fears or misapprehensions the parent has about talking with their child – commonly to do with how one or the other of them might react. Parents may say that they do not know how to talk to their child, or would not know what to say if he or she asked such and such a question. The clinician may address these directly and explore and practise with the parent ways of responding to their child.

Having done some preparatory work of this nature with parents, at a certain point the clinician may wish to plan a joint session with parent and child together.

Initially, joint work may involve the parent coming into the child's therapy room at the end of the separate sessions. Children will invariably want to show off their drawings and memory book to mum or dad. Parents may need instructions and prompting to praise and reward the child for having done such work – but at this stage detailed retelling of the trauma is not needed. A little later, parents might be invited to stay with the therapist and child while the child is working on his or her memory book. It can be helpful to use family rooms if available, with the parent observing from behind a one-way screen. If this is not available, parents might take a seat in the therapy room. In this way, parents can observe how the therapist listens to the child and encourages detailed recall of the events of the trauma. Parents are often apprehensive about this, but usually surprised both at the amount of detailed recall the child shows and at how children are able to do this without the expected degree of distress or upset.

Modelling their behaviour on that of the therapist, the parent is then invited to listen to their child's narrative, structured around the memory book. Children will be keen to show the book to parents, and to talk through the cartoon strip scene by scene. The tendency of young children will be to rush through, so the task of the therapist (and parent) is to slow the pace. Parents are encouraged to use gentle questioning to help the child keep the story going. Parents will want to praise children for their work and for being brave in talking through what happened. It can be striking in these joint sessions how attuned young children are to possible distress in parents: they will often be closely watching mum or dad for signs of upset or avoidance. It is also common for new material to arise in joint sessions. It will be important to spend time with the parent in the next session, asking what the experience was like for them, whether it prompted further questioning or comments from the child during the week, and how the parent responded to them. It can also be useful to reflect on the parent's previous fears about the consequences of talking, and to probe for any changes in unhelpful beliefs.

Joint sessions will probably need to be repeated as the young child's memory book is worked on and elaborated. Joint work with parents here is invaluable as there will invariably be gaps or muddles in the memory which the parent can help to resolve. The clinician may want to repeat the process of using individual time with parents to clarify what has happened, or to help the parent find words to correct any misunderstandings that may have become apparent in the child's narrative. In subsequent joint sessions, the child and parent are helped to work collaboratively in constructing a joint narrative. It will be far more salient for young children if muddles and misunderstandings are unravelled and sorted out by mum or dad than if this is done by the therapist.

In summary, the process of facilitating therapeutic discussion of the trauma within the family, or between child and parent, needs to be handled with skill and care. Attention needs to be paid to engagement and separation issues from the outset. Children and parents should be seen separately at the beginning so that each can tell the therapist details of the event. After preparation, support, instructions and advice, parent and child are then brought back together and the therapist can facilitate listening and talking about the trauma and its aftermath. This process is repeated as the trauma memory is elaborated and clarified. This procedure is aimed primarily at the child. However, processing of the memory is likely to be beneficial for parents too. Importantly, parents are recruited as co-therapists – a process which is likely to restore a sense of being a competent, skilled parent.

> Work towards involving parents or carers in talking about the trauma with their child.

In vivo exposure with young children

As with older children and teenagers, having completed some memory work first, in vivo exposure to the site or to triggers may be helpful. Just as with memory work, the clinician will want to recruit the parent as a co-therapist for this task, and will therefore need to ensure that the parent understands the rationale and procedures, and is ready to embark on this sort of work. Stimulus discrimination techniques described above are likely to be rather complex for young children to understand and carry out. Instead, exposure with younger children tends to take a graded approach and is combined with relaxation skills to promote habituation to reminders.

A list of triggers may be drawn up with parents and children. In doing this, it helps to enquire about what things the child avoids, and what things seem to upset him or her. These triggers are then graded into a hierarchy, with parental help. Depending on their age, children may be more or less involved in drawing up the hierarchy – the more the child is involved the better. It will be necessary to make sure that the parent is willing and able to confront reminders and to provide help and support for their child in doing so.

Either within session alongside the therapist, or as homework tasks later in therapy, deliberate planned exposure to distressing and avoided reminders is carried out. The child is asked to report on their SUDS level if possible, and to practise relaxation while in the situation to bring their anxiety down. Encouraging comments from mum or dad and pre-rehearsed coping self statements can be useful here. The parent and therapist can provide plenty of praise and pre-agreed tangible rewards for the young child for their bravery. Of crucial importance for young children here is the response of the parent to reminders. It may be helpful to prepare or rehearse in vivo exposure with the parent alone first so that they can practise modelling calm coping behaviour for their child.

> Graded exposure to traumatic reminders accompanied by relaxation training is helpful for younger children.

Difficulties around bedtime, sleep problems, bedwetting, fear of toileting alone and clinginess are common in younger children who have been exposed to trauma. These sorts of difficulties are sometimes what prompt referrals of young children – parents' understandable worry is that the child is regressing in some way. During the initial assessment, it is important to take a detailed history in order to discover the extent to which current problems represent a change from pre-trauma functioning. Equally important, the clinician will want to assess parental attitudes and beliefs, particularly with regard to separation and overprotection. Separation anxiety and clinginess often decline once work on the memory has progressed. If parents appear overprotective, then addressing issues related to over-generalised fear within the family, or perhaps issues around guilt and responsibility, with parents alone may be helpful. If two carers are living at home, it is useful to invite both for a parent session so that a consistent approach at home can be developed. If some symptoms of separation anxiety remain following trauma-related work with the child and carers, then tackling separation anxiety directly may be needed. A graded approach to separation, with contingent rewards, is often effective.

Similarly, night-time problems may resolve following trauma-focused work. If they persist, then some direct work may be needed. Problems may be to do with difficulty settling initially, frequent waking, coming into the parents' bedroom during the night, or frequent nightmares. The importance of a regular bedtime routine can be emphasised, with parents encouraged to implement ways of soothing children prior to getting them off to sleep. Sticker charts with contingent rewards can used. Parents may be helped by a written plan for managing their child if they come into the parents' room upon wakening. Some young children will enjoy decorating their bedroom or bed with drawings or stickers of favourite superhero characters who will help them to stay in their bedroom if they wake up in the night. The clinician might practise with the young child how he or she can make use of imaginary superhero helpers.

> Behavioural methods and contingent reinforcement are helpful ways of addressing separation anxiety and night-time problems.

6

Cognitive therapy for PTSD with adolescents

Therapeutic work with adolescents – roughly defined here as secondary school age – can present unique challenges. These include issues of independence and autonomy in the context of parental involvement in treatment; the impact of trauma on self-evaluation and identity; and the importance of peer relationships and evaluation by others. Account needs to be taken of important goals and transitions. Compared to younger children, the presentation of PTSD symptoms in adolescence more closely resembles that of adults. Patterns of co-morbidity also differ: depression, for example, is relatively more common and separation anxiety relatively less common (although by no means absent) than in primary school age and pre-school children. Unlike younger children, common traumatic events for adolescents include exposure to interpersonal violence of some kind (assaults at school, violent street robbery), requiring therapists to find a way of making accurate judgements about the realistic level of danger encountered by young people – ensuring that therapeutic exposure is always safe.

Three cases are presented in some detail to illustrate some of these important aspects of adolescent work, to contextualise some of the treatment components described in Chapter 5, and to describe the therapeutic process from first assessment to post-treatment follow-up. They are based on real referrals to a specialist tertiary trauma clinic for young people, but have been altered to preserve anonymity.

Case 1: Joshua (17 years old)

Joshua was referred by his general practitioner (GP) for assessment and treatment of possible depression following a motorbike accident some six months previously.

Assessment

Joshua was accompanied to the first assessment appointment by his mother, and each of them was interviewed separately. Joshua said that he had been feeling down ever since his motorbike accident, and didn't know how to 'shake it off'. His mother complained that he was a 'changed character' who had dropped out of college and now spent most of his time at home, frequently arguing with her.

The accident had happened six months previously. He had been riding along a suburban street early one summer evening when a car on a side road ahead of him pulled out. Joshua hit the wing of the car and was thrown off his bike on to the road ahead. He was taken to hospital by ambulance where he was found to have sustained some minor injuries and was discharged the same day.

Interviewed using the Anxiety Disorders Interview Schedule (ADIS; see also Chapter 3, p. 30), Joshua reported having frequent intrusive recollections of the accident during the day. Intrusive images were of two main sorts: of the car, moments before impact; and of himself lying in the middle of a busy road after the impact. These images often arose when he was bored or underoccupied and were frequently accompanied by depressive rumination about the causes and consequences of the accident. He had occasional bad dreams of the accident, became upset when reminded of it and was quick to anger if his mother or girlfriend tried to raise the issue with him. He attempted to suppress memories of the accident when they came to mind (cognitive avoidance) and he had neither been back on a motorbike nor to the accident site since it happened (behavioural avoidance). He had given up football, dropped out of college and saw far less of his friends because he felt that they did not understand what had happened to him. He was gloomy about the future. Joshua's mother was not aware that he was experiencing intrusions and nightmares, but confirmed that he avoided all reminders of the accident. He tended to 'flare up' if the issue was raised, and in general was more irritable. Mother in turn frequently became angry with Joshua. She was disappointed that he was 'lazing around at home' rather than attending college.

Formulation

Joshua was suffering from chronic PTSD and co-morbid depression. Detailed chronology revealed that depressive symptoms emerged after PTSD symptoms. The primary disorder in need of treatment was PTSD. Collaborative formulation was started in the second session and was developed as sessions progressed. Joshua's memory did not appear to be particularly disjointed, but was heavily laden with sensory detail and easily triggered by physically similar cues. In terms of appraisals, two key peri-traumatic misappraisals were identified early on. First, when lying on the road after the impact, he believed that he had broken his neck and was paralysed. Second, when lying on the road, he thought that an approaching bus was about to run him over and kill him. Other important misappraisals related to the accident (bad things always happen to me; I can't stop bad things from happening) and its effect (I'm weak, I can't cope), and were often rehearsed in depressive-type rumination. His avoidant coping style was preventing change in these key misappraisals, thereby contributing to the maintenance of symptoms. The reciprocal relationship between Joshua's sense of current threat and his unhelpful coping strategies is illustrated in Figure 6.1. He believed that the occurrence of intrusions meant that he was going crazy. This belief motivated his attempts to suppress the intrusions.

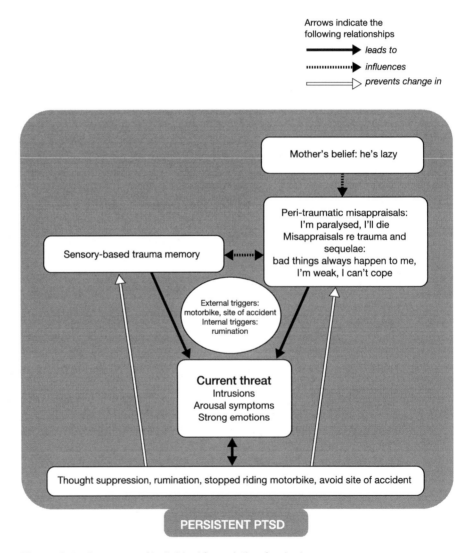

Figure 6.1   Summary of individual formulation for Joshua

The inadvertent effect of such thought suppression was to increase his intrusion frequency, which in turn strengthened his belief that he must be going crazy, which led to further efforts at control, and so on. Key family factors included a lack of discussion of the accident and its aftermath with his family, and a relationship with his mother which was now overshadowed by anger and irritability.

Treatment

This formulation, worked out collaboratively with Joshua in initial sessions, suggested a number of targets for treatment, which included:

- modifying his beliefs related to the accident and its aftermath
- modifying his peri-traumatic misappraisals and updating his trauma memory accordingly
- dropping dysfunctional avoidant coping and rumination
- facilitating discussion of the accident and its aftermath with his mother.

Psycho-education and normalisation

Early sessions included work on normalising Joshua's reactions to the accident, with the aim of beginning to modify his belief that he was weak and could not cope. He read the handout describing PTSD symptoms (see Appendix B) and expressed surprise that 'it's all me, written there in black and white'. Further psycho-education on the nature of anxiety and its protective function helped Joshua to view his reactions as essentially normal and common, and not indicative of weakness. Messages about Joshua being weak and unable to cope also arose in his relationship with his mother, who frequently criticised him for 'not doing anything'. Mother was therefore invited to the clinic in order to carry out some joint work, but she chose not to attend.

Reclaiming your life

Behavioural activation was started early on. Joshua was helped to generate a list of previously enjoyable activities that he had dropped since his accident. This was distressing initially because it showed him just how much he had been affected by the accident. However, he readily grasped the vicious cycle between reduced activity and lowered mood (accompanied in his case by depressive rumination), and was prepared to try out new strategies to break the cycle. The therapist's main task at this stage was to help break down seemingly daunting tasks into manageable chunks. Reclaiming life activities were monitored throughout therapy and discussed in following sessions as behavioural experiments in which he was discovering the effect on mood and rumination of increasing activity levels. Progress was patchy initially. The main block for Joshua in recontacting old friends was his shameful feelings about his reactions to the accident. This was addressed by tackling shame issues directly with him and by practical discussion, with 'scripting' and role play, of how he could deal with friends' questions.

Reliving

Joshua easily understood the rationale for reliving. He was quite sceptical that it might help because he felt that he thought about the accident 'all the time' already. His therapist made a distinction between ruminative thinking about the causes and consequences of the accident (which he often did) and thinking directly of the events as he had experienced them (which he did very rarely). Joshua remained unconvinced, but was prepared to give reliving a try. In his first full reliving, he stayed in the present tense with little prompting, spoke slowly and recalled many sensory details. In discussing the reliving in detail afterwards, Joshua said that it was upsetting but manageable – it felt 'weird' and his body felt strange. He was shocked at how much he could recall, particularly how 'real' it felt, and at how different it was to non-traumatic autobiographical memories. A discussion followed about the differences in quality between regular autobiographical memories and trauma memories. This was helpful for Joshua in seeing how his current difficulties were due to the memory, not to any inherent weakness on his part. It proved a boost to his engagement and motivation in therapy. Following this first full reliving, later sessions used a written narrative in order to capture and integrate new information that was emerging.

Cognitive restructuring

Reliving was used to identify misappraisals around hotspots. The most distressing part of the memory was when he was lying on the road after impact. He could not feel any pain and thought that he must have broken his neck. His thoughts at the time were along the lines of: 'I'm paralysed, I'll never play football or walk again, my life is over.' Second, he recalled thinking at the time he was lying on the road that he could not move out of the way of an oncoming bus and he thought, 'I'll get run over and killed.' These thoughts were written down using a version of the form described in Chapter 5. Although he now knew that he had not been paralysed, Joshua remained perplexed as to why he did not feel any pain at the time of the accident. A discussion followed about the extent of injuries and the role of endorphins in pain, with illustrations relevant to him, including footballers who continue playing without pain despite injury. Joshua was able to remember that he had indeed felt some pain once the danger was over. Second, he now knew that he had not been run over by a bus – but he still felt that he 'might have been', even though he could not remember having seen a bus. He and his clinician were initially puzzled as to why this thought had occurred to him since no buses were present. Joshua later recalled a conversation with a nurse in hospital. In an attempt to be helpful, the nurse had told Joshua how lucky he was not to have been run over by an oncoming bus. Recalling this conversation was a turning point for Joshua and he reasoned with the clinician that the comments from the nurse, occurring so soon after the accident, had been integrated into Joshua's trauma memory. (More straightforward in gathering information to update this 'hot cognition' was the later discovery from a site visit that the accident spot was not on a bus route!).

Reliving with cognitive restructuring

The next task was to integrate this new information into the trauma memory. This was done initially by writing new information into the narrative at the appropriate point. Later, this new information was recalled and spoken out loud in verbal reliving of hotspots. That is, during a reliving, Joshua recalled his hot cognition ('I think I'm paralysed') and then articulated out loud the new information ('What I know now is that I am not paralysed. The reason I cannot feel any pain is because I have no major injuries. My body's automatic reaction is to release natural painkillers so that I can keep myself safe, and this is why I cannot feel the injury to my wrist.'). Additionally, while still in the reliving, Joshua was asked to demonstrate to himself that he was not paralysed by moving his shoulders, arms and legs.

A similar procedure was used for the second hotspot. He recalled his original cognition while doing a verbal reliving ('A bus is going to come and run me over.'). He was then asked to say out loud the new information ('What I know now is that there was not a bus coming. Buses do not come down this street.'). Additionally, he was asked, while still in the reliving, to imagine that he was looking down on the scene from above. He could describe the layout of the street below and noted that there was no bus coming. Joshua carried out two full verbal relivings over the course of ten sessions, one at the beginning of therapy and one at the end (a probe reliving). Other memory work utilised written narratives, or verbal reliving of hotspots in order to integrate new information.

Working with triggers

As Joshua had not been to the accident spot in more than six months (because it would 'bring me down'), a visit to the site was an important step for him. He noted that there were many differences between the scene in his memory and the road in reality, and he was asked to be alert to these differences in order to update his memory and point them out to his therapist. By this stage, the site visit did not trigger excessive anxiety. Joshua was asked to rate and record his mood over the subsequent week and was pleased to find that the visit did not result in low mood (i.e. counter to his prediction, the visit did not 'bring him down'). The other main trigger for intrusions and upset was his motorbike, which he had not yet ridden. A hierarchy was constructed. Sitting on the bike was the first step, riding the accident route was the final step, and increasingly longer journeys were intervening steps. However, in the event, the hierarchy was not used. Having carried out reliving and a site visit, Joshua quickly began to use his bike again regularly and attended his final few sessions on his bike.

Other interventions

As Joshua's intrusion frequency diminished and his level of activity increased, his sleep improved. His sleep remained poor occasionally, so he was given some advice and sleep management and night-time routines. Rumination also improved as he made progress in therapy. He was able to see that this sort of thinking had been unhelpful in the past. In later sessions, he was asked to be alert to rumination and to practise switching from a ruminative mode to a memory-processing mode of thinking: that is, from a 'why?' mode to a 'how?' mode. Specifically, when he found himself going down a familiar mental route of abstract thinking about the causes and consequences of the accident, he was asked to recall his accident in detail from beginning to end including, at this stage, the integrated results of cognitive restructuring.

Outcome and discussion

Joshua responded well to a ten-session course of CT for PTSD. At the end of therapy, he had no significant symptoms of PTSD and his depression had lifted. He had begun to ride his motorbike regularly, was seeing his old friends again and was investigating new college courses. Notable aspects here included the prominent initial depressive symptoms. While depression sometimes suggests a poor prognosis, in this case it was clearly secondary to PTSD – the decision was made to target PTSD first, and this resulted in a lifting of depression. Cognitive restructuring with reliving included standard techniques, but also used other methods such as making body movements that were incompatible with the hot cognition, and taking a 'bird's eye perspective' on the trauma scene. Family factors seemed all-important at the outset. However, mother did not attend any of the treatment sessions: direct individual work with young people may be beneficial even without the involvement of parents or carers.

Case 2: Seema (15 years old)

The second case illustrates a course of CT for PTSD with a teenage victim of a violent street robbery. The process of carrying out reliving was quite different to Joshua's and there was scope here for using stimulus discrimination techniques.

Assessment

Seema was referred by her family doctor for help with 'stress' following an assault three months previously. She had been punched to the ground and kicked in the head in an attempt to steal her mobile phone. She was taken to hospital where she was found to have some bruising and lacerations and discharged the same evening.

At assessment, Seema said that she was scared to go out, became upset and angry at the slightest thing and was worried that 'there is something wrong with me'. She experienced frequent and upsetting intrusive images of the assault – in particular an image of someone stamping on her face. She had bad dreams about being assaulted several times a week. She avoided discussion of the assault with anyone because it upset her, and she did not like to talk to her mum and dad about it for fear of upsetting them. Marked behavioural avoidance was apparent: she would cross the street to avoid stepping on the stretch of pavement that she had been assaulted on. She had kept up with many of her previously enjoyed activities, but felt as if her friends did not really understand her any more. Her sleep was poor, she had considerable trouble concentrating and remembering at school and she was highly irritable. When Seema's parents were interviewed alone, they were unaware of most of her symptoms of PTSD. Their main concern was that she could have sustained a head injury during the assault and that this was causing her headaches and irritability.

Formulation

Seema was suffering from clear-cut PTSD as a result of the assault. She did not meet criteria for diagnosis of any other disorder. A cognitive formulation was worked out with Seema in sessions two and three and further developed in later sessions (see Figure 6.2). First, her memory of the event was basically intact, but she could remember neither how the assault finished, nor how she managed to get home afterwards. She had a significant chunk missing in her memory of the assault. Second, the Post Traumatic Cognitions Inventory (PTCI) was completed and discussed in some detail, revealing a number of important misappraisals. Having previously considered herself to be streetwise and tough, Seema now felt weak and unable to cope. Her frequent intrusions and marked behavioural avoidance coupled with her emotional lability had led to her feeling 'out of control' and to the belief that she must be 'going crazy'. The nature of her assault, combined with her headaches, the missing chunks in her memory, and problems she experienced in concentrating and remembering at school underpinned a belief that she had sustained some sort of permanent brain damage – a belief shared by her parents. Third, her marked cognitive and behavioural avoidance was hypothesised to be preventing a change in these key misappraisals. Fear of upsetting her parents led Seema to try to hide her reactions from them. Her parents' fears of brain damage, often repeated to Seema, had contributed to a strongly held family view about permanent physical injury.

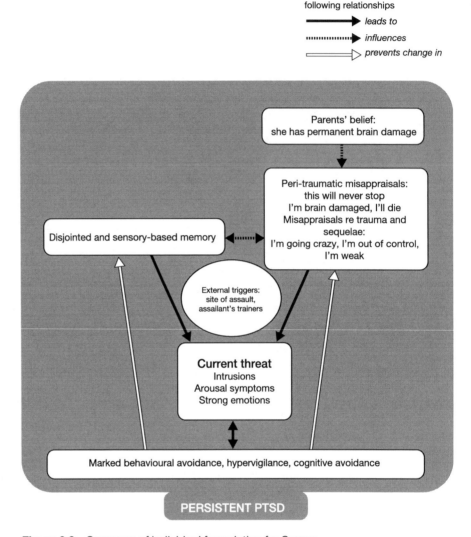

Figure 6.2   Summary of individual formulation for Seema

Treatment

This initial formulation suggested a number of treatment targets including:

- gathering information to address disjointedness and missing chunks in her trauma memory
- modifying beliefs about herself ('I'm weak') and her symptoms ('I'm going crazy')
- modifying shared family beliefs about permanent brain damage
- dropping unhelpful avoidant coping.

The process of therapy was quite different to the previous example. Whereas Joshua suffered from depression, appeared flat in sessions and needed considerable motivation to continue, Seema was lively and talkative in sessions, but easily upset and tearful. From the outset, she was highly motivated and determined to 'fight back' against her problems. Many issues common to working with adolescents arose, including the limits of confidentiality in relation to her parents' knowledge of her boyfriend and other activities.

Treatment rationale

It was important to establish a firm rationale early on, given Seema's quite marked avoidance and her fear of the consequences of remembering ('I'll really make myself go crazy'). The first full verbal reliving did indeed result in considerable upset, so it was crucial to have an agreed rationale in place beforehand.

Beliefs about herself and her symptoms

Seema's beliefs about being weak and going crazy were also addressed early on – and returned to in later sessions. The information handouts (see Appendix B) were helpful for her to see that, rather than being signs of impending madness, her symptoms were actually common and normal reactions to a severe assault. She was asked to keep a diary to help her spot triggers to her intrusions and upset, with attention paid to low-level sensory triggers such as colours and sounds. This helped her to see that intrusions and upset rarely arose out of the blue, but were usually related to subtle trauma triggers. Her beliefs regarding weakness were related to her actions at the time of the assault (she had tried to curl up into a ball rather than fighting back), which stood in contrast to her view of herself as a 'tough streetwise kid'. After some discussion, she was able to see that it was not helpful to judge herself on the basis of an 'unfair fight'. She was helped to explore the likely consequences of having reacted differently (trying to fight back, using a weapon), and concluded that she had done the best that could be done in the circumstances. She concluded that 'I did everything I could to protect myself', and later checked this out with friends who agreed with her.

Reliving with cognitive restructuring

Seema was highly anxious about carrying out a reliving, although she understood the rationale clearly. She appeared to 'get stuck' in the memory towards the end of the assault (when she could not remember what had happened next), and needed gentle encouragement to continue by 'fast-forwarding' to the next part she could remember. She was very tearful and upset at the end. However, the key point for Seema was that, although the reliving had been highly distressing, it was not as bad as she had predicted: in particular, it did not result in her 'going crazy'. She was pleased with herself for having done it and this proved to be an important early step in freeing her up to recall further details of the assault.

A number of key peri-traumatic misappraisals related to memory hotspots were uncovered via reliving. For example, she had thought when curled up on the ground, 'This is going on forever, it will never stop.' This was associated with considerable distress and sometimes resulted in her getting 'stuck' in the memory at this point when deliberately recalling the assault. This was tackled in two main ways. First, information and examples were provided about the common time-distorting effects of severe stress. Second, she was encouraged to talk to friends who had witnessed the assault. She asked them how long it lasted for and how it ended. She was surprised to find that her friends reported the whole event as lasting a matter of minutes. She also discovered that her friends and a passing motorist had rushed to help, at which point the assailants ran off. She had been unaware of this previously because she had avoided talking to friends about the assault at all. In this way, Seema was able to begin to piece together the missing part of the memory.

Second, she had thought at the time, 'This is going to give me brain damage, I'll never recover.' Seema was asked to outline her evidence for the thought. There were a variety of things, including the belief that she had not been assessed properly at hospital. To address this, she was accompanied to the hospital to talk to helpful nursing staff about triage procedures in emergencies. Seema was surprised and relieved to learn that her medical examination on the day of the assault had in fact been very thorough. In addition, she wanted to know how she could have survived such an assault, so part of the following session was spent examining how well the brain is protected, by studying the anatomy of the skull using medical textbooks and models. Last, despite understanding the medical procedures on the day of the assault and learning about how well the brain is protected, Seema still needed to account for her headaches: if she was not brain damaged, what was causing them? Her headache diary revealed that they were very clearly triggered by stress and had dropped off considerably in frequency since the start of therapy. She reasoned that this would not be possible if she had some permanent physical brain damage. Considerable time was devoted to identifying and then shifting these sorts of key misappraisals. The results of cognitive restructuring were then integrated with reliving, first via a written narrative and later through verbal reliving of hotspots, and finally in a verbal reliving of the whole trauma.

Working with triggers

By the final weeks of therapy, Seema had completed memory work and a visit to the site of the assault. She was doing very well overall, but was occasionally very upset by reminders. Discussion and diary keeping revealed that upsetting intrusive images were often triggered by seeing trainers similar to those worn by her attacker, and by fast movements in her visual field which resembled the movement of the sole of the trainer stamping on her face. Using the sorts of techniques described in Chapter 5, Seema realised that a harmless object (trainers) had been linked with danger in the past (during the assault). She was aware that it would be helpful to break the link between the trainers and danger. To do this, a pair of trainers similar to those her assailant had worn were brought into the session. At first, she found that looking at the trainers in their box triggered intrusions. She was encouraged to allow the images to arise, to describe them to herself or her therapist, and then to contrast the images with the current context – that is, to look around the room and orient herself to time and place, out loud. This was repeated a number of times. When she was accustomed to looking at the trainers in their box, she was asked to look at them out of box, and the procedure was repeated. The next step was to look at the sole of the trainers, repeating the 'breaking the link' procedure. After several more steps she was able to tolerate her therapist moving the sole of the trainers at speed very close to her face, as had happened during the assault. Again, she was asked to allow any intrusive memories to arise, to acknowledge them as memories, and then to contrast the memory with the current context.

Outcome and discussion

Seema also responded well to CT for PTSD. As with Joshua, imaginal reliving with cognitive restructuring was at the core of treatment. However, the process was quite different in each case. Seema was highly anxious about carrying out a reliving, became very upset when doing it and needed time to recover. It was quite draining for her, and initially a little concerning for her therapist (who wondered if he had paced therapy too quickly). Ultimately, however, this first reliving was a turning point because it was a powerful demonstration for Seema that her worst fear – that she would drive herself crazy by remembering – was disconfirmed. For her therapist, it was an equally powerful demonstration that expression of strong emotion is not to be avoided and can be highly beneficial. Considerable time was devoted to cognitive restructuring and updating particularly idiosyncratic misappraisals by gathering information from friends and hospital staff. Stimulus discrimination techniques were useful in tackling remaining symptoms.

Case 3: Nick (11 years old)

With older teenagers such as Joshua and Seema, family factors are clearly important in the formulation, but for a variety of reasons treatment is often with the young person alone. With younger people, families are more often involved. Our final example illustrates some family work in the treatment of an 11-year-old boy who had been caught up in a violent attack in a shopping mall two years previously.

Assessment

The attack had happened in a crowded shopping mall two years previously while Nick was out shopping with his parents and younger brother. A man with a knife had run amok in the mall and Nick saw a number of injured people and lots of blood. Nick's father was injured, although Nick did not see this because they had become separated. Father was rushed to hospital with others, while Nick and his brother were dropped off at a friend's house.

Nick presented as a bright, shy boy. He was reluctant to separate from his parents initially, but agreed after some encouragement from them. He was anxious about recounting the shopping mall attack and gave only the briefest of summaries. More ready to describe his current symptoms, he told of nightmares in which the event was replayed, sometimes with variations (of him and his family being attacked by a group of men armed with guns). He thought about the event during the day, sometimes believing that he could see the attacker at school or outside his home. He said that he tried very hard to keep such thoughts out of his mind (by thinking of 'good thoughts' instead), and had refused to go back to the mall since the attack, although other members of the family shopped there regularly. Having previously been keen on after-school clubs, he had dropped these in the last years of his primary school, preferring to be at home with his family. Nick reported sleeping poorly and being constantly on the lookout for the attacker. School had noted a drop-off in his attainment generally. Parents confirmed Nick's account, also reporting that he was withdrawn, 'over-sensitive' and worried about his family when apart from them. This was in the context of previous separation anxiety difficulties for which he had received help from child and adolescent mental health (CAMHS) services. His parents had been exposed to the same incident, but neither of them had sought help for any problems arising from the attack, and self-report screening questionnaires suggested that they had coped well.

Formulation

Nick's history of anxiety difficulties, and his family's efforts to cope with them, was a likely predisposing factor in his reactions to the traumatic event. They had previously tried to deal with his separation anxiety by providing reassurance and 'not pushing him too much'. A similar family coping style in the aftermath of the trauma meant that the event was rarely discussed at home, and his avoidance of the shopping mall was not challenged. In terms of the cognitive model of PTSD, Nick's memory of the event was somewhat patchy. This appeared partly to be a function of his young age at the time of exposure and the length of time since the event, and partly because he still did not know what had happened to his father on the day of the attack. Peri-traumatic misappraisals at the time of the event related to his father's well-being ('Dad must be hurt or dead.'), a thought which had generalised ('It's dangerous outside, no one's safe.') and now recurred when he was separated from his family. This over-generalised fear resulted in avoidance of the site of the incident, which in turn prevented change in his beliefs about danger. Nick had also dropped any sort of physical play with dad, such as football. Again, this appeared to be driven by beliefs about dad's well-being and consequently prevented change to these beliefs. Nick's cognitive avoidance – pushing intrusive images out of mind and trying not to think about the event – was also preventing processing of his trauma memory.

Further important appraisals were identified early on in therapy. Nick's marked cognitive avoidance initially appeared to be driven by beliefs about the personal emotional consequences of remembering ('thinking about it will get me really upset'). In the first treatment session, Nick said that he thought his intrusive memories might be a warning that the attacker would reappear. He believed that if he thought about the event, the attacker would reappear and another attack would happen, but 'worse this time'. Further questioning revealed that Nick recalled having thought on the morning of the event that something bad was going to happen. Not only had he thought that the event would happen, but he believed that *having the thought caused the event*. This was reminiscent of thought–action fusion in obsessive compulsive disorder (OCD) and is an example of 'omen-formation' identified by Terr (1991) in her seminal studies of traumatised children. This key appraisal meant that Nick felt responsible and guilty for what had happened, and he was consequently spending considerable energy in monitoring his thoughts. It was the main reason that he suppressed all thoughts of the event and it was clearly important to address this early so that work on his trauma memory could proceed in sessions (see Figure 6.3).

Treatment

The formulation suggested a number of promising targets for treatment including:

- changing Nick's beliefs about responsibility for the event and his potential to cause bad things to happen by thinking about them
- working with his parents to encourage family discussion of the event and to drop avoidant patterns of coping with anxiety
- reducing the disjointedness in his memory for the event
- updating peri-traumatic misappraisals
- reducing cognitive and behavioural avoidance.

Some of the treatment components used to address these targets are discussed in more detail below.

Omen formation

Psycho-education in early sessions emphasised that Nick's intrusive memories were in fact classic symptoms of PTSD rather than warning signs of another attack. Similarly, his first retelling of the event was construed as a behavioural experiment to test the consequences of remembering. However,

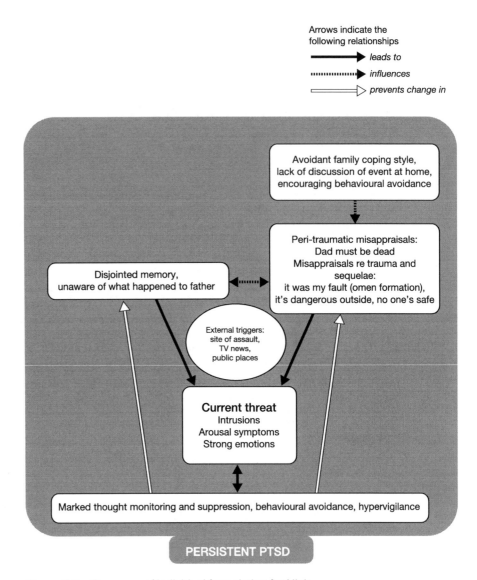

Arrows indicate the
following relationships

→ *leads to*

▸ *influences*

⇨ *prevents change in*

Avoidant family coping style,
lack of discussion of event at home,
encouraging behavioural avoidance

Peri-traumatic misappraisals:
Dad must be dead
Misappraisals re trauma and
sequelae:
it was my fault (omen formation),
it's dangerous outside, no one's safe

Disjointed memory,
unaware of what happened to father

External triggers:
site of assault,
TV news,
public places

Current threat
Intrusions
Arousal symptoms
Strong emotions

Marked thought monitoring and suppression, behavioural avoidance, hypervigilance

PERSISTENT PTSD

Figure 6.3   Summary of individual formulation for Nick

Nick was unconvinced by the outcome of the experiment: although no attacker appeared, he thought that he may have been lucky and 'got away with it this time'. His belief about the power of thoughts to cause things to appear was therefore tackled head on, using behavioural experiments of the sort described in Chapter 5. He was asked initially to bring up an image of a computer console and money to see if they would appear. He engaged readily with this, but became visibly more anxious when progressing to deliberately bringing up an image of the attacker to see if he would appear. When the attacker did not appear in the room, Nick wondered if he might be lurking elsewhere in the clinic, outside in the car park or hiding down the street, so he and his therapist went to look for him. The procedure was repeated several times in one session – Nick becoming less anxious and more animated each time. By the end of the session he could deliberately bring up his 'worst' image of the attacker, but not worry that he was about to appear. Nick's therapist was concerned that despite this rapid shift during the session, Nick's beliefs might revert in the coming week. For homework, he was therefore asked to let images of the attacker arise naturally and to deliberately recall an image – and in both cases to test out the prediction that the attacker would reappear. His mother helped him in carrying this out. The following week Nick showed up for his session looking both relieved and excited.

Guilt

This work on changing Nick's beliefs about the power of thoughts to cause things to happen was quickly followed up by addressing his guilt feelings. Nick now felt that his thoughts on the day could not have caused the attack to happen – and his mother was helpful in supporting this. The task then became one of working out who or what had been responsible for the attack. In a joint session with mum, using pie chart techniques, Nick could see that he bore no responsibility at all for what had happened and – very important for him – that his parents did not blame him for it.

Imaginal reliving

Tackling Nick's beliefs about omens early on freed him up to carry out detailed reliving of the attack itself. As in the previous two cases, a combination of verbal and written methods was used. During and after verbal reliving, Nick was prompted for ratings of anxiety using his 'feelings thermometer' (see Appendix C) as an explicit test of his prediction that it would be 'too scary and last for ages'. Ratings were charted on a graph and it proved helpful for him to see that his anxiety was not as bad as he had expected, and that he recovered very quickly. His main peri-traumatic misappraisals were to do with his father being injured or killed. While Nick knew that his father had survived, he did not know what had happened when they were separated on the day of the attack, nor whether dad had fully recovered from any injuries. It was clear that the planned work on updating Nick's misappraisals would overlap with interventions aimed at reducing memory disjointedness. That is, it seemed important that Nick hear from his father and mother what had happened on the day and how he was currently affected by any injury.

Family work to update trauma memory

Rather optimistically, this was first set for homework. Nick and his mother agreed to discuss with dad what had happened, and for Nick to have the chance to ask dad any questions he wanted to ask. However, this did not happen so dad was invited back in for a joint family session. With both parents and Nick in the room, mother and father read Nick's narrative of the attack, and the therapist helped Nick to ask his father what had happened. Mum and dad were shocked by the apparently gruesome level of detail that Nick was curious about. The therapist's task in this joint session was therefore to encourage dad to be open and honest about what had happened, while managing the overall pace of the session and the level of intensity of feelings expressed. New information from dad's point of view was added to Nick's written narrative in the session. Nick was relieved that dad's hospital procedures were actually quite mundane, in contrast to what he had imagined and he was proud that he had had a 'grown up' discussion with his father. For his parents, one of the important outcomes of the family session was that they realised it was not harmful for Nick to hear about the details of frightening events, and that he could tolerate exposure to far more detail than they had hitherto supposed. Finally, Nick was concerned that dad's injuries meant that he remained physically vulnerable, so he had stopped any sort of physical activity, such as football practice, with his dad. In addition to telling his son about what had happened two years previously, dad therefore also told Nick about the extent of his current injuries (which were minimal). A schedule was agreed for dad and Nick to restart some of the physical activities that they had previously enjoyed together.

Site visit

Nick's cognitive avoidance was tackled via: challenging his beliefs about omens; allowing intrusions to come and go without suppressing them; imaginal reliving in sessions and for homework; and increasing discussion and questions about the event at home. His behavioural avoidance of the shopping mall was addressed in the latter half of the course of treatment by carrying out a visit, accompanied by his mother and therapist. Nick had not been back to the shopping mall in over two years. The rationale for carrying out the visit to the mall was essentially the same as for carrying out reliving and narrative work in sessions: to gather information to help update the memory. Despite his progress in memory work in sessions, which had been accompanied by a reduction in symptoms, Nick remained very anxious about the prospect of going to the mall. However, his anxiety very quickly dissipated once he had spent a few minutes there because it was so very different to how he had remembered it. The visit lasted longer than had been planned because there were so many things that Nick wanted to note in his role as a 'detective for differences', looking out for how his memory contrasted with current reality. As usual, further visits to the mall were set as homework for Nick and his mum for the following weeks.

Outcome and discussion

Memory work – mostly via written narratives, but including verbal reliving – was again at the core of treatment in this case, but was preceded by identifying and challenging Nick's beliefs about the power of his thoughts to cause things to happen. Reliving would probably have been unhelpful if his thoughts about omens and responsibility had not been changed first. Given Nick's young age and his parents' involvement in the attack, involving mother and father in joint family sessions to help reconstruct a full and coherent narrative was useful. Nick's therapist was struck by how quickly Nick's anxiety declined after a short time at the mall. Site visits after very long intervals in chronic PTSD can often be a revelation for young people and usually result in considerable shifts in the trauma memory. Finally, it was interesting that Nick's symptoms of separation anxiety responded well to trauma-focused treatment. As with Joshua, co-morbid conditions may respond well to CT for PTSD.

Summary

These examples illustrate some of the approaches to assessment and treatment, described in previous chapters, as they apply to secondary school children of various ages, with different histories of trauma and presenting problems. The three young people described here had all developed PTSD – but the details of clinical presentation were quite different in each case. Accordingly, individual formulations, specific to each young person, were developed. The relative importance of the possible maintaining factors under the extended cognitive model differed from case to case – for example, family factors were more important in understanding Nick's reactions than they were for Seema or Joshua. Of course, the details of these maintaining factors were unique to each young person – for example, Nick's misappraisals related to guilt, while Seema's concerned being weak. Given the wide variety in clinical presentation, and the importance of individualised cognitive formulations, a flexible and individually tailored approach to implementing the treatment components described in Chapter 5 is always needed.

7

Cognitive therapy for PTSD with younger children

In Chapter 2 we described how young children may show a broader pattern of responses to exposure to trauma. This requires a different set of diagnostic criteria and attention to particular patterns of co-morbidity. The nature of trauma exposure in young children means that parents and carers are commonly involved in the event, at least as witnesses; and, of course, young children rely relatively more on their caregivers. Family factors may play a greater role in younger children's responses to and recovery from trauma exposure. This chapter describes two examples of working with young children. They are based on real cases, but details have been altered to preserve anonymity. The first concerns a five-year-old boy and describes how individual and parent work were combined. The second summarises work with a seven-year-old girl who had witnessed a killing, and includes the interweaving of trauma and grief-focused work.

Case 1: Simon (5 years old)

Assessment

Simon was a five-year-old boy referred by his family doctor for assessment and treatment of sleep problems and behaviour difficulties that had arisen following a nasty accident nearly a year previously. Simon had been playing in a small playground near his home, supervised by neighbours. As he tried to clamber over a wall to retrieve a ball, the wall collapsed and fell on top of him, resulting in a compound fracture to his right leg and deep lacerations with considerable blood loss. The neighbours had immediately called an ambulance and carried Simon to his house where his mother waited with him in the hallway as she tried to keep him awake and conscious. His leg required numerous operations over the following months, but was healing well by the time of assessment.

Simon presented as a lively, talkative and apparently cheerful young boy at assessment. However, he held his mother's hand tightly, and did not want to separate from her, so they were seen together initially. Simon very carefully watched the clinicians talking to his mother for around 20 minutes, but then got rather bored and restless, so he was encouraged to go to an adjacent room to play and draw with one of the assessing clinicians. It was then possible to assess mother and Simon independently.

Simon happily made some drawings while he chatted away to the assessor. She encouraged him in his drawing, while pacing gentle enquiries about his family and then, taking the lead from him, about his accident. He drew his mother with a tear in her eye and said that she was sad sometimes – she got sad when she looked at his leg. Simon said that he was strong, but that his leg was broken and did not work properly. He spontaneously showed his leg, still obviously scarred and thin, to the assessor. With a little prompting about how his leg had been broken, Simon said a few words about the accident, but then quickly changed the subject. Asked about what made him sad or scared, he said that he had dreams about monsters chasing him, so he stayed in mum's room 'because of the monsters'. He said that he was 'mostly happy' and then talked about some games that he played with his friends.

His mother gave a detailed account of his current state, based on the Scheeringa *et al.* (2006) semi-structured interview for pre-school children. Since the accident, Simon had been having frequent nightmares which usually woke him up. He was often unable to tell his mother what he had dreamt of, but sometimes talked of being chased by ghosts and monsters, and occasionally said that he dreamt of being hurt by the wall again. During the day, he was upset at reminders – for example, he became distressed if alone in the hallway at home and complained that he could 'see blood' there. If they were walking past a wall, he sometimes commented to mum that it looked 'tired' and might fall down. He refused to be in the hallway alone and had not been back to the playground – although it was difficult to disentangle whether this avoidance was driven by Simon or his mum. Simon was more temper prone since the accident, at home and at school. He tried to delay going to sleep, which was causing considerable bedtime battles. Having acquired continence just prior to the accident, Simon now wet the bed and refused to go to the toilet alone. He was generally more clingy and grouchy. Simon did not meet criteria for PTSD according to *DSM-IV*, but fulfilled the developmentally more appropriate Scheeringa criteria. He was clearly suffering from a traumatic stress reaction that was adversely affecting his and his family's life. Simon also presented with symptoms of separation anxiety and secondary enuresis.

Simon's mother was quite tearful during the assessment. Screening using adult self-report scales showed her to be well above cut-off for both depression and PTSD, with prominent guilt feelings about the accident. At a subsequent meeting, structured clinical interview revealed that she did indeed meet criteria for major depression and PTSD.

Formulation

Case conceptualisation with this young child took greater account of family factors than in the cases of older adolescents described previously. Simon's mother was highly avoidant. Her restriction of his general activities was likely to be contributing to his irritability, and prevented each of them from (re)discovering that he could play safely in many environments. She also avoided all talk of the accident at home, so that he had not had the opportunity to begin to address the muddles and confusion in his memory of the event. Mum encouraged his avoidance of reminders and preferred him to sleep in with her. This was preventing him from re-establishing the more independent night-time routine that he had prior to the accident. Mum had become anxious about setting limits for Simon in general. He had become more oppositional as a result and she felt less effective as a mother. Much of the change in her relationship with her son was driven by her own symptoms of PTSD and depression, especially her accident-related guilt feelings. Despite the strong emphasis on family factors here, some aspects of the individual cognitive model appeared to apply. Simon's memory of the event was confused and muddled. He showed clear behavioural avoidance of reminders and seemed to present with some misappraisals which he had not had the opportunity to update or modify.

Sharing this formulation with Simon's mother was done thoughtfully and carefully, in a gradual manner, in order not to inadvertently reinforce her guilt feelings about the accident in particular, and her capacity as a mother in general (see Figure 7.1). The formulation suggested a number of treatment targets including:

- providing CT for PTSD for mother in her own right
- reducing mother's cognitive and behavioural avoidance
- enhancing mother's parenting skills
- reducing muddles in Simon's trauma memory
- reducing his avoidance of remembering and reminders
- changing his beliefs about walls being dangerous.

Treatment

Two therapists worked with mother and Simon in parallel from the outset. Once engaged in treatment, Simon was happy to spend time alone with his therapist. At the same time, mother was seen individually. Some time was always spent at the end in a joint meeting, where Simon was encouraged to tell his mother what he had been doing and homework tasks were agreed. Very broadly, the process was one of working with each of them individually over a number of sessions in preparation for bringing them together for some joint trauma-focused work.

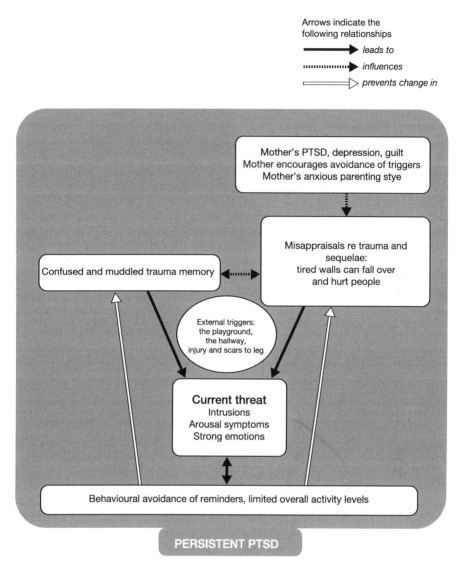

Arrows indicate the following relationships

→ *leads to*

⋯⋯▶ *influences*

⟹ *prevents change in*

Mother's PTSD, depression, guilt
Mother encourages avoidance of triggers
Mother's anxious parenting stye

Confused and muddled trauma memory

Misappraisals re trauma and sequelae:
tired walls can fall over and hurt people

External triggers:
the playground,
the hallway,
injury and scars to leg

Current threat
Intrusions
Arousal symptoms
Strong emotions

Behavioural avoidance of reminders, limited overall activity levels

PERSISTENT PTSD

Figure 7.1 Summary of individual formulation for Simon

Parent work

As usual, work started with psycho-education about the effects of trauma on children. Additional aims here were: to reattribute the causes of Simon's current problems to the accident, rather than to mum's parenting skills; and to help her to begin to see the similarities between Simon's and her reactions to the accident – such as unwanted memories, increased fears and marked avoidance. Simon's mum initially tended to use her individual time to tell the therapist about her own current problems. The therapist thought that this would be helpful at the beginning, but soon realised that it would leave little room for work focused on Simon. She therefore raised the idea of referring mum for help in her own right. Mother felt, however, that she would not be able to manage her own therapy, saying that she 'just wanted to stay strong for Simon'. Mother and therapist agreed instead that they would devote some time to mum's difficulties in each session, but that the bulk of time would be focused on Simon. It was not until towards the end of Simon's course of CT for PTSD that his mum decided that she would indeed like to see a therapist for treatment of her own.

A recurring theme in these initial sessions with mum was her guilt at having left Simon unsupervised. This was tackled early on because it seemed sufficiently overwhelming to be preventing mum from thinking about other accident-related issues. All of the possible factors contributing to the accident were listed, with mum being able to see that her role was minor. For homework, mother carried out a small survey among her friends about whether it was reasonable (versus irresponsible) to leave a boy of Simon's age with other adults. All of them thought it was perfectly reasonable. All of them had done it at various times with their own children, and a couple of them pointed out that it was in any case necessary and healthy to leave young children with trusted adults at times. An unplanned 'side effect' of carrying out this survey was that she enlisted the ongoing help and support of friends. Mum was also able to see that her guilt feelings were a sign that she was a good mother, rather than the reverse.

Work moved on to discussing Simon's day-to-day routines. Mum believed that she should restrict Simon's activity levels to give his leg a chance to recover. The therapist asked permission to contact Simon's hospital physiotherapist to see what exercises Simon could be doing. The physiotherapist was surprised to hear that mum thought Simon's activity should be restricted. While this had been true soon after the accident, what he now needed was plenty of activity. The physiotherapist was therefore invited into a session with Simon and his mother and a detailed activity diary, incorporating as much natural activity as well as specific exercises, was planned.

Of special concern to mum were Simon's refusal to use the toilet alone and the difficulties that she had in settling him at night. For toileting problems, a home visit was carried out. Simon said that there might be ghosts in the toilet. With some encouragement, he said that Superman would be able to get rid of the ghosts. He and his therapist spent some time drawing pictures of Superman and these were then pasted up in the toilet. Simon wanted to continue to make more pictures, so he and mum spent some time drawing extra pictures in the toilet. He was soon left alone, absorbed in his drawings. A sticker chart system was then set up, whereby Simon earned a sticker for each set period of time that he spent alone in the toilet. Having overcome his initial fear, he was easily engaged in earning stickers for time without mum in the toilet, and mum was consistent about providing rewards.

Night-time routines were tackled in a slightly different way. Again Simon worried about ghosts, and he suggested making some more drawings to stick around his bed. However, much of the work in managing his bedtime routines was carried out via instructions to mum. A clear and consistent routine was agreed. If he awoke during the night, mum was advised to comfort him, but then to settle him back in his own bed and stay with him as he fell asleep; and to repeat this if he woke again. A sticker star chart was set up to provide clear visible rewards for staying in his own bed. Mother found the latter part of this quite hard to implement, especially as her own sleep was disturbed and she was tired herself a good deal of the time. Although progress was not steady, mum persisted, and in line with improvement in other symptoms Simon's sleep gradually improved.

Simon's behaviour was by no means out of control, but he was playing up more than prior to the accident. Mum had held off in reasserting what had been very sound pre-accident parent management strategies because she felt that Simon had 'been through enough' and she did not want to upset him further. Following discussion, she was able to see that if she refrained from setting and enforcing limits, although this resulted in some short-term gain, it was unhelpful in the longer term. Mum was helped to recall what had been effective in terms of managing Simon's behaviour previously. Suggestions were made about how she could enhance these when necessary, and a behaviour management plan was made and monitored for the remainder of the sessions. As mother regained her confidence as a parent, she was able to rely on her own intuition as to what would be helpful for Simon.

Work with Simon

In parallel with this parent work, Simon was also seen alone each week for about 40 minutes. In order to reduce avoidance and begin to identify any muddles and gaps that he had in his memory of the accident, work was started on a 'memory book'. Prior to this, Simon was taught some brief relaxation techniques, which he enjoyed practising at the beginning and end of each session. Simon's rationale for doing the memory book was to 'get used to remembering' what had happened. Simon was given as much control over the process as possible. He chose the binder that the memory book was kept in, for example, and decorated it with stickers and with some help wrote his name on the front. Each week, he drew one or two scenes, in sequence, and was encouraged to talk about everything that he could remember, including what he had felt at the time. Feelings were rated on a simple thermometer (see Appendix C). When feelings were high on the thermometer, he was encouraged to stay with the picture until he 'got used to it', using relaxation strategies at the end if needed. In general, Simon enjoyed this process and was proud of his book, which he wanted to show to mum each week. The therapist's work was in trying to elicit as much detail as possible, including accessing 'scary feelings', while still making the process as positive as possible. When mum had begun to discuss the event in her individual sessions, she was able to go through Simon's book in some detail with him. She was shocked at how much he remembered and was able to fill in some missing details for him, having discussed in her individual sessions what might be an appropriate level of detail. One session was devoted entirely to joint work in which Simon and his mother discussed the accident, using his memory book. By this time mum was able to tolerate such a discussion and it proved a turning point in allowing them to discuss the accident at home when the subject arose.

Another home visit was carried out towards the end of the course of CT for PTSD, in order to go to the playground. By this stage, Simon was able to talk freely about the accident and he was not reluctant to visit the playground. He readily showed how the accident had happened, paying close attention to his mother's reactions. By this stage, the wall had been repaired. Simon said that he thought it did not look tired, like before, and would not fall down. To test this out, he was helped to touch the wall and then to try to push it over, showing himself and his mother that it was indeed stable.

During this site visit, Simon mentioned again that although this wall seemed okay, some walls were tired and 'could fall on you'. His mother confirmed that he appeared to remain vigilant of old-looking walls and stayed away from them when he could. A series of behavioural experiments was then planned to test out the thought that 'old-looking walls are tired and can fall over'. Simon and his mother, along with the therapist, went for a walk to find old-looking walls and investigated them by looking, touching and ultimately trying to push them over. This was anxiety-provoking for Simon initially, but it soon became more of a game for him when he quickly discovered that he could not push over any walls.

Outcome and discussion

Simon attended for more than a month before he appeared to be more settled in sessions, and his mother began to report changes in his behaviour at home. This may have been because more time was spent preparing Simon for trauma-focused work before beginning work on the trauma narrative itself. Equally, given mum's crucial role, it may have been that some changes in the way she responded to his difficulties were needed before symptomatic improvement would be seen. Last, given young children's limited concentration span and memory, therapeutic work is necessarily broken into smaller chunks and must proceed at a pace appropriate to the young child. Of particular importance in this case was the careful pacing of work with Simon and his mum. Clinical impression was that considerable progress was made after the joint session in which Simon and his mother went over his storyboard narrative in detail. However, this work could not have been rushed. Mum needed to have made some progress in her individual sessions before being able to discuss what had happened in the joint session with Simon.

Case 2: Lisa (7 years old)

The second case illustrates the interplay between trauma and grief in a seven-year-old girl. Intervention included work with her bereaved mother, some school liaison and carefully paced trauma- and grief-focused work with Lisa herself.

Referral

Lisa's primary school referred her to the clinic because she was falling behind in her learning, was often disruptive in class, was easily upset and frequently tearful. School were aware that an uncle had died recently and enquired whether 'bereavement counselling' might be appropriate.

Assessment

Assessment was carried out over two sessions. As usual, a family meeting was held first with Lisa, her mother and – on this occasion – one assessor. The assessor made sure to ask Lisa, in mum's presence, whether it would be okay to talk about her uncle later, and she agreed. After the usual explanations about the nature of the assessment procedure were given, Lisa chose to wait with a family friend while mum was interviewed first.

Interviewed alone, mum tearfully described how Lisa's difficulties had started after the death of her uncle abroad. He had been shot dead in front of Lisa during a bungled burglary. Lisa and her mother were interviewed by police, but no one was ever arrested. Lisa did not attend the funeral. Mother felt that their neighbourhood was so unsafe that she left within a few months to 'make a new start' in the UK. Mother's main concerns were that Lisa became upset easily when reminded of her uncle. Lisa asked questions about her uncle 'all the time', leaving mum feeling exhausted and helpless. Lisa was fearful and avoidant of graveyards and cemeteries. She was sleeping poorly and often woke up with nightmares. Mother reported that Lisa had nightmares about the shooting, avoided reminders and spent less time playing with friends. She was easily startled by loud noise and was on the lookout for danger (often telling mum that she thought a robber would get into their house). Additionally, Lisa was showing some signs of separation anxiety. She refused to sleep alone, worried about mum when they were apart and often asked to phone mum several times a day to check if she was okay. According to mum's report alone, Lisa met *ICD-10* criteria for PTSD, complicated in this case by her prolonged traumatic grief reaction. Lisa's mother was distressed during much of the initial interview. She scored above clinical cut-off on self-report questionnaires of depression and PTSD.

Despite the separation difficulties mentioned by mum, Lisa was quite happy to be seen alone. In contrast to her silence in the initial family meeting, she needed little encouragement to talk when seen without her mum. Lisa said that she missed her uncle. Without prompting, she said, 'A robber killed him and I saw it,' and became tearful. Rather than stopping the interview because she was upset, the assessor gently asked Lisa if she remembered what had happened. She was able to give an account of the shooting, describing the burglar's face, the very loud noise of the gun, and saying that he had also pointed the gun at her before running away. She had thought that she was going to die. Lisa was given plenty of praise for her bravery in talking about what happened. Asked systematically about her current memories of the shooting, she described 'scary pictures' of a bad man with a nasty face pointing a gun at her, and of her uncle covered in blood. She had bad dreams of killing and blood. She thought the man would come to get her and mum. She tried to think happy thoughts instead, to get rid of the 'bad pictures'. She didn't like to talk about it because it was scary and made her mum cry. She said that she did not know what a funeral was, but her uncle was 'under the ground with the ghosts'. She looked scared and muddled when talking about this.

Over two assessment sessions, Lisa was giving a fairly clear report of traumatic stress symptoms, which was more detailed than her mother's report. She was also having trouble accessing positive memories of her uncle, due to prominent intrusive recollections of the killing. She appeared to be very muddled in her understanding of death in general.

Formulation

A preliminary formulation was worked out after the first two sessions and used to guide treatment planning and progress. Lisa's memory of the event appeared intact but muddled and was easily triggered by sensory cues and reminders of death, such as passing nearby a cemetery. Her core peri-traumatic misappraisal had been that she was about to die. This appraisal, seemingly accurate at the time, had not yet been updated. Indeed, there was now, some two years on, an over-generalised sense of danger, very clearly linked to the belief that 'the man' was coming to kill her and mum. Lisa was trying to cope by suppressing intrusive memories and by not talking about what had happened.

As in the previous case, family factors were highly relevant. Mother had been exposed to the same trauma, had lost her brother, and developed PTSD herself, with probable co-morbid depression. Her reactions meant that she was unable to talk about either the killing or the uncle with Lisa: that is, she was reinforcing Lisa's unhelpful avoidant coping.

Lisa had been exposed to the killing at a young age when her understanding of death was developing, and she had not been involved in the funeral or other rituals afterwards. The lack of opportunity to participate in the funeral or to ask questions about death meant that her understanding remained muddled and frightening. It appeared that her intrusive memories of the killing were overshadowing any other memories of her uncle, and she had had little chance to mourn his death. This formulation (see Figure 7.2) suggested that to enable her to grieve for her uncle, Lisa's PTSD would

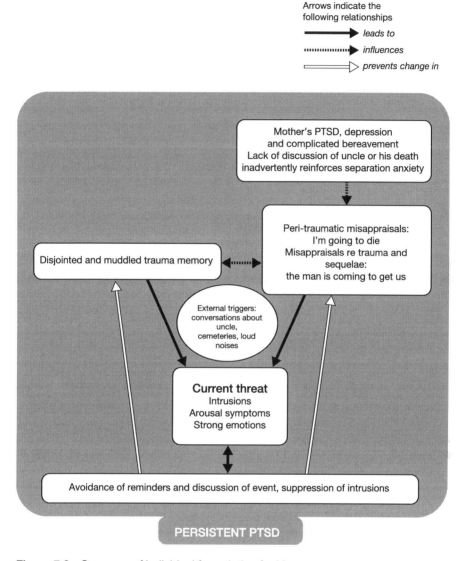

Arrows indicate the
following relationships

→ *leads to*

┅┅┅⋯▶ *influences*

═══▷ *prevents change in*

Mother's PTSD, depression
and complicated bereavement
Lack of discussion of uncle or his death
inadvertently reinforces separation anxiety

Peri-traumatic misappraisals:
I'm going to die
Misappraisals re trauma and
sequelae:
the man is coming to get us

Disjointed and muddled trauma memory

External triggers:
conversations about
uncle,
cemeteries, loud
noises

Current threat
Intrusions
Arousal symptoms
Strong emotions

Avoidance of reminders and discussion of event, suppression of intrusions

PERSISTENT PTSD

Figure 7.2 Summary of individual formulation for Lisa

need to be tackled first. Treatment of her PTSD included targeting the
hypothesised maintaining factors, including:

- reducing the confusion in her memory for the event
- updating her peri-traumatic threat misappraisals and the related over-
  generalised sense of current threat to her and mum
- reducing her cognitive avoidance of the memory.

Reversing Lisa's avoidance was more likely to be achieved by working
directly with mum to change her own avoidant coping. Lisa's limited

understanding of death could be improved and she required help to mourn her uncle's death.

Treatment

Intervention was carried out over six months and included individual work with Lisa and her mother, joint work with both of them and school liaison.

Work with Lisa

The course of CT for PTSD started with psycho-education for mum and Lisa about PTSD and its treatment, goal setting and socialisation to the treatment model. By the second treatment session, imaginal reliving was started using the sort of storyboard technique described above in detail for Simon. The aim was to reduce confusion in Lisa's memory, to reduce avoidance and to identify and update misappraisals. Prior to beginning this storyboard work, Lisa was taught relaxation skills and 'safe place' techniques, as well as learning how to rate her distress using a feelings thermometer (see Appendix C). She understood that the reason for making the storyboard was to get the memory 'out in the open' so that she could 'get used to it'. Lisa included some words or short sentences for each picture in the storybook, although her literacy skills were limited due to her disrupted schooling. The storyboard was worked on each week and the folder was left at the clinic between sessions.

Work on the storyboard revealed a number of details that Lisa had not previously told her mother. For example, she said that when she first saw the man in the hallway of her home, she had screamed: hearing her scream, he had turned around, pointed his gun at her uncle and shot him. Lisa thought it was her fault that her uncle had been shot. Without recourse to complicated pie charts, Lisa's therapist simply told her that anyone else would have screamed, that the shooting was entirely the robber's fault, and that no one believed she had done anything wrong. In the joint meeting at the end of this session, Lisa was helped to tell her mother that she had screamed, and mother also explained that this was to be expected and was not the reason the man shot her uncle. Lisa was quite tearful and mum comforted her. The new interpretation ('It wasn't my fault, the bad man did it.') was integrated into the storyboard narrative by having Lisa write underneath the picture in subsequent individual sessions.

The two main hotspots were when she saw her uncle on the ground with blood coming out of him and when the man pointed the gun at her. After the full storyboard had been completed, Lisa was helped to go through the narrative again in detail, and to pause at the hotspots, looking at the pictures she had drawn until her Selective Units Discomfort Scale (SUDS) rating declined. Lisa was at first highly distressed when telling that she thought the man would kill her. Her therapist responded with empathy, support and praise for her bravery (at the time and currently), encouraging Lisa to stay with the memory before rushing to change it. Making it very clear that this was a very frightening event which would have scared anybody, the therapist asked Lisa what actually happened. After some discussion, she said that she didn't die, 'he didn't get me, he ran off, I beat him!'. As before, this 'updated meaning' was written by Lisa underneath the picture of that hotspot.

In this way, using a combination of drawing and writing appropriate to her abilities, Lisa was helped to write down the traumatic events in order, to recall and articulate the worst details of what had happened, and to develop and integrate new or updated meanings and interpretations of what had happened. This led quite quickly to some symptom reduction. Nevertheless, she continued to experience intrusions of the man's face. In sessions, Lisa was helped to 'stay with' her drawing of the man's face until her SUDS thermometer reading reduced. She spontaneously reported that the image itself changed as her distress declined, becoming smaller and less clear. She was helped to use the sort of image-changing techniques described in Chapter 5 to gain further control of the image. In particular, her therapist helped her to draw out the changed image while expressing her feelings of anger towards the 'bad man'.

Lisa's over-generalised sense of danger was based in part on the belief that the man would come after her and mum. After discussion with her and mum, it was apparent that she thought the man had deliberately come after her uncle, and so would do the same for her and mum. Several attempts to explain that he was a robber who had been disturbed unfortunately seemed to be confusing for Lisa, and did not help to address the problem. More effective for her were sessions in which she was helped to see how long ago the death was (by constructing a picture calendar, marking special events which had happened in the intervening two years), and how far away it had happened.

As Lisa's PTSD symptoms improved, she began to talk more of her uncle. She remained sad and sometimes tearful when doing this work, but her upset did not have the same fearful and distressed quality as previously. Her therapist helped Lisa to recall some facts about her uncle and she talked of things they had done together. Lisa wanted to be able to remember her uncle so she constructed a second memory book. This contained some of her drawings of him, copies of photos that mum brought in, notes about some of his favourite things and lists of what she liked best about him.

In conjunction with this move towards more grief-focused work, psycho-education around death was carried out. This included information about the physical processes of death – especially helpful for Lisa was learning that dead bodies cannot feel any pain – and about the rituals and ceremonies after death. After suitable preparation, a visit was made to a local church with a small cemetery, as a 'discovery trip' to find out about graves. This trip also proved useful as a way of helping Lisa to break the link between cemeteries and distressing memories. Although she had not been allowed to go to the funeral, Lisa's mother had some photos of the funeral, coffin and grave. A session was spent jointly with mum and Lisa in which mum told about what had happened at the funeral. Lisa put some copies of the funeral photos in her memory book.

Work with mother

Individual and joint work with mother were carried out from the beginning. Unlike the previous case example, Lisa's mother was keen to seek a referral to adult services. As she was treated, she was increasingly able to discuss the event and her brother with Lisa. As is invariably the case in family work, it was important to pay close attention to timing. That is, one aim of Lisa's sessions was to support her in discussing the killing of her uncle with her mother, but this was only carried out after mother had made sufficient progress in her own right to enable her to talk with her daughter without becoming overwhelmed. This was achieved through carefully paced sessions in which Lisa showed her storyboard book to mum as a means of discussing and elaborating the details of what had happened, and correcting any misunderstandings and muddles. When sessions with Lisa moved from a trauma focus to a grief focus, the process of joining together with mother was similar in that mum was supportive in helping Lisa to work on her memory book.

In addition to trauma and grief work, advice was given to mum about tackling the remaining symptoms of separation anxiety. Lisa was generally less fearful as sessions continued, but she did not sleep alone. Straightforward advice about sleep hygiene, night-time routines and star charts with contingent tangible rewards proved helpful.

Outcome and discussion

Despite the nature of the traumatic event and the length of time between exposure and treatment, Lisa made good progress. Once engaged, she showed a reduction in cardinal PTSD symptoms after about two months. She benefited from having made some progress with her PTSD symptoms and from education about death before moving on to grief-focused work.

Most clinicians would agree that intrusive trauma memories (and the individual's response to them) impede the natural process of grieving, and that PTSD symptoms should therefore be at least partially alleviated before embarking on grief work. Broadly, Lisa's sessions followed such a plan, with trauma-focused work carried out initially and grief work later. However, this was a matter of emphasis, rather than of carrying out two sequential blocks of treatment. That is, in the initial trauma-focused phase, Lisa would talk about her uncle more broadly and ask questions about death, funerals and about what happens after a person dies. When possible, the therapist encouraged talk of such memories and provided a safe environment for her to begin to remember her uncle. When Lisa asked questions about death, the therapist answered them with honest, simple information appropriate to Lisa's level of development. Equally, in the latter stages of intervention when Lisa was making her memory/grief book, some time in sessions was still spent on practising image rescripting techniques to tackle residual intrusions.

In summary, while the emphases changed during the course of intervention, there was from the beginning a close interweaving of trauma- and grief-focused work. Last, family factors were crucial and Lisa's recovery was no doubt facilitated by her mother's own progress in her individual sessions.

Summary

These examples illustrate some of the aspects of clinical work with younger traumatised children. As with the adolescents described in the previous chapter, we hope it is clear that detailed assessment, individualised formulations and a flexible approach to implementing treatment components are always necessary. With younger children, detailed understanding of the wide variety of ways that traumatic stress reactions may be expressed at different ages is needed if a thorough assessment is to be carried out. Attention should be paid to developmentally influenced patterns of co-morbidity – such as the separation anxiety shown by Simon. In contrast to some older children, family factors are invariably crucial in formulating younger children's problems and in carrying out treatment – as illustrated in various ways above. The principles of the CBT approach to treatment seem to apply well to young children and families. However, the pace of therapy will necessarily be different. Creativity and imagination are needed in finding appropriate and appealing ways to engage and intervene – such as the use of drawings and cartoon strips, in place of written narratives.

8

Real-world hurdles in treatment

The approaches described earlier can be implemented flexibly across a range of situations. Nevertheless, broader issues sometimes need to be considered when making decisions about treatment including:

- the timing of interventions
- dealing with ongoing threats
- adapting treatment for children exposed to multiple traumas
- working with interpreters
- delivering treatment in a group format.

Each of these issues is addressed in turn below.

When is it appropriate to start treatment?

There is considerable debate in the literature about the efficacy of early intervention in PTSD. In adults, some forms of universally delivered single-session debriefing in the immediate aftermath of a trauma have been found to impede natural recovery (Ehlers and Clark 2003), whereas a brief course of cognitive behaviour therapy (CBT) delivered within the first two weeks to adults with significant symptoms of acute stress disorder appears beneficial (Bryant *et al.* 1998). Unfortunately, there are still very few studies of early intervention in children. Single-session universal debriefing for children does not appear to be harmful (Stallard *et al.* 2006), but clear benefits have yet to be demonstrated. The effect of a course of treatment (in contrast to one-off debriefing) delivered early to symptomatic children (in contrast to universal intervention) is not yet known.

The National Institute for Clinical Excellence (NICE, 2005) recommended that trauma-focused cognitive behavioural treatments should be provided for children and young people if moderate to severe PTSD symptoms are present, regardless of whether reactions are acute or chronic. If mild symptoms are present in the first four weeks, the NICE guideline recommends 'watchful waiting' initially, followed up by an appointment within four to eight weeks of the trauma. The reason is that many trauma-exposed individuals will experience some PTSD symptoms initially, but for the majority these will largely remit without treatment within four weeks of the trauma (see Chapter 2).

> 'Watchful waiting' is recommended for mild symptoms in the first four weeks post trauma.

In clinical practice, however, a formal course of trauma-focused CBT will rarely be started within the first four weeks post trauma, if for no other reason than referrals are seldom made so soon. The exception is when there have been highly publicised traumatic events involving other agencies, such as in cases of sudden parental death, or accidents involving many children. At such times, clinics are often contacted by the police, schools or social service departments within days of a traumatic event for advice about what help to provide for children.

If contacted by families or other professionals in the first few days after a trauma, telephone consultation is often the first response. This provides parents with the opportunity to express any concerns, allows a brief assessment to be carried out if appropriate, and is a chance for advice and information to be given. This sort of support is just what is needed by many families. It establishes contact and face-to-face appointments can be scheduled for later as needed. For other families, more immediate face-to-face meetings may be appropriate, and if so arrangements can be made to see the adults and children as soon as is practical. The role of such a meeting in this early phase is not to initiate a formal course of trauma-focused CBT, but to listen to children and parents; and to provide information and advice, both about self-care and about how to support children who may be showing a range of acute reactions. Establishing contact in this way early on allows follow-up appointments to be scheduled. At follow-up several weeks later, a course of trauma-focused CBT may be offered if needed. Treatment is not always necessary at this stage, however. Families sometimes find that the initial meeting (which gave them the opportunity to describe the event and its aftermath, and to receive normalising information and practical advice) led to substantial improvement.

For traumatically bereaved children, Yule (2005) describes how the first few days and weeks are far too soon to begin formal therapy. What children need at that point is comfort and security and for their basic needs to be taken care of. Instead, advice for the surviving parents or foster carers can be provided early on. This might include: information and reassurance about the range of common reactions in traumatised and bereaved children; suggestions as to how adults can support and encourage children to talk about what has happened and their reactions if they choose to do so; and advice about managing behaviour and re-establishing routines. Similarly, liaison with schools in the immediate aftermath of a sudden bereavement can help to explain to teachers why the child may have problems concentrating, for example, or why they might become upset when something in a lesson reminds them of what happened. Dyregrov (2008) provides detailed and practical guides for parents, teachers and therapists on how to help bereaved children – including help that might be given early on. Harris-Hendriks *et al.* (2000) have written extensively about help for children who have witnessed the murder of one parent by the other.

> The initial goal in working with traumatically bereaved children is to help adult carers to increase the child's sense of safety and security.

Parents, carers and other agencies involved may question whether it is a good idea to let the child attend the funeral of any lost loved ones or friends, or attend severely injured relatives in hospital. Often, their worry is about retraumatising the child in some way. While such worries are under-standable, a trauma involves, by definition, exposure to actual or threatened death or injury to the self or others. Attending a funeral or hospital may be upsetting for children, but it will not be retraumatising. Indeed, the benefits to the child of participating in most aspects of the mourning process (such as wakes, memorial services, cremations or burials) far outweigh any short-term upset that may occur by attending. In the aftermath of a traumatic bereavement, children will often report that they very much wanted to attend ceremonies and feel bad that they did not. Likewise, there is little benefit to the child of preventing them from seeing an injured relative in hospital. In the case of funerals and hospital visits, the key issue is one of preparation. In the main, this will involve explaining to the child what will be happening and answering the child's questions in a frank and age-appropriate way.

> Attending funerals or making hospital visits may be upsetting, but will not retraumatise the child.

Finally, schools may seek advice when many children have been caught up in a traumatic event, such as a bus accident or witnessing the sudden death of a teacher or schoolfriend. In this case, seeing the group of children together initially makes sense. Dyregrov (2008) suggests a structured format for carrying out such an initial meeting in school. Aims include helping to clarify the facts of what happened and sharing and normalising reactions. As noted above, this need not be a single one-off 'debriefing', but it provides the opportunity for longer term monitoring and structured interventions for those who need it.

What can be done to help children who are reluctant to attend?

Avoidance is such a prominent feature of PTSD that is it is not uncommon to encounter children and young people who simply do not want to attend for treatment. The first assessment appointment, described in detail in Chapter 3, is therefore crucial in beginning to engage young people. In practice, a thorough yet sensitive interview often provides great relief for many, and is sometimes the first chance children have had to ask questions about their reactions, and to hear that PTSD is a common, well-understood and treatable condition.

For children and young people who are reluctant to attend, part of the engagement process includes asking them how they have dealt with symptoms so far, and how successful their coping strategies have been. With careful questioning, children are able to see that while avoidance may have provided some short-term relief, it has not solved the problem. As described in Chapter 4 (see Socialisation to the Treatment Model), the use of metaphor (such as the jigsaw puzzle or the overfull cupboard) and behavioural experiments (such as thought suppression) can help to demonstrate why avoidance has been unsuccessful. This can lead naturally to the idea that if avoidance has not worked so far, then it makes sense to try thinking about and processing the trauma instead.

For younger children who do not want to attend for further sessions, parents are the key to successful engagement. Enough time must be set aside to discuss treatment options with carers, and for them to ask any questions they may have. Anxious parents may have doubts about the value of talking. It is important for these to be discussed openly if they are not to impede treatment. Occasionally, it may help to see parents of young children alone for a session following the initial assessment. This is a chance to address any concerns that parents may have, for specific advice about handling upset or separation anxiety to be given, and to explain in more detail what treatment may entail. Initial sessions can then be paced as appropriate, and if parents and young children remain anxious about separating, then joint sessions may be tried to start with. Having said that, it is often the case that concerned parents of young children are very willing to follow clinicians' advice and commit to a course of CT for PTSD.

For older children and teenagers, the issues are different. Those who choose to attend often do so without their parents. Parents have less influence over teenagers' behaviour in general – including whether or not they choose to engage in treatment. Again, sufficient time must be made following the assessment for young people to express any concerns they may have, and for clinicians to respond to these honestly. Clear explanations about what treatment is likely to entail (and what it definitely does not entail), its collaborative and short-term nature, and the emphasis on concrete goals which are relevant and meaningful for the young person will help. Practical issues such as the timing of appointments may be important. Most young people who attend for assessment recognise that whatever they have been doing so far to try to cope has not been very effective – their dilemma is whether to risk trying something different. For those who are unsure, it can be beneficial to specify a limited number of sessions to start, with a planned review after four to six weeks. This 'try it and see' approach is true to the collaborative nature of CT for PTSD and gives the young person some much needed control over what is happening to them. Often, sufficient treatment gains are made in the first four to six weeks that the young person is then ready to renew the treatment contract. For teenagers who do not want to commit to a limited number of initial sessions, it may help to give some specific advice about coping, with a follow-up appointment in about a month. Sometimes, if the young person has experienced little improvement over the month, then they may be ready to start a course of treatment.

What happens if there are real threats or other major ongoing stressors?

In the aftermath of a trauma, children are sometimes confronted with genuine threats to their physical safety or basic needs that might affect the decision to provide treatment. Examples include a genuinely dangerous living environment, threats from an offender (or their friends) to try to stop the child or family giving evidence in court, or efforts by offenders to intimidate or drive the family from their home. For asylum-seeking families, there is often the real and imminent risk of forced deportation or relocation to a refugee centre.

The difficulty arises for the therapist in trying to determine whether the threats reported by the child or family are realistic, or reflect anxiety arising from the trauma. When the threat is realistic, treatment is unlikely to be effective. Under such circumstances, clinicians may decide that the best approach is to engage the family in an ongoing assessment of threat, liaising with the appropriate services (police, social services, Home Office, solicitors), and offering some advice on coping skills.

> If the clinical issue is really one of safety, then this should be the focus of the intervention.

For children who have been the victim of or witness to a crime and are waiting for further interviews by the police or a court appearance, reliving should not be undertaken without first having spoken to the police about the implications of this for the legal case. Police will be able to give specific advice about Crown Prosecution Service guidelines for child witnesses. It might also be helpful to ask about the specific procedures for the child giving evidence (such as one-way screens, videotape, presence of parents, etc.). Again such information can often be passed back to the family and can help alleviate any fears about testifying. Excellent witness liaison services are available in many Crown Courts, and pre-trial visits can be arranged to help allay young witnesses' fears about testifying.

In cases where offenders are not apprehended, assuming that there is no actual risk to the child or family, treatment can be offered. Some work will often be required to help the child to consider whether there is any rational reason for the offender to threaten them. This often takes the form of conversations about offenders not wanting to return to the scene of a previous crime for fear of being caught. It can also be helpful to talk about the possibility that the offender may not even remember who the client is and the unlikelihood that they would recognise the child if they saw them again. In the main, encourage the child not to let the offender get away with upsetting them more by getting back to their normal life.

Other significant threats or stressors that a clinician should consider are major medical interventions involving the child or immediate family, and mental or physical health problems in the parents. In the case of ongoing parental mental or physical health problems, CT for PTSD with the child can still be effective. Work with the child to help them understand their parents' difficulties better. Often this involves helping the child to identify and challenge any fears that their parents are permanently damaged, are at imminent risk of dying or abandoning them, or are angry or blame them in some way for their difficulties. The child can also be helped to consider how being engaged in treatment may help their parents to worry less about them. Invite the parents into a session or two to talk about their difficulties; the seriousness, permanence and implications of these difficulties; and how they are trying to overcome or cope with them. It will be important in most instances to talk to the parents separately first before bringing them into the session for such a discussion. The clinician needs to be confident that the parents feel able to be positive and to gauge their language (and content) to the child's needs rather their own.

Finally, it is sometimes the case that the trauma has led to a serious physical injury to the child which involves surgery to correct fractures, to remove scar tissue, or carry out reconstructive plastic surgery. Such procedures necessarily involve exposure to reminders of the trauma, as do seeing their injuries or scars on a daily basis. These reminders can trigger intrusive recollections, worries and anxious avoidance, and result in an increase in general distress. Injuries or surgeries to correct them should not prevent the implementation of treatment. The important point is to help the child consider the difference between having an injury now and what their injury meant at the time of the trauma.

> CT for PTSD can be implemented alongside ongoing medical interventions.

What issues arise when the young person has been exposed to multiple traumas?

A history of more than one trauma is not uncommon in young people presenting with PTSD. However, not all children will have symptoms (of intrusions or avoidance) relating specifically to each traumatic event. They may re-experience only one of their multiple traumatic events. In such circumstances, the content of the intrusions, nightmares or flashbacks should guide the clinician to the traumatic event to be processed through CT for PTSD.

Alternatively, children with a history of multiple traumas may have nightmares, intrusions or flashbacks related to more than one of these traumas. When there are relatively few traumatic events that continue to give rise to PTSD symptoms, then CT for PTSD is often still feasible. Additional sessions are usually required in order to carry out reliving and restructuring relating to multiple events. Under such circumstances, the therapist's task is to help the child choose the event-specific re-experiencing symptoms they want to work on first, and then proceed with treatment techniques related to that event until re-experiencing symptoms are significantly decreased. Success in reducing re-experiencing symptoms tied to one traumatic event may generalise to another. Importantly, clinicians should be alert to any meaning themes that bind together the different traumatic events which are giving rise to intrusions: for example, related to guilt, shame or competence. Much of the treatment can then be organised around dealing with these common themes. However, the clinician may need to proceed in a sequential fashion through each of the traumatic events that the child is re-experiencing. Recent work with adults (Duffy *et al.* 2007) shows how this approach can be successfully used for treating people who have been exposed to multiple traumas.

The principles of CT for PTSD may be applied to young people who experience PTSD symptoms relating to more than one traumatic event. The main adaptation of the treatment in this case is to extend the number of sessions in order to provide time to address multiple events. Of course, in most clinical services sessions cannot be extended indefinitely. If there are a great many traumatic events, then CT for PTSD may prove impractical to implement (see Grey and Young 2008). This occurs most often when working with young refugees and asylum seekers. In this case, an adapted form of CBT, Narrative Exposure Therapy (termed KidNET for children)

(Schauer *et al.* 2005) can be both practical and effective (see Ehntholt and Yule 2006).

> CT for PTSD can be used to help children who have experienced multiple traumatic events.

Can this treatment be implemented via a translator?

The simple answer to this question is yes, but it will depend upon the skill of the translator and a good working relationship between therapist, translator and the family. The intervention is less likely to be effective if a new translator shows up to every session. Children must feel comfortable and safe with the translator. The skill of the translator will be partly dependent upon their understanding of the treatment and the terms used. Some clinicians will set aside a session for training with the translator in which they will run through the model of treatment and explain the aims of the various interventions to be used. Alternatively, the start of each treatment session might be used to meet the translator to review the agenda for that session and briefly describe the interventions to be used. It can be helpful to provide the translator with a list of frequently used treatment terms (reliving, hotspots, exposure) for translation and then ask them to explain what the translations mean in other words, so that you can obtain a better sense of their understanding. The nature of CT for PTSD is such that verbatim translation is often needed. For example, the clinician will want to know the young person's exact words when carrying out memory work – and translators need to be aware of this.

However skilled or experienced translators are, they are not clinicians and do not have access to the same level of support and supervision as most clinicians. It is therefore helpful to spend some time with the translator after a session – especially when there has been intensive reliving – to check out and discuss their reactions to the session.

> CT for PTSD can be conducted through translators, but care should be taken to explain commonly used procedures and to highlight the importance of verbatim translation.

Can this treatment be implemented in a group format?

The current treatment was specifically developed for use in an individual format. Many of the interventions (reliving, reliving with restructuring, in vivo work and behavioural experiments) are very time consuming, taking 60 to 90 minutes in a single session for one child. Most interventions need to be revisited each session to facilitate improvement. As such, the interventions described here may not lend themselves easily to group work where intensive weekly work with each and every member would be prohibitive time-wise.

However, a careful look at the published trials for PTSD in children reveals that many have evaluated trauma-focused CBT approaches delivered in group formats. In the majority of these treatment trials, children were selected from a clinical population because they had symptoms (of PTSD and other disorders) related to sexual abuse (Deblinger *et al.* 1990, 1999; King *et al.* 2000; Cohen *et al.* 2004), community violence (Stein *et al.* 2003), or cancer (Kazak *et al.* 2004). In such trials, the group treatment protocols emphasised coping skills more than exposure, although children are often pulled out of the groups for individual exposure work as necessary. In general, treatment effect sizes for group approaches are somewhat smaller than for individual treatment.

If many children have been exposed to the same traumatic event – as in transport disasters (Yule and Williams 1990), accidents at school (Misch *et al.* 1993), or natural disasters such as earthquakes (Giannopoulou *et al.* 2006) – then group approaches, often delivered in schools (Yule and Gold 1993), can be beneficial. For example, listening to others describe their similar traumatic experiences and reactions, and developing adaptive coping skills in a group format, can be particularly helpful.

In the event of large-scale disasters and war, many children may be affected, while local resources are often scarce. This means that individual treatment is not practical so group approaches are preferred. Through the Children and War Foundation (www.childrenandwar.org), the authors have developed a manualised six-session group CBT treatment protocol (Smith *et al.* 1999) for use following natural disasters and war. This has been used to good effect with child survivors of an earthquake in Greece (Giannopoulou *et al.* 2006) and with young refugees and asylum seekers in the UK (Ehntholt *et al.* 2005).

> CT for PTSD as described in this book is best suited for use with individual children.

What if clinicians start to burn out while providing treatment?

For most clinicians, burn-out is a subtle affair and generally a sign of compassion fatigue. For example, having treated many people with PTSD, overworked clinicians may sometimes think, 'You just need to face up to what happened. The quicker you do it the sooner we will finish.' Such thoughts are often accompanied by subtle and not so subtle cues to the client to hurry up. Clinicians may find themselves telling clients how they should be thinking or feeling, under the guise of cognitive therapy, rather than working with the client collaboratively to facilitate change with behavioural experiments or through Socratic questioning. The clinicians may even find themselves minimising symptom reports from the client that contradict their expectations of improvement. Sometimes the clinician on the verge of burn-out colludes with the client's avoidance strategies by agreeing with the highly symptomatic client when the latter asserts that they are better enough and can stop treatment now.

The best protection against burn-out is effective clinical supervision and variety in clinical work. Leave enough time between clients to have a break, collect your thoughts and if necessary talk to another team member. If you are running groups, make sure that at least some of the groups are co-led with another professional. Try to ensure that there is a variety of assessment, treatment and supervision sessions, so that no team member is spending the whole day in back-to-back treatment sessions. Provide co-workers with regular peer supervision, and when necessary seek outside supervision on difficult cases.

Over the long term, an important part of burn-out prevention is to see a range of clients, not only traumatised individuals or those with PTSD. Try to share work amongst team members so that no one clinician carries the most difficult cases. Make sure that each team member devotes a portion of their time to teaching, research and training, and is supported in attending conferences. Perhaps most importantly, recognise in an overt way that burn-out is a real issue and that clinicians should be active in trying to prevent it. If clinicians sense that they are starting to burn out, they should not hesitate to seek support from their team or another professional.

> Openly discuss the effects on the clinician of working with traumatised children, and ensure that adequate team support and supervision is available.

9

Co-morbidity

Introduction

Leo Kanner, the doyen of American child psychiatry and the person who first recognised infantile autism, once gave a lecture entitled 'But the children do not read the textbooks'. By this he meant that no matter how well we define childhood disorders through research studies and careful clinical practice, the next child we see in the clinic will not fit any diagnosis precisely. This is only too true of PTSD in children.

Classificatory systems such as *DSM* and *ICD* are very helpful as short-hand ways of ensuring more accurate communication between professionals and roughly pointing the way to appropriate interventions, but the clinician needs to go well beyond this in making sense of the individual presentation of each patient. Only careful observation and interviews with the child and the family can help to pinpoint how best to help the child. The different classification systems have their own rules. *DSM* presents a series of algorithms that can result in the same presenting reactions or symptoms being used to decide that the child has met criteria for a number of different diagnoses – what is currently termed 'co-morbidity'. At the same time, if a child is deemed to have met criteria for PTSD, then the clinician is not supposed to diagnose, for example, a simple phobia. Under *ICD* rules, the clinician has to match the presenting symptoms to a complex exemplar and has to try to give only one main diagnosis. In both cases, children may have additional distressing symptoms that may not fit the diagnostic picture but that do need treatment.

In one large follow-up study of adolescents caught up in the sinking of the cruise ship *Jupiter* (Bolton *et al.* 2000), 41 per cent of survivors had developed an anxiety disorder (excluding PTSD), one-third had developed major depression, nearly a quarter had developed a specific phobia, 7 per cent had developed separation anxiety and 6 per cent had developed substance misuse. Altogether, 57 per cent had developed at least one major disorder in the five to eight years after the disaster – and this is without considering PTSD that had developed in 51 per cent of the group. Those with PTSD had considerably increased levels of other anxiety disorders and major depression compared to those without PTSD: 82 per cent of those with PTSD as compared with 30 per cent of those without had developed one of the major disorders.

In summary, this study indicates that after a major life-threatening event, such as the sinking of a ship where four people died, half the adolescents who survived developed PTSD, mostly within the first year and with very few developing it later. Some five to eight years later, 15 per cent still met rigorous criteria for a diagnosis of PTSD. Many others had what other clinical researchers sometimes term 'partial PTSD' – that is where they miss the strict diagnosis by one or two symptoms. When presented with a child with 'partial PTSD' following a traumatic experience, it is important to assess the impact that the symptoms are having on the child and family and offer treatment as appropriate.

This study also shows very clearly that PTSD is not the sole disorder that young people develop after a disaster. It was the single commonest reaction, but in four of the five cases of PTSD, the surviving adolescent also had an additional serious disorder. Thus, while concentrating on developing better treatments for PTSD, clinicians still need to be knowledgeable in treating other common disorders such as specific phobias, separation anxiety, social phobias, obsessive compulsive disorders and major depression.

> PTSD often presents alongside anxiety or depressive disorders.

There is also considerable overlap with some conduct or behavioural problems. One of the symptoms of increased arousal is an increase in aggression and temper. This can, if not addressed, escalate to being a disorder in its own right. As illustrated in the case of five-year-old Simon in Chapter 7, parents can sometimes relax their normal disciplinary strategies in the belief that the child already has too much to cope with. A helpful approach is to be sympathetic to the dilemma facing the parent, but to help them reinstate good behavioural management practices, setting up contingencies for appropriate behaviour. This is also discussed with the child – so that they realise they are behaving this way as a result of the traumatic event.

> Encourage the maintenance of good behaviour
> management practices.

Another difficulty is the increase in problems of concentration and activity levels – also both symptoms of hyperarousal – being seen as part of attention deficit disorder (ADD) or attention deficit hyperactivity disorder (ADHD). These days, some clinicians are too quick to prescribe methylphenidate to control the activity levels without taking a proper trauma history and realising that the problems stem from a traumatic experience and need to be treated as such.

In younger children, the pattern may be even more diverse with aggression, destructiveness, anxiety disorders, separation anxiety and phobias featuring strongly. It is a matter of clinical judgement as to which problem to target first, although this is best undertaken with the child and their parents so that they can share an understanding of all that is involved. This way, one can negotiate a hierarchy of problems to be tackled.

Separation anxiety

Separation anxiety often manifests during the first meeting, as was illustrated in the case of Simon (Chapter 7) when it took quite a bit of gentle persuasion to allow one clinician to interview mother while the other played with Simon. It is strongly recommended that parents and child be interviewed separately, as experience has shown that each party may be trying to avoid upsetting the other. Children are very sensitive to the ways that parents react to them when they try to talk about the traumatic event. If they have seen that such discussions lead to mum or dad getting upset, they may stop talking about it in front of them. Usually, the child welcomes an opportunity to discuss all the details with a sympathetic outsider. But first, one has to separate them from the parents.

One way of doing this is to make sure that the parents have given the child proper permission to talk to the stranger they are meeting at the clinic. The child can be shown where the interview rooms are and where they can play under supervision while the parents tell the boring bits of what they were like as little ones. Given that most survivors feel they have lost control of their lives, then it can be a good idea to see all the family together to clarify what is going to happen and then give the child the choice of who talks first to the clinician. Children often surprise themselves (and their parents) by wanting to be seen alone and first – the first step to treating the anxiety about separating.

With younger children, separation anxiety may well present as the child being very clingy and never wanting to let the parent, usually the mother, out of their sight. Reassurance may have been tried already at home and not worked. Discussing or uncovering some of the underlying worries that the child may have about the safety of the parent can be a useful first step. Thereafter, one may have to teach the child strategies for relaxation and work out a systematic desensitisation approach whereby the child spends longer time apart from the parent while being busy with interesting activities.

The parent will also need considerable reassurance that being firm as well as sympathetic is the right approach.

The separation anxiety is very likely to show at bedtimes. It can be anything from a reluctance to go to bed without a parent present, to refusing to sleep in their own bed and insist on sleeping in the parental bed. Once established, the latter takes considerable time and ingenuity to alter. This is where the need to re-establish sensible bedtime routines comes into its own. Winding down at the end of the day means not watching scary movies and not drinking caffeinated drinks. When appropriate, a bath followed by a bedtime story and a firm goodnight gets off to a good start. Discussions about what to do if the child has a nightmare or bad dream mean that when one occurs, everyone knows how to respond.

Separation anxiety is also quite common among teenagers where, at least in the *Jupiter* study (Bolton *et al.* 2000), one in ten of adolescents with PTSD also had a separation anxiety. It is a somewhat different experience when an adolescent needs to have the comfort of sleeping in the parental bed. It is important to have parents and young person recognise that this can be a common reaction to any major scary event. Instead of trying to ban the young person from the parental bed, a discussion about what is going on, how to relax so as to counter any anxiety, and how to reassure without leading to incessant requests for reassurance can be utilised.

> The development of a sound bedtime routine and anxiety management techniques can help with separation problems at night-time.

Specific phobias

Clinicians as well as survivors need to be constantly aware that children can re-experience much of the distress when it is triggered by stimuli, usually in the external environment. Sometimes, the specific phobia is not recognised until long after the event. The child may not encounter any reminder and so show no avoidance or distress until one day, 'out of the blue' as it is so often described, they suddenly experience overwhelming distress. Teenagers often experience such an unexpected distress as evidence that they are 'going mad'. The clinician can usually convince them that they are not, but that something in their immediate environment just before the distress was evident had triggered off the memory of the traumatic incident.

Many adolescents who survived the sinking of the *Jupiter* cruise ship developed specific fears of the sound of running water. They had been below decks when the other ship holed the *Jupiter* and they heard water rushing in. Later, they experienced fear when they heard similar noises – such as the sound of a shower. Recognition of the trigger and some advice on relaxation and gradual exposure are often sufficient to deal with the fear.

There was no obvious explanation of why some pupils who had apparently settled back into school suddenly developed fears of going to the school assembly after the summer holidays, having been comfortable doing so for many months beforehand. This looked like an emerging, specific phobia. However, a careful piece of detective work soon uncovered the trigger for the altered behaviour. One pupil was asked to describe in detail everything she saw from entering the school to taking her seat in assembly. She described climbing up into the gallery and then she froze as she described looking down the steep steps which had a railing at the bottom – both obvious reminders of standing on the quickly sloping decks of the sinking ship when she had feared that she might drown. It turned out that after the summer holidays she had moved up a class year and now had the privilege of sitting in the gallery, whereas before she had sat in the body of the hall. Once identified, the triggers held no threat and the pupils' behaviour returned to normal.

> A mixture of CBT techniques with relaxation and graded exposure is usually sufficient to tackle any phobias developed during the traumatic incident.

General anxiety

Threat appraisals in children with circumscribed PTSD are usually fairly clearly related to the traumatic event. Those who have been involved in a car crash will perceive travelling by car as dangerous and will worry about another crash happening. Those who have been assaulted may worry that they will be attacked again if they revisit the site of the assault. For a minority of trauma-exposed children, these worries about harm may generalise to domains beyond the traumatic event. Children may worry about harm coming to others (as in separation anxiety, described above), about their health, family finance or other family issues, upcoming events, performance at school, or about events in the news such as wars and disasters. Such children may appear to have excessively high 'perfectionist' standards, their worries are often characterised by 'what if . . .?' thoughts about future events, and frequent reassurance is sought. When worries are frequent, uncontrollable, extend to a number of domains (beyond the traumatic event) and are accompanied by a number of physiological symptoms, then a diagnosis of generalised anxiety disorder (GAD) is likely.

A history of anxiety difficulties (including GAD) is known to be a risk factor for PTSD in adolescence (Udwin *et al.* 2000), and clinical experience suggests that if GAD is present, its onset often pre-dates trauma exposure and the development of PTSD. Treatment of GAD using cognitive behaviour therapy (CBT) techniques may be more difficult if PTSD is present, so CT for PTSD is recommended initially. For children whose PTSD responds well to treatment, it then becomes clearer what the remaining (non-PTSD) worries are. Further intervention is likely to be needed and it is possible that this may build upon some of the principles learned in CT for PTSD. For example, for younger children, CBT for GAD might include: psycho-education about the relationship between thoughts, feelings and behaviour; identification of worrisome thoughts; modifying these thoughts; behavioural experiments to test out worries; and relaxation training. Older children and adolescents may benefit from cognitive interventions aimed at helping them to identify and change their general beliefs about worry and its function (see Stallard, this series).

Social anxiety

After any traumatic event, the surviving child will do better if they have good social support from family and peers. The latter can be tricky. Friends can be very supportive, but can also be intrusive. In the early days after an incident, especially one that has had a lot of publicity, the survivor may be in a state of shock and not want to discuss what happened. At times they may feel a great impulse to offload everything on whoever is nearest. Both reactions can inhibit friends from listening and so impair social support. It can be useful for the clinician to check with the parents and the school about what advice has been given to friends about supporting the child. Quite often, if the child has been off school for some time after the accident, they may dread going back because they do not know what to say. Suggesting that they meet up with one or two trusted friends and discuss what happened can be one way of bridging the gap. In addition, some role play to anticipate questions and reactions can be helpful.

Sometimes, a child may have been injured. If there is any visible injury, especially any scarring to the face, then the child will need help in facing up to the stares and enquiries of others. Once again, discussion about why others may be interested or curious, discussions about the motivation of the curiosity – in other words that the other children are not necessarily malevolent but just curious – will help prepare the child for re-entry to what might otherwise be a difficult social situation. When there has been permanent scarring or other disability, then the survivor may need to return for help with predictable problems later on when appearance becomes even more important. This is not directly related to traumatic stress, but the stress of weathering teenage angst over dating and sexual relations can be anticipated from the outset and steps taken to ensure that help is available when needed.

> Social anxiety can be reduced through role play and cognitive techniques.

Major depression

Among adults, depression is a common diagnosis following exposure to trauma, often occurring alongside PTSD. Similarly, among adolescents, up to two-thirds of those who develop PTSD can also present with a co-morbid depressive disorder (Yule *et al.* 2000). This common co-occurrence may be due to a number of factors. First, as described in Chapter 3, there is a degree of symptom overlap: for example, loss of interest in previously enjoyed activities, social difficulties and poor sleep are common to both conditions. Indeed, intrusive memories are now known to occur in depression as well as PTSD (Brewin 1998; Williams and Moulds 2007). Second, PTSD and depression may share predisposing or vulnerability factors. Previous exposure to trauma and/or adverse life events and demographic factors are relevant in this context (Ozer *et al.* 2003). Third, there are likely to be common maintaining factors: rumination, behavioural inactivity and social withdrawal, for example, are all implicated in both disorders (see Harvey *et al.* 2004). Last, depression is often seen to arise as a clear consequence of PTSD itself. Symptoms of PTSD and their adverse effect impact on functioning (such as experiences of failure at school or college) can lead to hopelessness and a major depressive episode.

Given the common co-morbidity of depression and PTSD, careful assessment is required. Depression is distinguished by prominent low mood (or irritability in younger children) and low self-worth, which may be accompanied by biological symptoms. Because depression may precede exposure to trauma (i.e. it may be a vulnerability factor for developing PTSD) and may arise following exposure to trauma (i.e. it may be a secondary consequence of PTSD), a detailed and precise history is also needed. Following a thorough assessment, the key question for the clinician is when to prioritise treatment for depression over that for PTSD.

In cases when secondary depression has developed as a consequence of (sometimes chronic) PTSD, it is suggested that PTSD is targeted first. Smith *et al.* (2007) found that CT for PTSD resulted in significant improvement in symptoms of depression. Successful treatment of PTSD will often lead to remission of depression, as illustrated by the example of Joshua in Chapter 6. Treatment will be individually tailored and may include an initial emphasis on reclaiming life activities (see behavioural activation in CBT for depression), interventions to reduce depressive rumination and techniques to counter hopelessness. When a detailed history shows that depression preceded exposure to trauma, then treatment of PTSD first may still be advisable. In such cases, clinicians should be especially alert to cognitive themes that may characterise both disorders: pre-existing thoughts of hopelessness, helplessness and guilt, for example, may have been strengthened by the trauma and its sequelae, and more extensive cognitive restructuring may therefore be required. Further treatment of residual symptoms of depression may be needed once the PTSD has remitted.

On occasion, depression in young people is of sufficient severity to warrant treatment in its own right before beginning CT for PTSD. This occurs most clearly when the initial assessment indicates that the young person is at risk of self-harm or suicide in the context of a depressive disorder. It is unlikely that the vulnerable young person will be able to tolerate intensive reliving, and such procedures may even be harmful. Other symptoms of depression, if sufficiently severe, may also disrupt CT for PTSD. For example, sustained concentration is needed to engage in reliving and other procedures; a degree of motivation is required to continue with a course of CT for PTSD; and a level of general functioning which allows the young person to test out predictions in behavioural experiments is helpful. If the clinician's judgement is that depression is of a severity to warrant treatment first, then a variety of options is available. Cognitive behavioural therapy (see Verduyn *et al.* this series) and interpersonal psychotherapy for adolescents (IPT-A) (Mufson *et al.* 2004) are both recommended by the National Institute for Clinical Excellence (NICE) as evidence-based treatment for depression in young people.

Clinicians should also be alert to the possibility of depression in parents or carers (see suggested screening measures in Chapter 3), and should make referrals to specialist adult services as appropriate.

Traumatic grief

Symptoms of PTSD not only overlap with symptoms of depression, but also overlap with grief reactions when the child has been bereaved. The co-occurrence of stress reactions and grief reactions can require careful handling, but is very common among children who have experienced war and major natural disasters. Indeed, they are extremely common among minors seeking asylum. Numerous studies have confirmed clinical impressions in finding that when a young person witnesses a death, particularly one that is violent, then that person is at greater risk of developing difficulties in grief reactions. The consensus is that normally when people are grieving they get considerable comfort from recalling good interactions with the dead person. They take opportunities to remember the dead person through discussions with friends and family. However, when a death is traumatic these normal mechanisms can be compromised. In particular, the probability is that whenever the bereaved young person starts to think about the dead person, their thoughts immediately switch to graphic memories of how the person died. In these circumstances, it is usually suggested that the traumatic memories should be treated in the first instance before the person can begin to grieve properly. Having said that, there are always exceptions as the following case illustrates:

> *Anne was ten years old when she went with her family on a Christmas shopping expedition. Her beloved grandfather was driving them along the high street when he had a fatal heart attack. The car careered across the street into the path of an oncoming vehicle. On impact, Anne was thrown forward and hit her head. There was a lot of blood. People rushed to get them all out of the car in case it caught fire. Anne was taken to hospital and her head wounds were treated. The next day, her grand-mother visited. Gran was wearing granddad's favourite crucifix. This confirmed for Anne that granddad had died, but no one told her. A week later, Anne was allowed home in the afternoon only to discover that her grandfather had been buried that morning. The family's concern not to upset her had denied her the right to participate in the funeral and to start grieving properly.*
>
> *Six years later, Anne was referred to our clinic for help. Sadly, it is far from uncommon that there should be such a delay. In the interim, she had developed both a chronic PTSD and a complex, unresolved grief reaction. She was carefully interviewed and then offered therapy, but she decided she did not want to confront the issues and so declined. A further year later, she was re-referred, re-interviewed and again offered help. This time, she accepted.*
>
> *On the day of the first treatment session, she was asked how things had been and she surprised the therapist by saying, 'A lot better. I have decided to do what you suggested.' The therapist had not at that time made any suggestions as to what treatment would be appropriate, but asked, 'So what have you decided to do?' Anne replied that she had decided to go back to the high street where the accident had happened. (In the intervening seven years none of the family had been down the street, such was the degree of their avoidance.) She would take a bunch of flowers, lay them at the spot where granddad had died and say a little prayer. Then she would go into the betting shop! This latter was to thank the staff of the shop who had come out to rescue her.*
>
> *So here was the young person having decided on a plan of action. The therapist had not made any direct suggestions, but the careful inter-viewing that had asked her whether she had visited the scene and whether she had said goodbye to her grandfather had suggested a course of action. Whatever the advice of the experts, it is always best to listen to the child and so the therapist backed Anne's own plan.*
>
> *A few weeks later, Anne had organised her family to accompany her to the high street. They laid flowers and said a prayer. They could not go into the betting shop as it had long since closed. Then she was able to*

go to the cemetery on her grandfather's birthday and lay more flowers – the first time she had been able to visit his grave.

As if this were not enough, on reassessment all her grief and PTSD symptoms had vanished. One could argue that the therapist had empowered Anne to confront the major avoidance, and by supporting her to do so at her own pace had achieved a good result. But the way of doing it flew in the face of the generally accepted advice (which, it must be said, is far from evidence based). So the lesson learned is to realise that systematic assessment is part of treatment and that one should follow the instincts of the client.

> Traumatic memories may need to be treated before the child can grieve properly.

10

Future issues

Recent years have seen considerable advances in our understanding and treatment of traumatic stress reactions in young people. However, much remains to be discovered. A selection of issues that are likely to become a focus of clinical and research attention in the near future are highlighted below.

Delineating children's traumatic stress reactions

Building on the early clinical descriptions of children's reactions to extreme stress, recent studies have employed multi-informant, multi-mode methodologies to assess high-risk samples using prospective longitudinal designs (Bryant *et al.* 2007; Meiser-Stedman *et al.* 2007). This work has helped to define more precisely the natural history of children's reactions to trauma, not only in terms of PTSD but also including other reactions such as anxiety, depression and grief. However, progress in our understanding of children's reactions has also raised a number of important questions. Most obviously, the *DSM-IV* criteria for PTSD, which were developed for adults, may not capture fully the reactions of young people. When working clinically, the *DSM-IV* requirement for at least three symptoms of avoidance/ numbing results in many young people being formally categorised as below diagnostic threshold, despite presenting with cardinal PTSD symptoms and clear impairment in functioning. This is most apparent in work with very young (pre-school) children, where the utility of the current diagnostic criteria is doubtful (Scheeringa *et al.* 2006; Meiser-Stedman *et al.* 2008). Ongoing and future research will benefit from a focus on refinement to the criteria for making diagnoses in children across the age range, especially younger children. For example, further detailed prospective studies with high-risk young children, assessing both symptoms and functioning over time, can make an important contribution to the issue of developmentally sensitive diagnostic validity.

> Developmentally sensitive criteria to assess young children's traumatic stress reactions are required.

In addition to this sort of work on documenting younger children's PTSD reactions over time, future research focusing on describing acute stress reactions is also likely to be fruitful. For example, while there is no evidence that universal single-session debriefing in the immediate aftermath of a trauma is beneficial for children (Stallard 2006), current UK national recommendations are that young people who show severe symptoms in the acute phase (roughly the first four weeks post trauma) should be offered a course of trauma-focused CBT (NICE 2005). But what counts as 'severe symptoms' in the acute phase? Clinicians are ill-advised to use *DSM-IV* acute stress disorder (ASD) diagnosis to help make such decisions about which early reactions are pathological. This diagnosis relies heavily on dissociative symptoms, which have now been shown to have very little utility or predictive value over and above early symptoms of PTSD (Meiser-Stedman *et al.* 2007). If dissociation indeed turns out to be of little relevance in the early days following a trauma, then further research aimed at identifying acute symptom profiles (that require early treatment) and/or acute risk factors (for later pathology) are likely to be practically helpful to clinicians who are often required to make treatment decisions in the first few days following a trauma.

> Identification of acute symptom profiles and acute risk factors are required to better inform treatment decisions.

Finally, while considerable progress has been made in describing children's reactions to single-incident, one-off traumatic events, relatively little is known is about children's reactions to the sorts of multiple or repeated trauma exposure that commonly occurs during war and mass disasters. Several cross-sectional surveys of high-risk or community samples have reported that children exposed to multiple traumatic events may develop PTSD symptoms (alongside considerable co-morbidity), but there is far less information about risk factors, patterns of co-morbidity, natural history and treatment response among these groups. More fine-grained knowledge about likely stress responses, especially the interplay between grief and trauma reactions, will be helpful for clinicians who work with particularly vulnerable groups such as young refugees and asylum seekers, or with young people who have been caught up in natural disasters.

> Further research is required to better understand the effects of repeated or multiple trauma exposure.

Refining our understanding of children's stress reactions

Paralleling the growth in knowledge of the phenomenology and natural course of children's traumatic stress reactions has been a development in our understanding of these reactions. As described throughout this book, the most significant development in recent years has been the application of cognitive models to understand children's PTSD reactions.

Further work in testing aspects of established cognitive models will be required in the future. For example, while the important role of misappraisals and avoidance has now been confirmed in a number of studies, there has been less research attention to other aspects of the cognitive model – such as the disjointed nature of trauma memory and the role of the family. Ongoing work is building on questionnaire-based studies to test theory-driven hypotheses about autobiographical memory and family interactions, using a broader range of methodologies. For example, detailed narrative analysis of children's early accounts of traumatic experiences (see Pennebaker 1995) may shed light on whether a disjointed representation of the traumatic event in memory is indeed a risk factor for later PTSD. Equally, such an approach will be useful in testing the clear prediction from cognitive models that the nature of the trauma memory will change following successful trauma-focused CBT (see Foa and Rauch 2004). Family factors have been implicated in a number of questionnaire-based surveys of traumatised children (e.g. Smith *et al.* 2001; Meiser-Stedman *et al.* 2006), confirming that child and parental reactions are associated. But the precise mechanisms underlying or maintaining this association remain poorly understood. Detailed assessment of interactions between parents and children, using coding of video-taped behavioural observations under standardised conditions, may help in specifying the important components in complex family interactions (see Bogels and Brechman-Toussaint 2006).

Again, while cognitive models have been tested in older children and teenagers, the extent to which they are applicable to younger children is not yet clear. Studies testing the role of avoidance, misappraisals, memory quality and family factors in young children are needed. Appropriate methodologies will need to be developed, and it is likely that models will need refining – perhaps with greater emphasis on family factors. When children are exposed to trauma at a very young age, the question of ascribed meanings and memory representations becomes highly complex and will present an important challenge for future research.

> Studies are required to test specific aspects of the cognitive model across the age range.

In addition to testing the predictions from cognitive models more thoroughly across the age range, there is scope for developing and extending these models. The aim is to understand better children's reactions, and in so doing to highlight reversible maintaining factors that may offer additional avenues for intervention. This may include investigation of basic processes, such as perception, memory and attention, as well as higher order factors, such as thinking styles, judgements, attributions, interpretations, executive control and emotional regulation (Dalgleish *et al.* 2005). Promising candidate factors include over-general autobiographical memory and depressogenic or trauma-related rumination. Vasey *et al.* (2003) and Dalgleish *et al.* (2005) provide up-to-date summaries of this literature, with key recommendations for future research into cognitive factors. Even more broadly, attachment theory has been used to investigate young adolescents' reactions to sexual trauma (Stubenbort *et al.* 2002), and young children's reactions to a wide range of other interpersonal trauma (Lieberman and Amaya-Jackson 2005). As with research into cognitive factors, this work is at an early stage, but is likely to be a useful and productive area for future study.

As work continues in the cognitive arena, investigations of neurophysiological factors in children's stress reactions are also progressing. Driven by contemporary neuroscience accounts of fear and stress, there is now growing evidence that children with symptoms of PTSD may show complex alterations to a number of interrelated neurophysiological systems, including the catecholamine system (i.e. adrenaline, noradrenaline and dopamine) and the hypothalamic-pituitary-adrenal (HPA) axis (for reviews see De Bellis 2001; Cohen *et al.* 2002; Pine 2003). Further work will help to develop a better understanding of the complex interplay between physiological and psychological responses to traumatic events (Yule and Smith 2008).

> The nature and extent of the relationship between neurophysiological systems and stress reactions requires further investigation.

Developing and evaluating interventions

The focus of this book, and the ultimate aim of many of the sorts of research programmes referred to above, is on developing more effective treatments for traumatised children and young people. What is the future likely to hold in terms of developing and evaluating interventions for traumatised youth?

Critical Incident Stress Debriefing (Mitchell 1983) – a form of secondary prevention – initially appeared promising as an effective intervention for survivors of mass disasters, including children (Dyregrov 1997). However, research with adults indicates that some forms of debriefing may actually slow down recovery, relative to those who receive no intervention (Mayou *et al.* 2000). While there is no evidence that debriefing is harmful in this way for young people, recent research with young traffic accident survivors shows that it does not improve recovery either (Stallard *et al.* 2006). It is now widely agreed that one-off, brief interventions administered in the days immediately following a trauma do not help to reduce later PTSD. However, this does not rule out all forms of early intervention. Further carefully controlled trials of early administered courses of trauma-focused CBT (in contrast to one-off debriefing meetings), possibly only for those who are highly symptomatic or otherwise at risk (in contrast to universal intervention for all), are needed. Such trials would benefit from including untreated control groups so that the effects of intervention can be evaluated relative to natural recovery, and from using repeated measures over time so that the rate of recovery (as well as post-intervention and follow-up outcome) can be gauged.

A stepped care approach to childhood PTSD might include interventions which are effective yet resource-efficient for children who develop mild to moderate difficulties following trauma. One such option is symptom monitoring. There is some evidence from adult (e.g. Tarrier *et al.* 1999) and child studies (e.g. Smith *et al.* 2007) that simple, structured, daily monitoring of PTSD symptoms (using a paper and pencil diary format) is associated with a reduction in PTSD symptoms. In relation to children, Smith *et al.* (2007) found that around a quarter of young people who completed such daily diaries over a four-week period improved sufficiently to lose their PTSD diagnosis. The young people who responded to this simple intervention had less severe PTSD symptoms initially, better psychosocial functioning and were less likely to have a co-morbid diagnosis. This approach holds promise as an effective intervention for those who are less severely affected initially – but further work is needed. In order to test whether symptom monitoring has an effect over and above that of the passage of time, a controlled trial comparing symptoms monitoring to wait list is now underway.

Alongside symptom monitoring, a stepped care approach might include developing self-help packages, including computerised delivery of CT for PTSD. Although self-help along CBT lines (using bibliotherapy and homework tasks) proved ineffective in one study with traumatised adults (Ehlers *et al.* 2003), more promising results have been reported following internet-delivered self-help for adults (Lange *et al.* 2003). Advances in technology mean that appealing and interactive computerised packages for young people can be developed and made widely accessible: the challenge is to ensure that such approaches are rigorously evaluated.

Early intervention may speed up recovery for some. Symptom monitoring plus guided self-help may be effective for young people who are less severely affected by exposure to trauma. Nevertheless, there will still be a need for effective treatments for more severely affected young people. Apart from outcome studies with young people who have developed PTSD as a result of sexual abuse (e.g. Cohen *et al.* 2006), there is a dearth of well-conducted randomised controlled trials (RCTs) of treatment for paediatric PTSD (for recent reviews see Feeny *et al.* 2004; Stallard 2006). Further small-scale RCTs evaluating CT for PTSD relative to a wait list or untreated control group would make valuable contributions to the sparse outcome literature. A potential next step is to evaluate the efficacy of CT for PTSD relative to wait list plus other active comparison conditions. There is also a pressing need to adapt and develop CT for PTSD interventions for very young children – probably with an emphasis on parent and carer involvement in treatment – and to carefully evaluate these using a similar approach to that taken for older children and teenagers. More generally, once efficacy of CT for PTSD with children whose symptoms arise from single incidents is established, it will become important to adapt interventions to address PTSD symptoms that arise from multiple exposure to trauma, and to evaluate such interventions with a broad population of young people.

> There is a need to develop a stepped care approach involving a number of evidence-based interventions.

References

American Psychiatric Association (APA, 1980, 1987, 1994). *Diagnostic and Statistical Manual of Mental Disorders*, 3rd edn, 3rd edn rev., 4th edn. Washington, DC: APA.

Beck, A.T., Rush, A.J., Shaw, B.F. and Emery, G. (1979). *Cognitive Therapy of Depression*. New York: Guilford Press.

Bennett-Levy, J., Butler, G., Fennell, M., Hackman, A., Mueller, M. and Westbrook, D. (eds) (2004). *Oxford Guide to Behavioural Experiments in Cognitive Therapy*. New York: Oxford University Press.

Bernstein, D., Borkovec, T. and Hazlett-Stevens, H. (2000). *New Directions in Progressive Relaxation Training: A Guidebook for Helping Professionals*. Santa Barbara, CA: Greenwood.

Birleson, P. (1981). The validity of depressive disorder in childhood and the development of a self-rating scale: A research report. *Journal of Child Psychology and Psychiatry, 22*, 73–88.

Bogels, S. and Brechman-Toussaint, M. (2006). Family issues in child anxiety: Attachment, family functioning, parental rearing and beliefs. *Clinical Psychology Review, 26*, 7, 834–856.

Bolton, D. (2005). Cognitive theory. In P. Graham (ed.) *Cognitive Behaviour Therapy for Children and Families*, 2nd edn. Cambridge: Cambridge University Press.

Bolton, D., O'Ryan, D., Udwin, O., Boyle, S. and Yule, W. (2000). The long-term psychological effects of a disaster experienced in adolescence: II: General psychopathology. *Journal of Child Psychology and Psychiatry, 41*, 513–523.

Bolton, D., Hill, J., O'Ryan, D., Udwin, O., Boyle, S. and Yule, W. (2004). Long-term effects of psychological trauma on psychosocial functioning. *Journal of Child Psychology and Psychiatry, 45*, 5, 1007–1014.

Brewin, C.R. (1998). Intrusive autobiographical memories in depression and posttraumatic stress disorder. *Applied Cognitive Psychology, 12*, 4, 359–370.

Brewin, C.R. (2001). A cognitive neuroscience account of posttraumatic stress disorder and its treatment. *Behaviour Research and Therapy, 39*, 373–393.

Brewin, C.R., Dalgleish, T. and Joseph, S. (1996). A dual representation theory of posttraumatic stress disorder. *Psychological Review, 103*, 670–686.

Brewin, C.R., Andrews, B. and Valentine, J.D. (2000). Meta-analysis of risk factors for posttraumatic stress disorder in trauma-exposed adults. *Journal of Consulting and Clinical Psychology, 68,* 747–766.

Brewin, C.R., Andrews, B. and Rose, S. (2003). Overlap between acute stress disorder and PTSD in victims of violent crime. *American Journal of Psychiatry, 160,* 783–785.

Bryant, R., Harvey, A., Dang, S., Sackville, T. and Basten, C. (1998). Treatment of acute stress disorder: A comparison of cognitive-behavioural therapy and supportive counselling. *Journal of Consulting and Clinical Psychology, 66,* 862–866.

Bryant, R.A., Salmon, K., Sinclair, E. and Davidson, P. (2007). A prospective study of appraisals in childhood posttraumatic stress disorder. *Behaviour Research and Therapy, 45,* 2502–2507.

Children and War Foundation (1999). *The Children's Revised Impact of Event Scale, 13-Item Version (CRIES-13).* www.childrenandwar.org.

Clark, D.M. (2005). A cognitive perspective on social phobia. In W.R. Crozier and L.E. Alden (eds) *The Essential Handbook of Social Anxiety for Clinicians.* New York: Wiley.

Clark, D.M. and Ehlers, A. (2004). Posttraumatic stress disorder: From cognitive theory to therapy. In R.L. Leahy (ed.) *Contemporary Cognitive Therapy: Theory, Research, and Practice.* New York: Guilford Press.

Cohen, J.A., Berliner, L. and March, J.S. (2002). Treatment of children and adolescents. In E. Foa, T. Keane and M. Freidman (eds). New York: Guilford Press.

Cohen, J.A., Deblinger, E., Mannarino, A.P. and Steer, R.A. (2004). A multisite randomized controlled trial for children with sexual abuse-related PTSD symptoms. *Journal of the American Academy of Child and Adolescent Psychiatry, 43,* 393–402.

Cohen, J.A., Mannarino, A.P. and Deblinger, E. (2006). *Treating Trauma and Traumatic Grief in Children and Adolescents.* New York: Guilford Press.

Copeland, W.E., Keeler, G., Angold, A. and Costello, E.J. (2007). Traumatic events and posttraumatic stress in childhood. *Archives of General Psychiatry, 64, 5,* 577–584.

Costello, E.J., Erkanli, A., Fairbank, J. and Angold, A. (2002). The prevalence of potentially traumatic events in childhood and adolescence. *Journal of Traumatic Stress, 15, 2,* 99–112.

Dalgleish, T., Meiser-Stedman, R. and Smith, P. (2005). Cognitive aspects of posttraumatic stress reactions and their treatment in children and adolescents: An empirical review and some recommendations. *Behavioural and Cognitive Psychotherapy, 33,* 459–486.

De Bellis, M. (2001). Developmental traumatology: The psychobiological development of maltreated children and its implications for research, treatment, and policy. *Development and Psychopathology, 13,* 539–564.

Deblinger, E., McLeer, S.V. and Henry, D. (1990). Cognitive behavioral treatment for sexually abused children suffering post-traumatic stress: Preliminary findings. *Journal of the American Academy of Child and Adolescent Psychiatry, 29, 5,* 747–752.

Doherr, L., Reynolds, S., Wetherly, J. and Evans, E.H. (2005). Young children's ability to engage in cognitive therapy tasks: Associations with age and educational experience. *Behavioural and Cognitive Psychotherapy, 33, 2,* 201–215.

Dudley, R. and Kuyken, W. (2006). Formulation in cognitive-behavioural therapy: 'There is nothing either good or bad, but thinking makes it so.' In L. Johnstone and R. Dallos (eds) *Formulation in Psychology and Psychotherapy: Making Sense of People's Problems.* New York: Routledge.

Duffy, M., Gillespie, K. and Clark, D.M. (2007). Post traumatic stress disorder in the context of terrorism and other civil conflict in Northern Ireland: A randomised controlled trial. *British Medical Journal, 334,* 1147–1150.

Dyregrov, A. (1997a). *Barn og Traumer* [Children and Trauma]. Bergen: Sigma Forlag.

Dyregrov, A. (1997b). The process in psychological debriefings. *Journal of Traumatic Stress, 10,* 4, 589–605.

Dyregrov, A. (2008). *Grief in Children: A Handbook for Adults,* 2nd edn. London: Jessica Kingsley Publishers.

Ehlers, A. and Clark, D.M. (2000). A cognitive model of posttraumatic stress disorder. *Behaviour Research and Therapy, 38,* 319–345.

Ehlers, A. and Clark, D.M. (2003). Early psychological interventions for adult survivors of trauma: A review. *Biological Psychiatry, 53,* 817–826.

Ehlers, A., Clark, D.M., Hackmann, A., McManus, F., Fennell, M., Herbert, C. *et al.* (2003a). A randomised controlled trial of cognitive therapy, a self-help booklet, and repeated assessments as early interventions for posttraumatic stress disorder. *Archives of General Psychiatry, 60,* 1024–1032.

Ehlers, A., Mayou, R.A. and Bryant, B. (2003b). Cognitive predictors of post-traumatic stress disorder in children: Results of a prospective longitudinal study. *Behaviour Research and Therapy, 41,* 1–10.

Ehlers, A., Clark, D.M., Hackmann, A., McManus, F. and Fennell, M. (2005). Cognitive therapy for PTSD: Development and evaluation. *Behaviour Research and Therapy, 43,* 413–431.

Ehlers, A., Clark, D.M., Hackmann, A., McManus, F., Fennell, M. and Grey, N. (in press). *Cognitive Therapy for Posttraumatic Stress Disorder: A Therapist's Guide.* Oxford: Oxford University Press.

Ehntholt, K. and Yule, W. (2006). Assessment and treatment of refugee children and adolescents who have experienced war-related trauma. *Journal of Child Psychology and Psychiatry, 47,* 1197–1210.

Ehntholt, K., Smith, P. and Yule, W. (2005). School-based cognitive-behavioural therapy group intervention for refugee children who have experienced war-related trauma. *Clinical Child Psychology and Psychiatry, 10,* 235–250.

Feeny, N.C., Foa, E.B., Treadwell, K.R. and March, J. (2004). Posttraumatic stress disorder in youth: A critical review of the cognitive and behavioral treatment outcome literature. *Professional Psychology: Research and Practice, 35,* 466–476.

Foa, E.B. and Rauch, S.A. (2004). Cognitive changes during prolonged exposure versus prolonged exposure plus cognitive restructuring in female assault survivors with posttraumatic stress disorder. *Journal of Consulting and Clinical Psychology, 72,* 879–884.

Foa, E.B., Steketee, G. and Olasov-Rothbaum, B. (1989). Behavioral/cognitive conceptualizations of post-traumatic stress disorder. *Behavior Therapy, 20,* 155–176.

Foa, E.B., Rothbaum, B.O., Riggs, D.S. and Murdock, T.B. (1991). Treatment of PTSD in rape victims: A comparison between cognitive-behavioural procedures and counselling. *Journal of Consulting and Clinical Psychology, 59,* 715–723.

Foa, E.B., Riggs, D.S., Dancu, C.V. and Rothbaum, B.O. (1993). Reliability and validity of a brief instrument for assessing post-traumatic stress disorder. *Journal of Traumatic Stress, 6,* 4, 459–473.

Foa, E.B., Ehlers, A., Clark, D.M., Tolin, D.F. and Orsillo, S.M. (1999). The Posttraumatic Cognitions Inventory (PTCI): Development and validation. *Psychological Assessment, 11,* 303–314.

Foa, E.B., Johnson, K.M., Feeny, N.C. and Treadwell, K.R. (2001). The Child PTSD Symptom Scale: A preliminary examination of its psychometric properties. *Journal of Clinical Child Psychology*, *30*, 376–384.

Friedberg, R.D. and McClure, J.M. (2002). *Clinical Practice of Cognitive Therapy with Children and Adolescents*. New York: Guilford Press.

Giaconia, R.M., Reinherz, H.Z., Silverman, A.B., Pakiz, B., Frost, A.K. and Cohen, E. (1995). Traumas and posttraumatic stress disorder in a community population of older adolescents. *Journal of the American Academy of Child and Adolescent Psychiatry*, *34*, 1369–1380.

Giannopoulou, I., Strouthos, M., Smith, P., Dikaiakou, A., Galanopoulou, V. and Yule, W. (2006). Post-traumatic stress reactions of children and adolescents exposed to the Athens 1999 earthquake. *European Psychiatry*, *21*, 3, 160–166.

Green, B.L., Korol, M., Grace, M.C., Vary, M.G., Leonard, A.C., Glesser, G.C. *et al.* (1991). Children and disaster: Age, gender, and parental effects on PTSD symptoms. *Journal of the American Academy of Child and Adolescent Psychiatry*, *30*, 945–951.

Grey, N. and Young, K. (2008). Cognitive behaviour therapy with refugees and asylum seekers experiencing traumatic stress symptoms. *Behavioural and Cognitive Psychotherapy*, *36*, 3–19.

Grey, N., Young, K. and Holmes, E. (2002). Cognitive restructuring within reliving: A treatment for peritraumatic emotional 'hotspots' in posttraumatic stress disorder. *Behavioural and Cognitive Psychotherapy*, *30*, 37–56.

Hackmann, A., Ehlers, A., Speckens, A. and Clark, D.M. (2004). Characteristics and content of intrusive memories in PTSD and their changes with treatment. *Journal of Traumatic Stress*, *17*, 3, 231–240.

Harris-Hendricks, J., Black, D. and Kaplan, T. (2000). *When Father Kills Mother: Guiding Children through Trauma and Grief*, 2nd edn. London: Routledge.

Harvey, A.G. and Bryant, R.A. (1998). The relationship between acute stress disorder and posttraumatic stress disorder: A prospective evaluation of motor vehicle accident survivors. *Journal of Consulting and Clinical Psychology*, *66*, 3, 507–512.

Harvey, A.G. and Bryant, R.A. (2002). Acute stress disorder: A synthesis and critique. *Psychological Bulletin*, *128*, 886–902.

Harvey, A., Watkins, E., Mansell, W. and Shafran, R. (2004). *Cognitive Behavioural Processes Across Psychological Disorders: A Transdiagnostic Approach to Research and Treatment*. Oxford: Oxford University Press.

Horowitz, M.J. (1997). *Stress Response Syndromes: PTSD, Grief, and Adjustment Disorders*, 3rd edn. Lanham, MD: Jason Aronson.

Horowitz, M.J., Wilner, N. and Alvarez, W. (1979). Impact of event scale: A measure of subjective stress. *Psychosomatic Medicine*, *41*, 209–218.

Janoff-Bulman, R. (1985). The aftermath of victimization: Rebuilding shattered assumptions. In C.R. Figley (ed.) *Trauma and its Wake*. New York: Brunner/Mazel.

Kassam-Adams, N. and Winston, F.K. (2004). Predicting child PTSD: The relationship between acute stress disorder and PTSD in injured children. *Journal of the American Academy of Child and Adolescent Psychiatry*, *43*, 403–411.

Kazak, A., Alderfer, M., Streisand, R., Simms, S., Rourke, M., Barakat, L., *et al.* (2004). Treatment of posttraumatic stress symptoms in adolescent survivors of childhood cancer and their families: A randomized clinical trial. *Journal of Family Psychology*, *18*, 493–504.

Keane, T.M., Fairbank, J.A., Caddell, J. and Zimering, R. (1989). Implosive (flooding) therapy reduces symptoms of PTSD in Vietnam combat veterans. *Behaviour Therapy, 20*, 245–260.

Kendall, P.C. (2006). Guiding theory for therapy with children and adolescents. In P.C. Kendall (ed.) *Child and Adolescent Therapy: Cognitive-Behavioral Procedures*, 3rd edn. New York: Guilford Press.

Kessler, R.C., Sonnega, A., Bromet, E., Hughes, M. and Nelson, C.B. (1995). Posttraumatic stress disorder in the National Comorbidity Survey. *Archives of General Psychiatry, 52*, 1048–1060.

Kilpatrick, D., Ruggiero, K., Acierno, R., Saunders, B., Resnick, H. and Best, C. (2003). Violence and risk of PTSD, major depression, substance abuse/dependence, and comorbidity: Results from the National Survey of Adolescents. *Journal of Consulting and Clinical Psychology, 71*, 4, 692–700.

King, N.J., Tonge, B.J., Mullen, P., Myerson, N., Heyne, D., Rollings, S. *et al.* (2000). Treating sexually abused children with posttraumatic stress symptoms: A randomized clinical trial. *Journal of the American Academy of Child and Adolescent Psychiatry, 39*, 1347–1355.

Kinzie, J., Cheng, K., Tsai, J. and Riley, C. (2006). Traumatized refugee children: The case for individualized diagnosis and treatment. *Journal of Nervous and Mental Disease, 194*, 7, 534–537.

Lange, A., Rietdijk, D., Hudcovicova, M., van de Ven, J-P., Schrieken, B. and Emmelkamp, P. (2003). Interapy: A controlled randomized trial of the standardized treatment of posttraumatic stress through the internet. *Journal of Consulting and Clinical Psychology, 71*, 901–909.

Lieberman, A. and Amaya-Jackson, L. (2005). Reciprocal influences of attachment and trauma: Using a dual lens in the assessment and treatment of infants, toddlers, and preschoolers. In L. Berlin, Y. Ziv, L. Amaya-Jackson and M. Greenberg (eds) *Enhancing Early Attachments: Theory, Research, Intervention, and Policy*. New York: Guilford Press.

McFarlane, A.C. (1987). Family functioning and overprotection following a natural disaster: The longitudinal effects of post-traumatic morbidity. *Australia and New Zealand Journal of Psychiatry, 21*, 210–218.

McNally, R.J. (1991). Assessment of posttraumatic stress disorder in children. *Psychological Assessment, 3*, 531–537.

March, J.S. (1998). Assessment of pediatric posttraumatic stress disorder. In P. Saigh and J. Bremner (eds) *Posttraumatic Stress Disorder: A Comprehensive Approach to Assessment and Treatment*. Needham Heights, MA: Allen and Bacon.

Mayou, R.A., Ehlers, A. and Hobbs, M. (2000). Psychological debriefing for road traffic accident victims: Three-year follow-up of a randomised controlled trial. *British Journal of Psychiatry, 176*, 589–593.

Meiser-Stedman, R. (2002). Towards a cognitive-behavioral model of PTSD in children and adolescents. *Clinical Child and Family Psychology Review, 5*, 217–232.

Meiser-Stedman, R., Yule, W., Smith, P., Glucksman, E. and Dalgleish, T. (2005). Acute stress disorder and posttraumatic stress disorder in children and adolescents involved in assaults or motor vehicle accidents. *American Journal of Psychiatry, 162*, 7, 1381–1383.

Meiser-Stedman, R., Yule, W., Dalgleish, T., Smith, P. and Glucksman, E. (2006). The role of the family in child and adolescent posttraumatic stress following attendance at an emergency department. *Journal of Pediatric Psychology, 31*, 397–402.

Meiser-Stedman, R., Dalgleish, T., Smith, P., Yule, W. and Glucksman, E. (2007). Diagnostic, demographic, memory quality, and cognitive variables associated with acute stress disorder in children and adolescents. *Journal of Abnormal Psychology, 116*, 1, 65–79.

Meiser-Stedman, R., Smith, P., Glucksman, E., Yule, W. and Dalgleish, T. (2008). The post-traumatic stress disorder (PTSD) diagnosis in pre-school and elementary school-aged children exposed to motor vehicle accidents. *American Journal of Psychiatry, 165*, 1326–1337.

Meiser-Stedman, R., Smith, P., Bryant, R., Salmon, K., Yule, W., Dalgleish, T., *et al.* (2009). Development and validation of the Child Post Traumatic Cognitions Inventory (CPTCI). *Journal of Child Psychology and Psychiatry, 50*, 432–440.

Meltzer, H., Gatward, R., Goodman, R. and Ford, T. (2003). Mental health of children and adolescents in Great Britain. *International Review of Psychiatry, 15*, 185–187.

Misch, P., Phillips, M., Evans, P. and Berkowitz, M. (1993). Trauma in preschool children: A clinical account. *Association of Child Psychology and Psychiatry Occasional Papers, 8*, 11–18.

Mitchell, J. (1983). When disaster strikes: The critical incident stress debriefing process. *Journal of Emergency Medicine Services, 8*, 36–39.

Morgan, L., Scourfield, J., Williams, D., Jasper, A. and Lewis, G. (2003). The Aberfan disaster: 33-year follow-up of survivors. *British Journal of Psychiatry, 182*, 532–536.

Mufson, L., Dorta, K., Moreau, D. and Weissman, M. (2004). *Interpersonal Psychotherapy for Depressed Adolescents*, 2nd edn. New York: Guilford Press.

Nader, K.O. (1995). Assessing traumatic experiences in children. In J.P. Wilson and T.M. Keane (eds) *Assessing Psychological Trauma and PTSD: A Handbook for Practitioners*. New York: Guilford Press.

Nader, K., Blake, D., Kriegler, J. and Pynoos, R. (1994). *Clinician Administered PTSD Scale: Child and Adolescent Version (CAPS-C), Current and Lifetime Version, and Instruction Manual*. Los Angeles: UCLA Neuropsychiatric Institute and National Center for PTSD.

National Institute for Clinical Excellence (NICE, 2005). *Post Traumatic Stress Disorder: The Management of PTSD in Adults and Children in Primary and Secondary Care* (Clinical Guideline 26). London: Gaskell and the British Psychological Society.

Ohmi, H., Kojima, S., Awai, Y., Kamata, S., Sasaki, K., Tanaka, Y., *et al.* (2002). Post-traumatic stress disorder in pre-school aged children after a gas explosion. *European Journal of Pediatrics, 161*, 12, 643–648.

Ozer, E.J., Best, S., Lipsey, T. and Weiss, D. (2003). Predictors of posttraumatic stress disorder and symptoms in adults: A meta-analysis. *Psychological Bulletin, 129*, 1, 52–73.

Pennebaker, J.W. (ed.) (1995). *Emotion, Disclosure, and Health*. Washington, DC: American Psychological Association.

Perrin, S., Yule, W. and Smith, P. (2004). Treatment of PTSD in children and adolescents. In P.M. Barrett and T.H. Ollendick (eds) *Handbook of Interventions that Work with Children and Adolescents: Prevention and Treatment*. Chichester: Wiley.

Perrin, S., Meiser-Stedman, R. and Smith, P. (2005). The Children's Revised Impact of Event Scale (CRIES): Validity as a screening instrument for PTSD. *Behavioural and Cognitive Psychotherapy, 33*, 487–498.

Pfefferbaum, B., DeVoe, E., Stuber, J., Schiff, M., Klein, T. and Fairbrother, G. (2004). Psychological impact of terrorism on children and families in the United States. *Journal of Aggression, Maltreatment and Trauma, 9*, 3–4, 305–317.

Pine, D. (2003). Developmental psychobiology and response to threats: Relevance to trauma in children and adolescents. *Biological Psychiatry, 53*, 796–808.

Pynoos, R.S. and Eth, S. (1986). Witness to violence: The child interview. *Journal of the American Academy of Child Psychiatry, 25*, 306–319.

Pynoos, R.S., Goenjian, A., Karakashian, M., Tashjian, M., Manjikian, R., Manoukian, G., *et al.* (1993). Posttraumatic stress reactions in children after the 1988 Armenian earthquake. *British Journal of Psychiatry, 163*, 239–247.

Quakley, S., Coker, S., Palmer, K. and Reynolds, S. (2003). Can children distinguish between thoughts and behaviours? *Behavioural and Cognitive Psychotherapy, 31*, 2, 159–167.

Quakley, S., Reynolds, S. and Coker, S. (2004). The effect of cues on young children's abilities to discriminate among thoughts, feelings and behaviours. *Behaviour Research and Therapy, 42*, 3, 343–356.

Ramchandani, P. and Jones, D.P.H. (2003). Treating psychological symptoms in sexually abused children: From research findings to service provision. *British Journal of Psychiatry, 183*, 484–490.

Saigh, P.A. (1992). The behavioural treatment of child and adolescent post-traumatic stress disorder. *Advances in Behaviour Research and Therapy, 14*, 247–275.

Salmon, K. and Bryant, R.A. (2002). Posttraumatic stress disorder in children: The influence of developmental factors. *Clinical Psychology Review, 22*, 163–188.

Salmon, K., Sinclair, E. and Bryant, R.A. (2007). The role of maladaptive appraisals in child acute stress reactions. *British Journal of Clinical Psychology, 46*, 203–210.

Saylor, C.F., Swenson, C.C., Reynolds, S.S. and Taylor, M. (1999). The pediatric emotional distress scale: A brief screening measure for young children exposed to traumatic events. *Journal of Clinical Child Psychology, 28*, 1, 70–81.

Schauer, M., Neuner, F. and Elbert, T. (2005). *Narrative Exposure Therapy: A Short-term Intervention for Traumatic Stress Disorders After War, Terror, or Torture.* Cambridge, MA: Hogrefe and Huber.

Scheeringa, M.S. and Zeanah, C.H. (1995). Symptom expression and trauma variables in children under 48 months of age. *Infant Mental Health Journal, 16*, 4, 259–270.

Scheeringa, M.S., Zeanah, C.H., Drell, M.J. and Larrieu, J.A. (1995). Two approaches to diagnosing posttraumatic stress disorder in infancy and early childhood. *Journal of the American Academy of Child and Adolescent Psychiatry, 34*, 191–200.

Scheeringa, M.S., Peebles, C.D., Cook, C.A. and Zeanah, C.H. (2001). Toward establishing procedural, criterion, and discriminant validity for PTSD in early childhood. *Journal of the American Academy of Child and Adolescent Psychiatry, 40*, 1, 52–60.

Scheeringa, M., Zeanah, C.H., Myers, L. and Putnam, F. (2003). New findings on alternative criteria for PTSD in preschool children. *Journal of the American Academy of Child and Adolescent Psychiatry, 42*, 561–570.

Scheeringa, M., Wright, M., Hunt, J.P. and Zeanah, C.H. (2006). Factors affecting the diagnosis and prediction of PTSD symptomatology in children and adolescents. *American Journal of Psychiatry, 163*, 644–651.

Scheeringa, M., Salloum, A., Arnberger, R., Weems, C., Amaya-Jackson, L. and Cohen, J. (2007). Feasibility and effectiveness of cognitive-behavioural therapy for posttraumatic stress disorder in preschool children: Two case reports. *Journal of Traumatic Stress*, *20*, 631–636.

Silverman, W. and Albano, A. (1996). *Anxiety Disorders Interview Schedule (ADIS-IV) Child/Parent Version*. New York: Oxford University Press.

Smith, P., Dyregrov, A., Yule, W., Perrin, S., Gjestad, R. and Gupta, L. (1999). *Children and War: Teaching Recovery Techniques*. Bergen: Foundation for Children and War (http://www.childrenandwar.org).

Smith, P., Perrin, S., Yule, W. and Rabe-Hesketh, S. (2001). War-exposure and maternal reactions in the psychological adjustment of children from Bosnia-Hercegovina. *Journal of Child Psychology and Psychiatry*, *42*, 3, 395–404.

Smith, P., Perrin, S., Dyregov, A. and Yule, W. (2003). Principal components analysis of the Impact of Event Scale with children in war. *Personality and Individual Differences*, *34*, 315–322.

Smith, P., Yule, W., Perrin, S., Tranah, T., Dalgleish, T. and Clark, D.M. (2007). Cognitive-behavioral therapy for PTSD in children and adolescents: A preliminary randomized controlled trial. *Journal of the American Academy of Child and Adolescent Psychiatry*, *46*, 1051–1061.

Stallard, P. (2002). Cognitive behaviour therapy with children and young people: A selective review of key issues. *Behavioural and Cognitive Psychotherapy*, *30*, 3, 297–309.

Stallard, P. (2003). A retrospective analysis to explore the applicability of the Ehlers and Clark (2000) cognitive model to explain PTSD in children. *Behavioural and Cognitive Psychotherapy*, *31*, 337–345.

Stallard, P. (2006). Psychological interventions for post traumatic stress reactions in children and young people: A review of randomised controlled trials. *Clinical Psychology Review*, *26*, 895–911.

Stallard, P. and Smith, E. (2007). Appraisals and cognitive coping styles associated with chronic post-traumatic symptoms in child road traffic accident survivors. *Journal of Child Psychology and Psychiatry and Allied Disciplines*, *48*, 194–201.

Stallard, P., Salter, E. and Velleman, R. (2004). Posttraumatic stress disorder following road traffic accidents: A second prospective study. *European Child and Adolescent Psychiatry*, *13*, 172–178.

Stallard, P., Velleman, R., Salter, E., Howse, I., Yule, W. and Taylor, G. (2006). A randomised controlled trial to determine the effectiveness of an early psychological intervention with children involved in road traffic accidents. *Journal of Child Psychology and Psychiatry*, *47*, 127–134.

Stein, B.D., Jaycox, L.H., Kataoka, S.H., Wong, M., Tu, W., Elliott, M.N., *et al.* (2003). A mental health intervention for schoolchildren exposed to violence: A randomized controlled trial. *Journal of the American Medical Association*, *290*, 603–611.

Stubenbort, K., Greeno, C., Mannarino, A. and Cohen, J. (2002). Attachment quality and post-treatment functioning following sexual trauma in young adolescents: A case series presentation. *Clinical Social Work Journal*, *30*, 1, 23–39.

Tarrier, N., Pilgrim, H., Sommerfield, C., Faragher, B., Reynolds, M., Graham, E., *et al.* (1999). A randomised trial of cognitive therapy and imaginal exposure in the treatment of chronic posttraumatic stress disorder. *Journal of Consulting and Clinical Psychology*, *67*, 13–18.

Terr, L. (1991). Childhood traumas – An outline and overview. *American Journal of Psychiatry*, *148*, 10–20.

Udwin, O., Boyle, S., Yule, W., Bolton, D. and O'Ryan, D. (2000). Risk factors for long-term psychological effects of a disaster experienced in adolescence: Predictors of posttraumatic stress disorder. *Journal of Child Psychology and Psychiatry*, *41*, 969–979.

Vasey, M., Dagleish, T. and Silverman, W. (2003). Research on information-processing factors in child and adolescent psychopathology: A critical commentary. *Journal of Clinical Child and Adolescent Psychology*, *32*, 1, 81–93.

Vernberg, E.M., La Greca, A., Silverman, W.K. and Prinstein, M.J. (1996). Prediction of posttraumatic stress symptoms in children after hurricane Andrew. *Journal of Abnormal Psychology*, *105*, 237–248.

Wenzlaff, R. and Wegner, D. (2000). Thought suppression. *Annual Review of Psychology*, *51*, 59–91.

Williams, A.D. and Moulds, M.L. (2007). An investigation of the cognitive and experiential features of intrusive memories in depression. *Memory*, *15*, 8, 912–920.

Wolmer, L., Laor, N., Gershon, A., Mayes, L.C. and Cohen, D.J. (2000). The mother–child dyad facing trauma: A developmental outlook. *Journal of Nervous and Mental Disease*, *188*, 409–415.

World Health Organization (WHO, 1987/1988/1991). *International Classification of Diseases: 10th Edition (ICD-10)*. Geneva: WHO.

Young, A. (1997). *The Harmony of Illusions: Inventing Post Traumatic Stress Disorder*. Princeton, NJ: Princeton University Press.

Yule, W. (1998). Anxiety, depression, and post traumatic stress disorder in children. In I. Sclare (ed.) *The NFER Child Portfolio*. Windsor: NFER-Nelson.

Yule, W. (2005). Working with traumatically bereaved children. In B. Monroe and F. Kraus (eds) *Brief Interventions with Bereaved Children*. Oxford: Oxford University Press.

Yule, W. and Gold, A. (1993). *Wise Before the Event: Coping with Crises in Schools*. London: Calouste Gulbenkian Foundation.

Yule, W. and Smith, P. (2008). Post traumatic stress disorder. In M. Rutter, D. Bishop, D. Pine, S. Scott, J. Stevenson, E. Taylor, *et al.* (eds) *Rutter's Child and Adolescent Psychiatry*, 5th edn. Oxford: Blackwell.

Yule, W. and Williams, R. (1990). Post-traumatic stress reactions in children. *Journal of Traumatic Stress*, *3*, 279–295.

Yule, W., Bolton, D., Udwin, O., Boyle, S., O'Ryan, D. and Nurrish, J. (2000). The long-term psychological effects of a disaster experienced in adolescence: I: The incidence and course of post traumatic stress disorder. *Journal of Child Psychology and Psychiatry*, *41*, 503–511.

Zigmund, A.S. and Snaith, R.P. (1983). The Hospital Anxiety and Depression Scale. *Acta Psychiatrica Scandinavia*, *67*, 6, 361–370.

Appendix A

Self-report measures for children

Child PTSD Symptom Scale (CPSS)

Foa, E.B., Johnson, K.M., Feeny, N.C. and Treadwell, K.R. (2001). The Child PTSD Symptom Scale: A preliminary examination of its psychometric properties. *Journal of Clinical Child Psychology*, *30*, 376–384.

This scale is made up of 23 items. The first 17 items assess PTSD symptoms. The child is asked to rate how frequently the symptom occurred over the past week on a four-point scale (0, 1, 2, 3). The total score is the sum of items 1–17, ranging from 0 to 51. **A total score of 12 or more suggests PTSD symptoms in the clinical range** (Foa *et al.* 2001).

The last six items assess impairment in functioning. The child is asked to circle a Yes or No for areas of potential disruption: pleasurable activities; relationships with peers and family; school; chores; and general happiness. The impairment items are not scored, but are used to help the clinician gauge the degree of impairment over the previous week.

CPSS (children and young people)

Name:　　　　　　　　　　　　　　　　　　　　　　　**Date:**

Below is a list of problems that children and young people sometimes have after experiencing an upsetting event.

Read each one carefully and circle the number that best describes how often that problem has bothered you in the last week.

0	1	2	3
Not at all or only one time	Once a week or less/once in a while	2 to 4 times a week/half the time	5 or more times a week/almost always

(1)　0　1　2　3　Having upsetting thoughts or images about the event that came into your head when you didn't want them to.

(2)　0　1　2　3　Having bad dreams or nightmares.

(3)　0　1　2　3　Acting or feeling as if the event was happening again (hearing something or seeing a picture about it and feeling as if I am there again).

(4)　0　1　2　3　Feeling upset when you think or hear about the event (for example, feeling scared, angry, sad, guilty, etc.).

(5)　0　1　2　3　Having feelings in your body when you think about or hear about the event (for example, breaking out in a sweat, heart beating fast).

(6)　0　1　2　3　Trying not to think about, talk about, or have feelings about the event.

(7)　0　1　2　3　Trying to avoid activities, people, or places that remind you of the traumatic event.

(8)　0　1　2　3　Not being able to remember an important part of the upsetting event.

(9)　0　1　2　3　Having much less interest or not doing the things you used to do.

(10)　0　1　2　3　Not feeling close to people around you.

(11)　0　1　2　3　Not being able to have strong feelings (for example, being unable to cry or unable to feel very happy).

(12)　0　1　2　3　Feeling as if your future plans or hopes will not come true (for example, you will not have a job or get married or have kids).

(13)　0　1　2　3　Having trouble falling or staying asleep.

(14)　0　1　2　3　Feeling irritable or having fits of anger.

(15)　0　1　2　3　Having trouble concentrating (for example, losing track of a story on television, forgetting what you read, not paying attention in class).

0	1	2	3
Not at all or only one time	Once a week or less/once in a while	2 to 4 times a week/half the time	5 or more times a week/almost always

(16) 0 1 2 3 Being overly careful (for example, checking to see who is around you and what is around you).

(17) 0 1 2 3 Being jumpy or easily startled (for example, when someone walks up behind you).

Please indicate below if the problems you rated above have got in the way of any of the following areas of your life during the past week. Circle Y for Yes, N for No.

(18) Y N Fun and hobby activities.
(19) Y N Relationships with your friends.
(20) Y N Schoolwork.
(21) Y N Relationship with your family.
(22) Y N Chores and duties at home.
(23) Y N General happiness with your life.

Child Post Traumatic Cognitions Inventory (CPTCI)

Meiser-Stedman, R., Smith, P., Bryant, R., Salmon, K., Yule, W., Dalgleish, T. and Nixon, R. (2009). Development and validation of the Child Post Traumatic Cognitions Inventory (CPTCI). *Journal of Child Psychology and Psychiatry, 50,* 432–440.

The CPTCI measures the level of agreement with 25 trauma- and symptom-related appraisals. There are two subscales: 'permanent and disturbing change' (items 4, 6, 8, 13, 14, 16, 17, 19, 20, 21, 22, 23, 24); and 'fragile person in a scary world' (items 1, 2, 3, 5, 7, 9, 10, 11, 12, 15, 18, 25).

For each item the child is asked to rate their level of agreement on a four-point scale: *Don't agree at all* = 0; *Don't agree a bit* = 1; *Agree a bit* = 2; *Agree a lot* = 3. The scores for the 25 items are summed, with higher scores indicating unhelpful beliefs about permanent negative change, and about being a fragile person in a scary world. In the original study with N = 138 young people aged 6–17 years old who had been involved in an assault or traffic accident, the mean score of those with PTSD (N = 46) at six months post trauma was 64.26 (sd 15.18), while the mean score of those without PTSD (N = 87) was 40.11 (sd 11.04).

Child Post Traumatic Cognitions Inventory (CPTCI)
© Meiser-Stedman (2003)

How I've been thinking and feeling since the frightening event

We would like to know what kinds of thoughts and feelings you've been having after the frightening event.

Below is a list of statements. Please read each statement carefully and tell us how much you AGREE or DISAGREE with each statement by ticking one box.

People react to frightening events in many different ways. There are no right or wrong answers to these statements.

	Don't agree at all	Don't agree a bit	Agree a bit	Agree a lot
1 Anyone could hurt me.	[ ]	[ ]	[ ]	[ ]
2 Everyone lets me down.	[ ]	[ ]	[ ]	[ ]
3 I am a coward.	[ ]	[ ]	[ ]	[ ]
4 My reactions since the frightening event mean I have changed for the worse.	[ ]	[ ]	[ ]	[ ]
5 I don't trust people.	[ ]	[ ]	[ ]	[ ]
6 My reactions since the frightening event mean something is seriously wrong with me.	[ ]	[ ]	[ ]	[ ]
7 I am no good.	[ ]	[ ]	[ ]	[ ]
8 Not being able to get over all my fears means that I am a failure.	[ ]	[ ]	[ ]	[ ]
9 Small things upset me.	[ ]	[ ]	[ ]	[ ]
10 I can't cope when things get tough.	[ ]	[ ]	[ ]	[ ]
11 I can't stop bad things from happening to me.	[ ]	[ ]	[ ]	[ ]
12 I have to watch out for danger all the time.	[ ]	[ ]	[ ]	[ ]
13 My reactions since the frightening event mean I will never get over it.	[ ]	[ ]	[ ]	[ ]
14 I used to be a happy person but now I am always sad.	[ ]	[ ]	[ ]	[ ]
15 Bad things always happen.	[ ]	[ ]	[ ]	[ ]
16 I will never be able to have normal feelings again.	[ ]	[ ]	[ ]	[ ]
17 I'm scared that I'll get so angry that I'll break something or hurt someone.	[ ]	[ ]	[ ]	[ ]

	Don't agree at all	Don't agree a bit	Agree a bit	Agree a lot
18 Life is not fair.	[ ]	[ ]	[ ]	[ ]
19 My life has been destroyed by the frightening event.	[ ]	[ ]	[ ]	[ ]
20 I feel like I am a different person since the frightening event.	[ ]	[ ]	[ ]	[ ]
21 My reactions since the frightening event show that I must be going crazy.	[ ]	[ ]	[ ]	[ ]
22 Nothing good can happen to me anymore.	[ ]	[ ]	[ ]	[ ]
23 Something terrible will happen if I do not try to control my thoughts about the frightening event.	[ ]	[ ]	[ ]	[ ]
24 The frightening event has changed me forever.	[ ]	[ ]	[ ]	[ ]
25 I have to be really careful because something bad could happen.	[ ]	[ ]	[ ]	[ ]

Appendix B

Handouts for young people and for parents and carers

Getting over frightening experiences: information for young people

Introduction

Children and teenagers can get caught up in very frightening events from time to time. Very frightening events are things like car crashes, seeing someone get badly hurt or attacked, injuring yourself in an accident, getting badly burned, or getting bitten by a dog, for example. A very frightening event like this is a *trauma*. It is the sort of thing that everyone would be really scared by.

It is normal to be very frightened by these things, and normal to stay frightened for quite a while afterwards. After your frightening experience, you might find that you have problems sleeping and have bad dreams, or that you are really jumpy and stressed all the time, or that you keep remembering what happened to you even when you don't want to.

Many young people feel like this after they have been in a trauma. In this handout, you will find out how other children and teenagers have felt after frightening events. Take time to read the handout. You don't have to read it all at once, but try to read all of it over the next few days. You can see if you have felt the same way as other kids of your age. The handout is yours to keep, so write on it if you want to, to remind yourself of important parts. Next week, you can ask any questions about the things you've read.

The way you might feel after a trauma

There is no 'right or wrong' way to feel after a trauma. Everyone is an individual, and so will react in his or her own individual way. Below are some examples of ways that other young people have felt after a trauma. You might find that you have felt some of the same things recently.

1. Feeling scared

It's quite normal to feel fearful and anxious after a trauma. If you've been in car crash, for example, you might be afraid of going back to where the accident happened. You might become afraid of going anywhere in a car in case another accident happens.

Because you've been in a frightening event, it can seem as if there is danger everywhere now. You might find that you get scared for no obvious reason at all. This means that things which were no problem before the trauma can seem very frightening now, so you might get frightened of going out or going to school for example.

After a trauma, many young people get scared when they have to be on their own, so they always try to be with someone else, especially parents and family. Night-time can be especially frightening, so some teenagers want to sleep with the light on, or sleep in their parents' room.

You might find that as well as being frightened about what might happen to you, you get more worried about other people too. So it can be hard when you are apart from your family – you worry about what might happen to mum and dad, for example. After being in a trauma, lots of children and teenagers can worry that their parents are going to die.

2. Remembering the trauma

Many young people say that they keep thinking about the trauma, even when they don't want to. It's as if you can't get it out of your mind. Often, the memories come back in pictures, where you 'see' the event in front of your eyes all over again. These pictures and images are really clear, and it's as if the trauma is happening all over again. It might feel as if you have no control over these thoughts and pictures. They just jump into your mind. This could happen when you are reminded of the trauma, for example, if you see something similar on television or if you hear someone talking about your trauma. Many children also say that these memories jump into their minds when they are trying to drop off to sleep or when they are just quiet and relaxed. It's usually very frightening to have memories come back to you like this, and it often has an effect on your body too, where you get jumpy and feel shaky. Memories of the trauma can also come back in bad dreams or nightmares. Sometimes, the bad dreams might be like a 'replay' of the trauma, or sometimes they are nightmares about something else.

3. How your body feels

Many young people find that when they think about the trauma or when pictures of it pop into their mind, they feel shaky or trembly, feel sick or have 'butterflies' in their stomach, or that their heart races very fast. It's as if your body is in a constant state of 'red alert', prepared for danger everywhere, and it reacts automatically whenever you are reminded of the trauma.

Because your body is in this constant state of 'red alert', you might find that you are very jumpy and that you flinch or startle easily at loud noises, like a door slamming. Often, young people have sleep problems because it's hard to relax. You may have trouble dropping off to sleep, or find that you wake a lot during the night. Lots of children and teenagers find that they are much more moody or angry – they get into arguments and fights with brother and sisters and parents more often than they used to. Because it's hard to relax, you may find that you have trouble concentrating at school, for example, and you might find it hard to pay attention or to remember things.

Your body might also feel unwell. Young people sometimes get headaches, tummy aches, feel sick, or feel more tired than they did before the trauma.

4. *Staying away from things and not talking about the trauma*

Children and teenagers who have been in a trauma often say that they try to stay away from anything that reminds them of the trauma. They do this to stop themselves getting upset and having the pictures come into their mind. So, a boy who had been in a car crash got really frightened when going in a car. To stop himself getting frightened and upset, he stopped travelling by car. But this meant that he couldn't ever go out anywhere with his brothers and sisters in a car. He ended up staying at home a lot, and got more and more bored, and didn't see his friends so much.

As well as staying away from things that remind them of the trauma, kids who have been in a trauma often try not to talk about it. Talking about it brings back all the upsetting memories, so instead they keep their thoughts and feelings to themselves. Some children say that although they wanted to talk about it, their parents got upset when they tried to talk to them, so to stop upsetting their parents they just stopped talking about it. But it can be really hard to cope with things all on your own.

You might have tried to talk to close friends about what happened to you. Often, friends find it hard to know what to say for the best, so it can be awkward and again you end up keeping thoughts and feelings to yourself. Some young people say that this means they end up feeling 'different' from other kids, like no one else can really understand what they have been through.

You might have tried to stop thinking about the trauma too. This is really hard to do! Young people say that they try to keep themselves busy or that they try to think of happy things instead. This might work for a little while, but you probably find that the memories do come back in the end – you can't push them away for good.

5. *Feeling sad*

Some children feel low and sad after a trauma. They might cry or just feel like crying a lot. They stop going out so much. Nothing seems to be much fun any more. They lose interest in their friends and in the things they used to do before the trauma. Plans for the future don't seem to matter so much. They think that they will never get better, and so everything seems hopeless.

6. *Feeling guilty*

After a trauma, young people can sometimes feel guilty. So they might think that they were to blame for the trauma happening in the first place, even if that is not really true. Some children come to believe that it is their fault that people were injured or died in the trauma. If people have died, young people sometimes feel bad or guilty because they lived while others died. These guilty feelings, when you think that something was your fault, can make you feel sad and angry, and often make it harder to talk to others about what happened.

7. *Feeling embarrassed (silly)*

Many young people often feel embarrassed or silly at how they have reacted to the trauma. Some kids think that because they have pictures about the trauma coming to mind, it means that they are going mad (*it doesn't mean that!*). Some children feel silly and annoyed with themselves because their fear stops them doing things they used to enjoy. Some young people start to think that anyone else would cope better than them, and this makes them feel bad about themselves.

Summary

There are lots of different reactions to having been involved in a trauma, and no right or wrong way to feel afterwards. Some of the things that other young people said they felt were:

- feeling scared
- remembering the trauma when they didn't want to
- their bodies feeling very 'jumpy'
- not wanting to be reminded of the trauma
- feeling sad
- feeling strange or 'different'.

All these feelings can get very confusing and upsetting, and this just makes it worse. Lots of young people said they felt so strange, and it was so confusing, that they thought they must be going mad.

> **Remember that all of the things you've read about are normal feelings that many children have. If you've felt any of these things, then you are just like other young people. Your feelings are completely normal, and they don't mean that there is something wrong with you or that you are going mad.**

Your treatment

Your treatment will be talking to someone once a week. There won't be any pills to take or injections. Sometimes your parents will join us to talk about things too. In between your treatment sessions, you will be given activities and things to do as 'homework'. You will be shown how to deal with nightmares and pictures that pop into your mind. By talking about the trauma and facing up to it, you will learn how to win back activities that you have been missing out on since the trauma. This means that you will be able to put the trauma in the past where it belongs and get on with your normal life again, just as you did before the trauma.

Children and trauma: information for parents and carers

What are traumatic experiences?

A traumatic event is a severe emotional shock. For children and adolescents, traumatic experiences can include things like being involved in a road or rail accident, witnessing or experiencing violent crimes, or getting caught up in natural disasters like floods. Other accidents and events, like house fires, falls, accidents around the home, or dog bites can also be traumatic for young people.

Most traumatic events involve some sort of threat to life or threat of injury, and would cause distress and upset in almost everybody. Traumatic events in childhood and adolescence are fairly common: research suggests that between 10 per cent and 40 per cent of young people have experienced at least one traumatic event.

Everyone – children and adults alike – will react to trauma in his or her own unique way. Still, there are some common reactions that many young people will share. This handout describes some of these reactions. Please read the handout carefully and see which of these apply to your son or daughter. The handout is yours to keep, so feel free to make notes on it or underline particular passages. You will have the chance to ask any questions and talk about your reactions to this handout at your child's next appointment.

How do children react?

There is a wide range of responses after a trauma, and no 'right or wrong' way for children to react. From our experience of working with children and families who were involved in a variety of traumatic events, the following reactions are some of the most common.

1. Fear and anxiety

The most immediate and striking reactions that children show after a trauma are fear and anxiety. Feelings of fear are most obvious when the child is reminded of the trauma. For example, children who have been involved in a traffic accident might fear going back to the site of the accident, or might get very afraid when travelling by car. Sometimes, the thing that triggers fear and anxiety might be less obvious. For example, a child who has been badly mauled by a dog might develop a fear of dogs, but also of many other harmless animals. A teenager who was involved in a shipping accident might develop a fear of travelling by sea, but also become afraid of the sound of rushing water in the bathroom at home. Subtle triggers like this, which are only distantly related to the trauma, can nevertheless result in a very strong automatic fear reaction. These sorts of triggers are often hard for children themselves to spot, and can make it seem as if overwhelming fear just comes 'out of the blue'. This spread of fears from the original trauma to something distantly related can sometimes make it difficult for parents to spot the connection between the child's behaviour and the traumatic event too.

Children may often fear that another trauma is going to happen again. That is, they develop a heightened sense of danger and see the world as very risky place. Not surprisingly then, children and teenagers can develop a fear of being alone. Or they may fear for the safety of others, especially parents and brothers and sisters, and not want to be parted from them. When parents have been involved in the same trauma as their children, one of the most common fears of children is for the safety of their parents – and this applies to teenagers as much as to younger children. When asked, young people's worst fear is often that one of their parents will die soon in another trauma.

Typically, after a trauma, children's fear and anxiety is experienced in two main ways: continuing to re-experience upsetting memories of the trauma; and feeling physically jumpy, hyped up and alert to danger. Both of these common reactions are detailed below.

2. *Re-experiencing memories of the trauma*

Most young people who have been involved in a traumatic event are troubled by repetitive thoughts and images of what happened to them. These memories are intrusive – they just pop into mind whether the child wants them to or not, and he or she may feel that they have no control over them. Intrusive recollections of the trauma often come to mind when the child is faced with reminders, as in the section above. Many children also say that they are troubled by intrusive memories when they are quiet – for example, when lying in bed trying to fall asleep, or when they are bored, doing nothing in particular. Often, intrusive memories come in the form of very vivid visual images or pictures: the child 'sees' the trauma all over again.

When these vivid images pop into mind unexpectedly, it can seem very real, as if the whole event is happening again, as in a 'flashback'. Children may also relive the traumatic event in recurring bad dreams and nightmares. These sorts of intrusive memories are certainly very upsetting. Children may also feel as if they have no control over what they are thinking, feeling, or remembering, during the day or at night, and so some children start to fear that they are going crazy.

3. *Physical arousal*

Becoming physically anxious and over-aroused is one of the most common responses to having been involved in a traumatic event. Young people often say that they feel jittery, shaky and trembly, have 'butterflies' in their stomach, startle very easily (jump at loud noises, for example), and have problems getting off to sleep in the aftermath of a trauma.

These reactions are all a result of the body's natural response to threat and fear. When young people (and adults) are faced with danger, their bodies are mobilised to respond through the action of various hormones like adrenaline. After a very frightening trauma, one's body can stay constantly on the alert, ready for instant action in the face of danger. This state of being prepared for danger can persist for a long time – it is as if the body has failed to realise that the danger is in the past. This is why young people who have been involved in a trauma often feel constantly tense and jumpy and unable to relax for some time afterwards.

This state of physical over-arousal can show itself in a number of ways:

- *Sleep problems*. Having problems in getting off to sleep and having restless sleep when children wake at intervals during the night are very common after a trauma.
- *Irritability*. Many children find that they are much more snappy, bad tempered and moody, or even angry and aggressive with family and friends. Families often say that this is one of the most difficult changes to cope with after a trauma.
- *Jumpiness*. Another common sign of the body being on constant alert is that children find that they are much more jumpy. They startle very easily at loud noises like doors slamming or cars backfiring, for example.
- *Concentration difficulties*. During the day, children may have major problems concentrating on schoolwork. This can lead to enormous frustration, and its causes often go unrecognised by schoolteachers.
- *Memory problems*. Young people may have problems in learning and remembering new material, or even have difficulties in remembering old skills such as reading music.

Some young people also find that stress and over-arousal shows itself in health complaints such as: sickness, headaches, stomach problems, aches and pains, or skin problems like getting spots.

4. Avoidance

Because the emotions and bodily feelings that intrusive memories give rise to are so unpleasant and upsetting, children naturally try to avoid thinking about the trauma that they were involved in. This means that most children tend to avoid reminders of the trauma. For example, a child who was involved in a traffic accident may avoid the site of the accident, and might avoid going in cars altogether, as these are painful reminders of the accident. Although avoidance of reminders is a self-protective strategy, it can quickly become quite problematic. Gradually, the child's life becomes more and more restricted. They may find that they have lost interest in the sorts of activities and things they used to do before the trauma.

Young people often avoid talking about the trauma because it makes them feel upset to do so. Many young people do not want to talk about their feelings with their parents, so as not to upset them. This means that it can be hard for parents to know about the details of their child's suffering, although they can see that they are upset. There is often a much greater sense of frustration between parents and children at moments like this. Parents may feel much less close to their children, and it can seem as if the child is a 'changed character' since the trauma.

Children and teenagers often try to avoid talking with friends about their experiences too. It can be upsetting to talk and young people might be embarrassed at their reaction to the trauma, feeling that they are going crazy or that they should be over it by now. Children's friends often want to do all they can to help, but hold back from asking about the trauma for fear of upsetting their friend. Children who have been involved in a traumatic event can then feel rejected by friends, or feel 'different' and cut off from those around them.

5. Other emotions

Young people can experience a whole host of other confusing emotions after a trauma. Like adults, young people can sometimes feel *guilty* after a trauma. Children might feel guilty that they were in some way to blame for the trauma happening in the first place. They might feel guilty about things they did during the trauma to survive. If others have died in the trauma, young people may feel guilty about not having been able to save them, or even feel guilty that they themselves survived when others died.

Embarrassment and *shame* are common feelings after a trauma. Children and teenagers may feel embarrassed at the way they acted during the trauma: for example, wetting themselves or screaming and shouting during a car crash. More common is a feeling of shame at their reactions in the months after the trauma. Many children fear that they are losing control or going mad, or that they are somehow weak or not coping as well as other children would.

Many young people often *feel low and sad* after trauma. Nothing seems to be much fun anymore. Children can lose interest in their friends and in the things they used to enjoy before the trauma. Plans for the future don't seem to matter much. Children can be miserable, tired and weepy.

Summary

All young people will react differently to being exposed to a traumatic event, but the above reactions of fear and anxiety, physical over-arousal, re-experiencing memories of the event, and avoidance of places and thoughts to do with the trauma are all typical reactions.

It is important to emphasise that these are typical, common, normal reactions to having been involved in trauma. None of the above problems are signs of going crazy or losing control (although it may seem to be that way to the child you care for). In fact, they are normal reactions to an abnormal event. This is the main message: **the feelings, thoughts, and body sensations that your child has been experiencing are entirely normal**. They are a natural human response to extreme stress.

Your child's treatment

During treatment, we will work with you and your child to help you understand more about your child's reactions and how to deal with them. Vivid re-experiencing of the trauma, either in nightmares or during the day in intrusive mental pictures, coupled with the body being on a constant state of alert, can make it seem as if the trauma continues to happen over and over again in the here and now. The natural reaction is to avoid reminders of the trauma and to push away any thoughts associated with it. Although this strategy might help in reducing upset in the short term, we now know that it is unhelpful in the long term. Paradoxically, avoidance prevents things getting better, and may even make things worse. During treatment, we will work with you and your child to show your child ways of getting the trauma memory out into the open. This will help to take the heat out of the trauma memory and put the trauma in the past where it belongs. This in turn will allow your child to resume his or her regular activities, to get on with friends and family as they did before the trauma, and to restart their normal life.

Appendix C

*Activity diary, Updating my memory chart and
Feelings thermometer*

Activity diary

Name: _____   Date: _____

Write down what you have decided to do each day.

Afterwards, put a tick (✓) to say if you have done it, and a number (0–10) to say how much you enjoyed it.

	MORNING	AFTERNOON	EVENING
MONDAY			
TUESDAY			
WEDNESDAY			
THURSDAY			
FRIDAY			
SATURDAY			
SUNDAY			

Updating my memory

Situation	What I thought at the time	FEELING (0–8)	What I know now NEW INFORMATION	FEELING (0–8)

Feelings thermometer

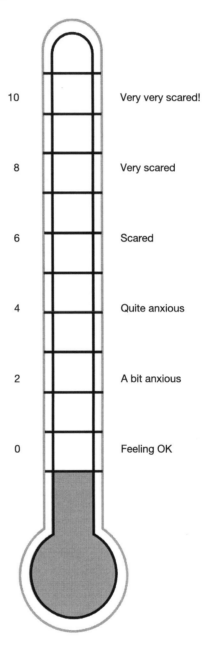

Appendix D

End of therapy letter and End of therapy diploma

End of therapy letter

Dear Michael,

I hope you have been keeping well.

At our last session, we agreed that I would write a short letter to you. This is to summarise some of things that you told me you have found helpful over the last couple of months.

When you first came to the centre with your mum, you told me all about the time that you and your friends had been attacked. It was a very severe attack that would have frightened anyone. I was really impressed by how brave you had been at the time, and by your courage in telling me about it the first time we met.

You also told me about what had been troubling you since the attack. This included having nightmares about what happened, and having pictures about the attack pop into your mind during the day. These memories were weird and scary, and so you tried to push them away and get rid of them. You also stayed away from the place where the attack happened, had stopped seeing your good friends who were with you that night, and you didn't like to talk about it to anyone because this just made it worse. You felt quite jittery most of the time, and you were getting in bad moods with other people (including teachers), and falling behind at school. This had all been going on for about eight months. You couldn't seem to get back to your old self, you didn't know what to do to make it better, and you wondered if you had 'lost it'.

Now you know that these reactions were 100 per cent normal. After really frightening events (traumas), most people have similar sorts of reactions. These reactions are so common that they have a name – Post Traumatic Stress, or PTSD for short. Your reactions were not signs that you were going mad or were weak – they were just a normal human response to being involved in a very frightening trauma. In our sessions over the last few months, you learned ways of overcoming your PTSD. In our final session last week, you told me what had been most helpful.

To start with, it helped to read the handout about trauma because you realised that there was nothing wrong with you and that you weren't going mad.

We then worked out that trying to push memories away seemed to be backfiring – it just made the memories bounce back more strongly (remember the pink rabbit?). So you experimented with other ways of coping, and found out that one of the best ways was to let the memories pass through your mind. This was hard to do at first, but when you did it, the pictures eventually went away by themselves.

After we had worked out that pushing the memory away was backfiring, you decided that you would try doing the opposite – you talked and wrote about the attack, in lots of detail, from beginning to the end. This was tough to do at first, and I really admired the courageous way you stuck with it. You said that it was really useful, for two reasons. First, you learned that nothing bad happened if you talked about the attack in detail. It got easier and easier the more you did it, and you found that your nightmares started to get less and less. Second, talking about it in detail helped you to 'update' the memory. There were many things that you 'updated', but the three most important were that: it wasn't your fault that you and your friends were attacked; that your screaming helped one of your friends to escape and get help; and that if you had fought back, it would almost certainly have been worse for you. Once you had updated the memory in this way, it was much easier to 'switch it off' when you wanted to.

Talking and writing about the attack in detail made it easier to talk to other people, too. You showed your mum your writing, and talked about it with her. You learned how concerned your mum had been (even if she didn't always show it!), and she said that she didn't blame you for the attack. In fact, she was a bit confused about what had happened, and it felt good to set her straight.

You also started seeing your old friends again. You said this was one of the most important things. You learned that they did not think badly of you – actually, they had been feeling guilty about running off, and so they were relieved to talk to you about it. John told you that he thought you'd been 'the hero' that night, which really helped in changing the way you saw it. You started to see your old friends more often, playing football again, and generally getting your life back on track.

Last, you chose to go back to the place where it all happened. This was also a big step, because you had not been back there since the attack. The place was not exactly the same as in your memory – again, this helped in 'updating' the memory. Going back to the place triggered some upsetting pictures at first, and as you expected, it made you feel more anxious. But these thoughts and feelings soon settled, and you were able to go back more and more over the next few weeks. It was your idea to get John and the others to go back with you – this worked out very well, and you knew afterwards that you had really 'beaten' it.

At our last session, you wrote down a plan for the future. You have learned a lot about dealing with stress, and this might be helpful for you in the future. You noted that if you or a friend get caught up in frightening events again, then you will:

- not try to push away the thoughts and feelings, but let the memory come and go instead
- if it continues to bother you, then you will write out what happened (including all the thoughts and feelings)
- talk to other people, friends and family
- stay active, and keep your life on track.

I am really pleased that you have made such good progress over the last few months. You worked very hard in all the sessions that we had together, and you now feel that you are back to your old self again. Your decision to come to the centre in the first place was a brave one. Choosing to stick with it even when it got tough showed how determined you are. You were keen to learn new ways of coping, and willing to take some risks in trying them out. And of course, you came up with plenty of good ideas yourself. Thank you for sharing these with me: I have also learned new things from you that will be helpful in my work with other young people.

I hope your exams go well this summer and I look forward to meeting you again in about six months to see how you have been getting on.

With best wishes,

End of therapy diploma

Index